Ashish Khetan is a journalist and a lawyer. In a fifteen-year career as a journalist, he broke several important news stories and wrote over 2,000 investigative and explanatory articles. In 2014, he ran for parliament from the New Delhi Constituency. Between 2015 and 2018, he headed the top think tank of the Delhi government. He now practises law in Mumbai, where he lives with his family.

UNDER COVER

MY JOURNEY INTO THE DARKNESS OF HINDUTVA

ASHISH KHETAN

First published by Context, an imprint of Westland Publications Private Limited, in 2021

1st Floor, A Block, East Wing, Plot No. 40, SP Infocity, Dr MGR Salai, Perungudi, Kandanchavadi, Chennai 600096

Context, the Context logo, Westland and the Westland logo are the trademarks of Westland Publications Private Limited, or its affiliates.

Copyright © Ashish Khetan, 2021

ISBN: 9789389152517

10 9 8 7 6 5 4 3 2 1

The views and opinions expressed in this work are the author's own and the facts are as reported by him, and the publisher is in no way liable for the same.

All rights reserved

Typeset in Dante MT Std by Jojy Philip, New Delhi 110 015

Printed at Thomson Press (India) Ltd.

No part of this book may be reproduced, or stored in a retrieval system, or transmitted in any form or by any means, electronic, mechanical, photocopying, recording, or otherwise, without express written permission of the publisher.

For Zoe, Tiya, Dani and Chris

The Big Nurse is able to set the wall clock at whatever speed she wants by just turning one of those dials in the steel door; she takes a notion to hurry things up, she turns the speed up, and those hands whip around that disk like spokes in a wheel. The scene in the picture-screen windows goes through rapid changes of light to show morning, noon, and night—throb off and on furiously with day and dark, and everybody is driven like mad to keep up with that passing of fake time; awful scramble of shaves and breakfasts and appointments and lunches and medications and ten minutes of night so you barely get your eyes closed before the dorm light's screaming at you to get up and start the scramble again, go like a sonofabitch this way, going through the full schedule of a day maybe twenty times an hour, till the Big Nurse sees everybody is right up to the breaking point, and she slacks off on the throttle, eases off the pace on that clock-dial, like some kid been fooling with the moving-picture projection machine and finally got tired watching the film run at ten times its natural speed, got bored with all that silly scampering and insect squeak of talk and turned it back to normal.

—Ken Kesey, *One Flew Over the Cuckoo's Nest*

Contents

Preface		ix
Introduction		1
1.	A Sting in the Tale	16
2.	Theatre of Masculinity	29
3.	The Ten-foot-tall Officer	46
4.	Painting with Fire	64
5.	Alone in the Dark	71
6.	Truth on Trial	81
7.	Conspirators and Rioters	99
8.	The Gulbarg Massacre	111
9.	The Killing Fields	131
10.	The Salient Feature of a Genocidal Ideology	154
11.	The Artful Faker	171
12.	The Smoking Gun	185
13.	Drum Rolls of an Impending Massacre	197

14.	The Godhra Conundrum	208
15.	Tendulkar's 100 vs Amit Shah's 267	233
16.	Walk Alone	251

Epilogue	268
Notes	286
Acknowledgements	308

Preface

Twelve-year-old Azar Mody loved cricket. On 24 February 2002, his team had won a match played in the cantonment area in Ahmedabad. Afterwards, they made offerings of sweets and coconuts at the city's famous Shree Camp Hanumanji temple. Ajju as his friends and family called him, brought home some sweets and a coconut for his mother Panaz, called 'Rupa' by his father and 'Rupaben' by neighbours and friends. Ajju's life was happy and relatively comfortable. His father, Darabhai, worked as a projector technician at a local cinema hall. Ajju would often tag along with his father to the theatre to watch films. The day before, on 23 February, it had been Bakr-Eid. Although the Modys were Parsis, they lived in a predominantly Muslim housing society called Gulbarg. Ajju had gone around the smart flats and spacious houses of the society to say 'Eid mubarak' to his friends and neighbours, stopping occasionally to taste the sweets and biryani on offer.

Later that week, on 28 February, Ajju got an unexpected day off from school because of the Gujarat bandh called by the Vishwa Hindu Parishad (VHP). He and his younger sister, eleven-year-old Binaifer, were glad, although they knew that something unpleasant had happened the day before. A train had burnt down. People had died. Still, Ajju could not help but be excited that he could stay home and watch WWF, the other 'sport' he loved. Rupa had made a

Gujarati favourite, muthia, for Ajju and his friends from the society to share. Ajju was a popular boy and always had friends over to play.

The Modys' neighbour, Shahzad, who lived in the apartment below, had advised Dara not to go to work that day because the city seemed on edge. Dara did not think it would be such a big deal, so he left for the theatre as usual, at around 9.30 a.m.

An hour later, a violent mob surrounded Gulbarg Society. Frightened, Rupa took Ajju and Binaifer to former member of parliament (MP) Ehsan Jafri's bungalow, situated in the same compound. Jafri was a man of considerable influence, he would know whom to call. But with every passing minute, the mob seemed to grow and become more violent. By the afternoon, the rioters were hurling stones and burning projectiles, gas cylinders and Molotov cocktails. Rupa knew there was nothing Jafri could do to keep anyone safe. Like much of the neighbourhood, his house was on fire too. At around 2 p.m., the mob had got its hands on Jafri, seizing him and tearing him apart. Rupa, her children, and a few other women and children from the neighbourhood were still hiding in the kitchen at the back of Jafri's house. When the fire spread to the kitchen, Rupa ran towards the terrace. She was holding Binaifer's hand and Binaifer was holding Ajju's hand. As they ran through the smoke and fire, Rupa tripped. Binaifer let go of her brother's hand to help her mother get to her feet. That was the last either of them would see of Ajju.

Rupa had burnt her hands and face in the fall. All around her, people were collapsing, as thick smoke bellowed from the burning houses, making it hard to breathe and even harder to see. The mob was still hurling stones, bottles and burning rags over the walls of Jafri's house. Rupa was hit by flying bottles a couple of times. But she kept going, making sure she had hold of Binaifer's hand, and calling out for Ajju. She thought maybe he had made it to the terrace already, but when she and Binaifer got there, he was nowhere to be seen. She turned to go back down to look for him, but the others seeking refuge there told her to stay put. Going back might tip off the Hindu mob that there were people hiding on the terrace.

Rupa and Binaifer survived what came to be known as the Gulbarg Society massacre, one of the most violent and horrifying episodes of the Gujarat riots. But Ajju was never found. In the last eighteen years, Rupa and Dara have put up hundreds of posters and distributed pamphlets with the last picture they had of Ajju in his school uniform and holding up an Indian flag. The picture was taken on 26 January 2002, just a month before the riots. Some of Dara's friends in the cinema business used their influence to have the posters pasted alongside those advertising hit movies. Dara and Rupa also put up posters at railway stations, bus stands and police stations. Rupa went around morgues, burn wards and every hospital in town, looking for her son. She looked at hundreds of bodies. Some of them were so charred that it was difficult to recognise they had once been human. She would focus on the feet. Ajju was a big boy and had large feet. 'Every few months, he would grow out of his pants and I would have to get a new pair stitched for him. His feet were bigger than even Dara's,' Rupa said to me in August 2020 when we spoke on the phone. She said that she had not given up; that the hope of finding Azar gave her purpose, kept her alive. 'Ajju's schoolteachers tell me that he was no naughty that he must have run away. One day, he will come back, just like that.'

⋯

As an investigative journalist, I went undercover in the state of Gujarat on three separate occasions. In the winter of December 2004, then again in April 2007, and once more in May 2007, which turned out to be a six-month journey deep into the insanity and mayhem of hard-line Hindutva. Assuming the identity of a Hindu fanatic, I penetrated deep into this hate-filled world. For six months, I shared meals and conversations with those who had committed the most gruesome crimes in the name of their faith. I heard stories of rape from the mouths of rapists, while casually sipping a cup of tea in their homes. I rejoiced with mass murderers as they boasted about their exploits—killing women, smashing small children against rocks while their parents watched, setting men on fire, slashing at the elderly and infirm with swords and machetes as they shrieked for help. For six months, I spoke the same hate-filled language as them. These mind-numbing, stomach-churning conversations sometimes stretched late into the night. I lived every day with the fear that I would be caught out, that they would see through my assumed identity, or that I would be frisked and they would find that I was wired. I lived with visions, nightmares that I too would be burnt alive, my corpse tossed into a mass grave in some godforsaken forest, like they had done to so many ordinary, innocent people back in the year 2002. But I was lucky. They never did find the wire. And I was able to return each time with new facts, with confessions caught on tape and with a little more evidence.

Each of my three undercover missions led to secretly recorded video footage and four books of transcripts that chronicled the darkest underbelly of the Narendra Modi regime in Gujarat.

More than a thousand people were killed in the 2002 Gujarat riots. The sting footage I captured juxtaposed the faces of the murderers with their monstrous deeds. I had footage of Hindu extremists admitting to planning and conspiring mass murder. I could not find out what had happened to Azar Mody. But I managed to put a few faces to the mob that perhaps killed him and sixty-eight others in the once idyllic Gulbarg Society. I could also film the extra-judicial confessions of those who lynched and burnt Jafri, those who burnt ten-year-old Aiyub alive in Naroda Patiya, those who killed nearly a hundred people in Patiya, and those who hacked to death Sugara, Raziyabanu, Karima and Jenab in neighbouring Naroda Gam.

The evidence I collected sketched out the contours of a larger conspiracy. It showed that the state of Gujarat created space for mass murder by deliberately retreating from its responsibilities and letting the Hindu mobs go on a killing spree, unchecked, unhindered and, at times, aided and abetted by the policemen on the ground. The sting footage contained strong evidence of the Gujarat government's role in subverting justice through the cynical appointment of card-carrying members of the Sangh Parivar as public prosecutors, among other things.

I suppose I was younger then, and audacious, and with a romantic view of the public good that reporters could do. I believed that once the story was published, my job as a journalist was done, and law would take over. Of course, once the tapes were out in the public domain, the stories took on a life of their own.

All three undercover operations—the investigation into the 2002 Gujarat riots, the investigation into the extra-judicial killings of Muslim men after they were branded as terrorists, and the sting operation on Bharatiya Janata Party (BJP) men who had bribed and coerced eyewitnesses—spurred fresh criminal investigations. All three stories were examined by Supreme Court-appointed Special Investigation Teams (SITs) or inquiry committees.

My investigative report on police custodial killings, which was published in April 2007, was examined and accepted by the retired Supreme Court judge, H.S. Bedi (though it took seven years for the investigation to be completed). Justice Bedi recommended the state of Gujarat to register criminal offences against the police officers whose names were disclosed in my report, but unsurprisingly, the Gujarat government has been contesting the Bedi report.

The sting operation I carried out in December 2004 was subject to inquiry by the then registrar general of the Supreme Court, B.M. Gupta. He carried out an eight-month-long judicial probe into the constant flip-flopping of Zahira Sheikh, a key eyewitness to a mass killing in Vadodara. Gupta relied on my story, among other things, to indict the Gujarat government and BJP leaders for influencing, threatening and bribing riot witnesses and denying them justice. I deposed before him and was cross-examined by the lawyers in one of the regal high-ceilinged court rooms of the Supreme Court. That was back in June 2005.

At that time, I did not know that I would going undercover once again, in May 2007. This undercover stint led to appearances as a prosecution witness in three separate Gujarat riot trials—the Naroda Patiya, Naroda Gam and Gulbarg Society massacres.

Between 2008 and 2013, I appeared and recorded my testimony before the Central Bureau of Investigation (CBI) in Mumbai, and then before the SIT in Gandhinagar. The CBI took possession of the sting tapes and sent them to the Forensic Science Laboratory (FSL) in Jaipur, which examined them over many months before concluding that they were genuine and not doctored or edited in any way.

A few years after the story was published, I deposed in the courts. I had to submit my work to the ultimate test to which a piece of journalism can be subjected—a forensic scrutiny, criminal investigations and finally a rigorous judicial cross-examination in three separate trials by a battery of aggressive defence lawyers who scrutinised, examined and doubted every word I had written and every fact I narrated. The wanted to diminish, if not destroy, my credibility so that the factualness of my work would also lie in tatters on the court-room floor, inadmissible as evidence. I had to become used to intimidation, insults and humiliation as a legal tactic, their contempt for me an extension of their contempt for my work.

In certain cases, the court-room environment was friendly towards the defence but hostile towards the victims and witnesses. For days on end, away from media glare and public attention, I testified and responded to every question, defended every accusation, addressed every insinuation, clarified doubts, laid bare the facts, over and over again. I did not want those who had confessed to me on camera, in graphic detail, to walk away free men, not after what they had done.

I told the courts how some VHP, Bajrang Dal and BJP leaders had admitted to their involvement in the riots. They had confided to me their roles in the maiming, burning and killing of men, women and children. Between them and their accomplices, they had killed over 175 people in a single day, in Ahmedabad alone. I produced before the presiding judges evidence I had marshalled of how the state machinery colluded with a mob drawn largely from right-wing Hindu groups. That the killing took place because the police allowed it. That the Gujarat government appointed public prosecutors who, as these men had told me triumphantly, instead of prosecuting the accused, focused on persecuting the victims. I told the courts what each of the accused had said about Narendra Modi and his role in the riots.

I identified Babu Bajrangi and his associates in court as killers. They had spoken to me of their role in the Naroda Patiya massacre, where close to a hundred people had died. The trial court judge, Jyotsna Yagnik, wrote a separate chapter in her judgement on the findings in my sting operation. She termed my evidence cogent, reliable, trustworthy, and used my testimony to convict Bajrangi and his cohorts. The Gujarat High Court upheld the convictions of three of the accused in the Naroda Patiya case on the basis of my testimony. It felt, to me, like a vindication of my journalism.

·◆·

In the years since the reporting I did in Gujarat, I have received many death threats and threatening phone calls. Anonymous letters have been delivered to my home. In these letters, faceless, nameless men (they must have been men because these sorts seem always to be men) claimed that they knew where my children went to school, that they had been following me, that after Gauri Lankesh, who had been murdered in Bangalore, it was now my turn.

Between 2010 and 2014, and then again between 2017 and 2018, I lived with round-the-clock security cover, provided on both occasions on the recommendation of the Supreme Court-appointed SIT. I was told by the police personnel who protected me to never follow a predictable routine, to leave home at a different time every day and to avoid taking the same road daily.

Worse than having to live with a Damoclean sword hanging over my head, was living with the bestial stories I had heard from these men. The images of children being sodomised and murdered, women raped, whole families burnt alive.

Violence alters your imagination.

I had a six-month-old daughter when I went undercover in 2007; the pain of the victims felt unbearably raw. And while the intensity of the trauma has receded over the years, there are still times when I tuck my young girls into bed at night and my mind travels to Naroda Patiya and Gulbarg Society—to the wailing of small children, the powerlessness of the parents, the terror they must have felt, the sound of all those fires...

Over the last fifteen years, I have told the Gujarat story in a fragmented, piecemeal way, in magazine stories, on TV programmes, in court depositions, in statements made to the CBI and SIT; some of it is in the public domain, but a lot of it is not. Most of all, the Gujarat riots seem to have faded from the collective memory. When the riots are brought up in public conversation, it is usually in bad faith, twinned now to 1984 and other communal riots, to prove some twisted point that we are all as bad as each other.

But I had always believed that, at some point, I would have to tell the full story of what I witnessed in Gujarat. Even though I went there a few years after the events of 2002, the riots have always been a reminder to me that an ideology built on hate can persuade ordinary people to become part of a murderous mob, can get them not only to kill but to kill with relish and then justify it as a long overdue assertion of communal power.

When western Uttar Pradesh erupted in a communal frenzy in 2013, I thought the time had come for writing this book. But that was when I embarked on my own political journey. I fought a parliamentary election, ran the campaign for the Delhi assembly elections, and became enmeshed in the running of a Delhi government think tank.

Then, in the last week of February 2020, riots broke out in northeast Delhi, the largest eruption of Hindu–Muslim violence in the capital since Partition. An eighty-five-year-old woman's house was surrounded by a mob and set on fire, and she was burnt alive, like so many Muslims in Gujarat eighteen years earlier. A group of rioters created a WhatsApp group called 'Kattar Hindu Ekta', where they bragged about killing Muslims and dumping their bodies in open sewers. They offered to supply fellow fanatics with weapons so that they too could kill Muslims. Between the afternoon of 25 February and midnight of 26 February, men from this WhatsApp group bludgeoned nine Muslims to death. They would stop passers-by and ask for identification, so they could confirm if the person was Hindu or Muslim; the latter would be forced to chant 'Jai Shri Ram' and then be battered anyway.

The 2020 Delhi riots left fifty-three people dead, most of them Muslims, and hundreds grievously injured. A Muslim doctor who attended to injured victims at a private hospital in Delhi described the horror before a citizen's tribunal: 'One man's legs had been ripped apart. Perhaps that was beyond the limits of brutality. Anger and hatred are one thing. Brutality is another.'

I knew then that I needed to write this book. That I had to begin straight away.

·•·

There is a price to pay if you stand up for human rights, if you believe in the notion of justice. As the years go by, those who champion the causes of others, particularly those of a demonised minority, will find themselves accused of being prejudiced, of having an agenda, of seeking to advance their careers, and of 'playing politics'. And if you insist on making something like an investigation into the 2002 Gujarat riots part of your life's work, you will repeatedly, aggressively, be asked: 'Why won't you let bygones be bygones? Why won't you let people move on? Why do you have to be so negative? Why don't you first talk about 1984 before you discuss 2002? Why don't you write about the riots during the Congress regime? Do you know the history of Gujarat? There have always been riots in Gujarat, don't you know that? The Muslims did this in

1947. The Hindus did that in 1984. The Muslims did this in Godhra in 2002.'

Every riot, every act of violence we have worked so hard to ignore, to 'get over' without a moment's reflection or any attempt to seek understanding and reconciliation, has made us more debased as a society. The mob now believes it can act with impunity. Not only will the rioters be protected, they might even be rewarded for their actions. Heinous acts become more and more normalised. The once malevolent is now unexceptional.

After watching a particularly vile Delhi election campaign by the BJP in 2020,[1] the Delhi riots were so much déjà vu, a replay of events in Gujarat. Communal speeches, followed by hate slogans, followed by riots. Select law officers appointed as special public prosecutors. A compromised bureaucracy in which the compliant rose to power and prestige, while the upright were hounded. A communal police force and a biased administration. An insipid media. A placid judiciary. If a judge dared to ask questions, he was immediately shunted out.

The Delhi riots show the dangers of never learning from our past. The dangers of decades of complacency, of feeling that we were an inclusive, multicultural nation proud of our diversity and openness, until one day we woke up to find out we were actually small-minded, resentful, parochial and violent. Because we do not remember, we repeat; because we do not look evil in the eye, we are always looking over our shoulder. The Gujarat playbook is now the India playbook. Surprise—it has nothing to do with good governance, prosperity and economic development, it is about sowing hate, division and anger. About picking on minorities and making a crude, poisonous rhetoric the vernacular of the national conversation.

'I am not so naïve as to believe that this slim volume will change the course of history or shake the conscience of the world. Books no longer have the power they once did. Those who kept silent yesterday will remain silent tomorrow,' wrote Elie Wiesel presciently in his book, *Night*.[2] I am not writing this book because I think it will change how people see the present times. It is a book to say, as much to myself as to you, that I was there and this is what I saw. It may seem as if it is a book about the past. But I hope that, by the time you finish reading it, you will be as convinced as I am that it is a book about our present and our future.

Introduction

To make sense of present-day India, one may want to begin on the warm and sunny morning of 27 February 2002, when a savage crime was committed on the railway tracks in Godhra, until then a nondescript town north of Vadodara. Fifty-nine Hindus, men, women and children, some of whom were VHP members—kar sevaks on their way back from Ayodhya after attending a temple ceremony—were burnt alive in an attack by a Muslim mob. Within hours, members of Hindu far-right organisations mobilised their own mobs, equipped them with weapons and inflammable liquid, and exhorted them to kill Muslims, burn down their properties, their businesses and their homes.[1] The carnage lasted a few days, until the pressure of non-stop media coverage and international opprobrium forced the state administration to stop the massacre. By then, nearly a thousand Muslims had been slaughtered and many more thousands had been made homeless, displaced from their own neighbourhoods, rendered refugees in their own country.

Years of actively cultivated hatred towards Muslims was manifest in the official machinery's response to this communal horror—first in failing to prevent the organised killing and then in failing to provide justice and restitution to the victims. No government institution, no organ of the state was untouched by communal bias. The Gujarat police fabricated evidence[2] to give the

Sabarmati train carnage—which was a horrifying but spontaneous riot—the appearance of a premeditated plot hatched by Godhra's most prominent Muslim residents. On the other hand, the state systematically subverted investigations into the actions of Hindutva hardliners in the post-Godhra massacres of Muslims. Even after the BJP-led National Democratic Alliance (NDA) was unseated in a surprise electoral defeat in 2004, the campaign for justice in Gujarat was largely confined to the work of a few human rights groups and even fewer journalists.

For ten years, the Congress party-led United Progressive Alliance (UPA) was in government. Under the watch of Prime Minister Manmohan Singh, a Cambridge and Oxford-educated economist, the Indian economy grew at an average of 8 per cent, though hidden beneath those surging aggregate numbers was extreme income and wealth inequality, rural distress, and growing numbers of unemployed and unemployable youth. The top 1 per cent walked away with almost 30 per cent of the national income. The top 0.1 per cent of Indians owned more wealth than the bottom half of the population. Meanwhile, the income of the middle 40 per cent remained stagnant, seeing very little growth in a period marked by accelerating GDP growth.[3] The full scale of the confusion, chaos and corruption within the UPA only came to be thoroughly exposed towards the middle of its second term, when telecom and coal-mining scandals sparked widespread anger and disgust among voters.

The relatively obscure subjects of coal blocks and spectrum allocations revealed the diseased heart of the UPA. Riven by factions and infighting, it appeared to have no charismatic mass leader, certainly not the putative prime minister whose power seemed to stem entirely from 10, Janpath, the home of Congress President Sonia Gandhi. Access to her was jealously controlled by a coterie of senior advisers and gatekeepers. There were such influential ministers as P. Chidambaram, Pranab Mukherjee, Kamal Nath and Anand Sharma, each of who was a kingdom unto himself. And then there were the leaders of the Congress allies, the patchwork of parties that formed the UPA, figures such as M. Karunanidhi, Shibu Soren, Prakash Karat, Sitaram Yechury, A. Raja, D. Raja, bidi baron Praful Patel, media baron Dayanidhi Maran and the leader of sugar barons Sharad Pawar. Never before, not even during P.V. Narasimha Rao's term in office in the 1990s, was the authority of the Government of India so disaggregated, the prime minister so diminished and cabinet ministers so unaccountable.

For its first six years in government, despite these inner contradictions and weaknesses, the UPA sailed smoothly forward, primarily because the BJP's own ship was in such disrepair. But in 2010–11, the Comptroller and Auditor General (CAG) reports on the 2G and coal scams, and then Anna Hazare's anti-corruption movement stripped the UPA of its legitimacy in the eyes of the people. From mid-2011 till 2014, the UPA, though formally in power, was a lame-duck government. In many ways, the Supreme Court replaced the executive, the CAG became the most powerful constitutional authority, while India Against Corruption—the movement led by Anna—and television news channels set the terms of the national conversation.

If the Congress-led UPA government was imploding, the alliance leaderless and rudderless, 500 miles to the southwest of Raisina Hill, one man was in complete control, not only of his state and its people, but also of his political destiny. Ruthless, and with an insatiable hunger for politics and power, he had been in charge of the narrative of the state, contorting its social fabric, for twelve years. If the UPA government was a series of accidents, one crisis following hard on the heels of another, Narendra Modi's reign in Gujarat was a triumph of choreography, each step meticulously charted, each move deliberated to advance his myth, the larger-than-life image of himself that he had superimposed on the state.

After his third consecutive electoral victory in Gujarat in December 2012, Modi, who was once a pariah in Indian politics, stormed onto the national stage to fill the vast political vacuum left by a lethargic, out-of-sorts UPA. It was a moment Modi had been waiting to seize.

When the national media called the 2002 massacre the shame of Gujarat,[4] Modi launched the 'Gaurav Yatra', invoking the pride of Gujarat. When human rights activists called for justice for the Muslim victims of that pogrom, he spoke only about bringing the 'merchants of death' behind the Godhra train-burning to justice. And when the media called him a mass murderer, Modi rallied his supporters to address him as the 'Lion of Gujarat'. In the face of national disgrace, Modi claimed it was a narrative that painted Gujarati Hindus as villains, and projected himself as the state's fiercest defender, its only hope against enemies.

Mounted atop his vehicle on the 'Gaurav Yatra', Modi roared at the crowd: 'They say Gujarat is full of rioters, looters and killers. This is a conspiracy to defame Gujarat.'[5] He had turned the widespread disgust over what had happened in Gujarat into a contest of 'us against them', motivating a supposedly besieged people to fight back, as they now saw it. In every town, he delivered this stump speech, as BJP workers heralded his arrival with the chant 'Look who is here, the lion of Gujarat'. In election after election, Modi would project the Congress as the party of the Muslims, in spirit if not literally. 'Let me ask a question to my Congress friends, if water is brought during Shravan month,' he said—at an event in the temple town of Becharaji in September 2002, referring to Congress criticism over the diverting of waters from the Narmada to the Sabarmati river—'then what is hurting them? Since we are here, we brought water to Sabarmati during the month of Shravan, when they are there, they can bring it in the month of Ramzan.'[6]

He would bellow: 'I warn the Congress, don't exploit the deaths of people for electoral victory.' But Modi himself turned the murder of kar sevaks into a major election plank in 2002. In village after village, rally after rally, speech after speech, he invoked the horrifying image of burnt bodies on the Sabarmati Express. There was no mention in these speeches of what had happened post Godhra, except to justify the pogrom as a reaction. Modi's second major poll plank was the threat of Islamic terrorism. Election campaign video ads would begin with a burst of loud gunfire, followed by the rhetorical question: 'Who will save Gujarat from the merchants of death?' The answer, of course, was 'Only BJP, Only BJP, Only BJP'. Modi positioned the carnage at Godhra as an act of terror.[7] His administration invoked the draconian provisions of the Prevention of Terrorism Act, 2002 (POTA) to try the Muslims accused of the attack on the Sabarmati Express. The state turned Godhra into a premeditated conspiracy, rather than a spontaneous communal riot, though it did not describe the subsequent pogrom in the same terms. Soon, the Gujarat police started gunning down Muslims in 'police encounters'. Subsequent court-monitored investigations showed that small-time criminals and underworld gang members from the Muslim community were passed off as Pakistan-trained terrorists before being killed in cold blood.[8] Whatever the compunctions and protests of civil society and even the courts, when Modi asked supporters at his rallies what he should do with 'terrorists' like Sohrabuddin Sheikh, killed by the police in 2005, 'kill him, kill him, kill him,' the crowds would chant.[9]

'Pay homage to the Godhra Martyrs. Cast your vote for BJP,' the poll advertisements screamed from every Gujarati newspaper on polling day in December 2002. 'Friends, when you all go to vote this time, if you press your finger on the hand symbol [Congress], you will hear the screams of Godhra, the pain of Godhra. I took a vow on the Godhra platform that I would not spare the sinners of Godhra,' Modi had said in his last campaign speech in 2002. Under Modi's leadership, the BJP not only retained Gujarat that year, it increased its tally by ten seats from 1998, winning 127 out of the 182 seats in the legislative assembly, a considerable majority.

Modi returned to power in Gujarat in 2007 and 2012, with thumping majorities. The fact that Modi's BJP never fielded a single Muslim as its candidate, the fact that Muslims never participated in BJP election rallies in any significant numbers, and the fact that, after the 2002 massacre, Muslims in Gujarat had been utterly marginalised, were the planks on which the BJP mobilised Hindus in Gujarat in election after election. During the 2012 Gujarat assembly election campaign, Modi himself, in a public speech, cautioned the voters of Gujarat that the Congress wanted to appoint Ahmed Mian Patel as the chief minister (CM) of Gujarat.[10] Modi's dog whistle, underlining for his base the faith of Sonia Gandhi's political secretary, was a ploy to consolidate his vote bank.

The Congress appeared to believe that though it did not, and would not, overtly stand up for the idea of justice or defend India's secular values, communalism would somehow disappear of its own volition. But the tentacles of an atavistic hatred for Muslims had spread across Gujarat and deep into the rest of India, tunnelling beneath the false euphoria of high GDP growth, booming stock markets and the expanding club of Indian billionaires.

In 2013, communal fighting broke out in western Uttar Pradesh (UP). Sixty-two people were killed, forty of them Muslim, and more than 50,000 were displaced, many of who are still living in relief camps seven years later. More than 570 riot cases were registered across five districts—Muzaffarnagar, Bagpat, Shamli, Meerut and Saharanpur. The police have closed dozens of cases of murder and loot, with the rest of the cases floundering in the morass of judicial subversion. Online trackers show a spurt in religious hate crimes since 2014.[11] Dozens of Muslims have been lynched by cow-protection vigilantes in different parts of the country. Nearly 3,000 'communal incidents' were reported in India between 2014 and 2017, in which 389 people were killed and 8,890 injured, according to home ministry figures presented before the Lok Sabha in February 2018.[12] In the last week of February 2020, communal violence broke out in Delhi, killing fifty-three people. Over 200 were grievously injured. Many independent observers have argued that there is clear evidence of police collusion with Hindu rioters in several instances.[13] Renowned police officer Julio Ribeiro, celebrated for effectively leading the Punjab police force during the period of militancy there, wrote to the Delhi police commissioner, S.N. Shrivastava, in September 2020 in a letter titled 'miscarriage of justice in northeast Delhi' that 'the Delhi Police has taken action against peaceful protesters but deliberately failed to register cognizable offences against those who made hate speeches which triggered the riots in Northeast Delhi. It troubles sane and apolitical persons, like me, why Kapil Mishra, Anurag Thakur and Parvesh Verma have not been arraigned before the courts of law while deeply hurt Muslim women, peacefully protesting against discriminations based on religion, were lodged for months together in jail.' Following Ribeiro's letter, nine more retired police officers, including former special director of the CBI, K. Saleem Ali, wrote to Shrivastava, calling the investigation into the riots as biased. 'We were sad to note that one of your Special Commissioners had tried to influence investigations claiming resentment among Hindus over the arrest of some rioters belonging to their community. Such a majoritarian attitude in the police leadership leads to a travesty of justice for the victims of violence and their family members belonging to minority communities. This would further mean that the real culprits of the violence belonging to the majority community are likely to go scot free ... Basing investigations on "disclosures" without concrete evidence violates all principles of fair investigation. While implicating leaders and activists, who expressed their views against CAA, all those who instigated violence and are associated with the ruling party have been let off the hook,' wrote the retired officers. Many human rights activists and young student leaders who, through public speeches and writings, exhorted people to protest peacefully against the CAA and the National Register of Citizens (NRC) have been charged as kingpins of this so-called conspiracy to foment communal violence and rioting.

India's body politic is now poisoned. An institutional bias, a repulsion towards Muslims, appears to permeate all branches of government. In many cases, judicial processes have been weaponised to deny Muslims equal rights, freedom and dignity.

In October 2020, while delivering a lecture on 'Preserving and Protecting Our Fundamental Rights', former judge of the Supreme Court of India, Justice Madan B. Lokur, said that 'freedom of speech is being eroded and mauled through twisting and turning the law' and 'almost every state seems to have weaponised sedition as a means of silencing critics'. Justice Lokur cited the case of Dr Kafeel Khan, who was kept in preventive detention under the National Security Act, without trial, for more than six months, as 'a classic instance of cooking up a case against a person with the intention of putting him behind bars for several months'.[14] Numerous villages and towns, where once Hindus and Muslims lived in harmony, are now shrouded in communal suspicion, even hate.[15] Death and prejudice loom over the fields of western UP, just as they do over residential neighbourhoods in northeast Delhi, and certain pockets of Jharkhand, Rajasthan, Madhya Pradesh, Maharashtra, Gujarat, Karnataka and Haryana.

•—•

How did we come to this?

My three undercover investigations into the 2002 riots and extra-judicial killings in Gujarat gave me an intimate insight into Hindu ethno-nationalism and Hindutva from the point of view of grassroots workers. Each riot-accused I met told me that he believed the Narendra Modi government had given him the freedom to kill. They said that the police looked the other way even as they went on a murderous rampage. After the violence was over, the state selected public prosecutors who were card-carrying members of the VHP or the Rashtriya Swayamsevak Sangh (RSS) to argue for the conviction of alleged rioters. Little wonder then that they failed to secure any for two years, until the Supreme Court stepped in, describing the Gujarat government as 'modern-day Neros' who looked elsewhere as men, women and children burnt. The police systematically weakened the evidence, did not charge many key accused, threatened victims and tried to prevent them from recording their true testimonies or naming the accused. Despite repeated petitions in the higher courts and intermittent interventions by the Supreme Court, the law enforcement machinery resolutely protected the rioters.

Arvind Pandya, the Gujarat government's special counsel before the Nanavati–Shah Inquiry Commission, who was handpicked by Modi to defend his government, told me (unbeknownst to him, I was filming him) that, because there was a Hindutva government in Gujarat, large-scale killings of Muslims could be achieved. 'The people were ready and the state was also ready,' he said. He added, 'The ruler was also strong in nature because he gave [the order] "just take the revenge and I am ready".' These tapes established that the killings of Muslims in 2002 was not a sudden outburst of communal violence.[16] Only Modi, a lifelong RSS pracharak, had sufficient courage and the ideological conviction to follow through on such a policy. It was remarkable how deeply the VHP and Bajrang Dal, and their mindset, had penetrated cities and urban settlements across Gujarat. These organisations were represented throughout Gujarati society, and either directly controlled or influenced the levers of power at every level.

After 2002, Narendra Modi emerged as an icon of hard-line Hindutva. For RSS and VHP cadres across Gujarat, there was only Modi, the embodiment of a muscular, assertive Hindu pride that was unafraid to show Muslims their place. He had catapulted past the likes of M.S. Golwalkar, V.D. Savarkar and L.K. Advani in the Hindutva pantheon, able to mobilise Hindu sentiment and able perhaps, like no leader before him, to establish India as the 'Hindu Rashtra' of which they dreamt.

In one of the charge sheets[17] filed by the Delhi police over the 2020 Delhi riots, there is a revealing thread of WhatsApp conversations among a group of Hindu rioters called 'Kattar Hindu Ekta'. At 9 p.m. on 25 February, when Muslims in northeast Delhi were under siege, one of the accused posted an inspirational message for the other accused in the WhatsApp group. Its English translation:

'A Muslim man challenged Modi to withdraw the police for fifteen minutes and then after that not one Hindu would be left alive. To that Modi replied, "I did withdraw the police in Gujarat for some time, after which your community was reduced to 10 per cent in my state."' The message ends with the exhortation: 'Build the Ram Mandir, kill at least twenty-two Muslims, else you are not a true son of the Hindu faith.'

Between 25 and 26 February, at least eighteen members of the Kattar Hindu Ekta WhatsApp group—all from poor economic backgrounds and between eighteen and thirty-five years old—killed at least nine Muslim men, who too were poor. They were bludgeoned, stabbed and shot, their corpses dumped in a *ganda nala* (dirty drain) flowing between the Bhagirathi Vihar and Ganga Vihar neighbourhoods in the Gokalpuri area of northeast Delhi. Ironically, the locations for these profane, murderous actions committed by supposedly devout Hindus are named after Hinduism's most holy river, the Ganges. The group chanted 'Jai Shri Ram' and 'Har Har Mahadev' as they lynched their victims, eyewitnesses told the police. The men's WhatsApp messages, though, were indiscreet, revealing their murderous plans and their discussions about logistics. The police were able to extract the chats and produce them before the courts as effective confessions, and set about arresting some of the killers.

There are frightening echoes between these messages and the almost boastful confessions of rioters in Gujarat that I captured on hidden camera. Just like these men, they too saw Modi as a hero, a Hindu leader who was not afraid to permit Hindus to unleash their pent-up fury on Muslim enemies. Modi has projected himself in a number of distinct ways before various audiences. Between 2002 and 2006, he was the 'lion of Gujarat' who would single-handedly save the Hindus from Islamic terrorism; he was the self-proclaimed *dharmarakhshak mahodaya*, or protector of the Hindu faith.

After 2006, he began to focus on his (again, self-proclaimed) prowess as an administrator—he was Modi, the vikasmuni, or saint of development. 'Vibrant Gujarat' summits replaced the rath yatras.

He wooed and charmed industry captains who were happy to traffic adulation for subsidised parcels of lands and tax breaks. Muslim-baiting was still high on the agenda, but the unsavoury details were left to leaders a few rungs below Modi. Instead, his silence that spoke eloquently on such matters.

For Modi, democracy seemed to mean majority rule. Electoral victories legitimised all actions, however unconstitutional, especially the social, legal, economic and political marginalisation of the Muslim population. Those decisive triumphs at the polls meant his supporters could drown out the voices of those, including some in Modi's own party, who demanded fairness, enforcement of individual rights, or rule of law. Anyone seeking to dissent from the Modi line was dismissed as a crank or contrarian, or worse, a Congress supporter. In Gujarat, the state legislature was sidelined, the administration was subordinate and the police was under Modi's thumb. Courts of law hardly seemed to matter. While refusing to implement a High Court judgement, the Gujarat government argued that rebuilding places of worship of minorities would be a violation of secularism.[18] Even strictures passed by the higher courts were routinely ignored.[19] When a criminal investigation into the killing of Sohrabuddin Sheikh was underway, under the direct oversight of the apex court, a key eyewitness named Tulsiram Prajapati was killed in another staged encounter.

After 2012, Modi projected himself as the man who had transformed Gujarat into the land of prosperity and development, and who was now ready to implement the Gujarat model in the rest of the country. Once in power, he allowed the communal agenda to simmer on the slow burner, the flame of which the BJP kept adjusting to the demands of an election at hand. On Modi's watch, the BJP and associate outfits created divisions over religion and nationalism.

Like in Gujarat, Modi has come to personify the state at the Centre. Criticism of Modi is akin to an attack on the nation. Through constant insinuation, dog-whistling and rabble-rousing, he and other BJP leaders seem to have succeeded in projecting Muslims as the natural enemy in the eyes of many Hindus. In the midst of a crumbling economy and social disorder, Modi's popularity continues to soar. Endemic hostility towards Muslims among the core vote bank perpetuates his rule, even as hate speech, toxicity and disinformation targeted at the minorities, dissenters and liberals continues to erode the social fabric.

Leo Tolstoy was dismissive of the importance of leaders in shaping nations' histories, seeing historic figures as mere ex post facto justifications for events that by their nature were wholly beyond any individual's influence. Karl Marx, in *The Eighteenth Brumaire of Louis Bonaparte*, argued that leaders must choose from a historically determined set of choices, which means that they have much less freedom to act than they think they do. To Tolstoy, Marx and other thinkers who argue that deterministic forces shape historical outcomes, leaders are merely symbolic: 'labels' to describe particular expressions of underlying social phenomena.

Is the ascendance of the Hindu right-wing and the annihilation of a liberal, tolerant, inclusive politics driven by deterministic forces?

It is true that much before Modi took over as chief minister, the political ideology of Hindutva had already permeated our society. Since Independence, India has seen sporadic outbursts of communal violence, particularly in UP, Bihar, Assam, Maharashtra and Gujarat. Beginning in the 1980s, when the BJP launched a strident campaign to destroy the Babri Masjid, a mosque in Ayodhya, the frequency of communal violence increased.[20] The mosque was allegedly built, on the orders of the Mughal emperor Babur, on top of a Hindu temple marking the birthplace of Ram. The dispute was long-running, but the BJP gave it fresh momentum, using the issue to gain a political foothold in India by demonising the country's Muslims and fostering a sense of grievance among Hindus.

Despite the BJP's best efforts, though, there were always counteracting political forces, social movements and competing ideologies that stripped Hindutva of any lasting mass appeal and kept the rise of the Hindu right-wing in check. What separates Modi from an L.K. Advani or a Syama Prasad Mookerjee is that he has effectively vanquished those ideological challenges to Hindutva, first in Gujarat, and now in large parts of central and north India.

The portrayal of the Congress party as a venal, dynastic party beholden to minorities found resonance with voters, laying the ground for the ascendance of Hindu nationalism. But without Modi's popular appeal, his oratorical skills and his flagrant abuse of state power, the Hindu right-wing would have never attained such complete hegemonic control over Indian democracy. Any flickering challenge to Modi's supremacy has come from civil society rather than any cogent political opposition. Tools honed and deployed over twelve years in Gujarat are now being used on a national scale to subvert, harass and demonise dissent, with critics of Modi characterised, and often jailed, as opponents of and threats to the nation.[21]

UP Chief Minister Yogi Adityanath appears to be taking Modi's Gujarat model a step further. In UP, Muslims with a criminal background are more likely to be killed in a police encounter than arrested.[22] His government has recommended the withdrawal of prosecution in over 200 cases of communal rioting in western UP. But now, there is almost no pushback from the higher levels of the judiciary, which was not the case even as recently as the mid-2000s.

The mainstream national media, which once tore apart the UPA, brick by brick, exposing corruption and complacency, as it should have, acts as Modi's handmaiden. News channels praise him incessantly, reserving their questions for the Opposition, papering over or explaining away the prime minister's failings on the economic and foreign policy fronts, while continuing to assail Congress politicians for foibles that may have occurred over a decade ago. Debates on news channels are noisy distractions—

shouting matches dedicated to the exchanging of insults rather than presenting a serious discussion on the considerable challenges facing the country or the government's largely poor performance in meeting those challenges.

The current course on which India finds itself suggests, contra Marx and Tolstoy, that a nation's historic path can indeed be radically altered and affected by just one individual. That these same set of circumstances, without Modi, might not have led to the hegemony of militant Hindu nationalism.

Many of his political opponents loosely call Modi authoritarian, a dictator, a tyrant, a fascist, and describe his rule as an 'undeclared Emergency'. These terms have distinct historical contexts and meanings. Certainly, Modi and his government display some of these characteristics. But such are his experiments on the public and political imagination that academics will have to find new ways to explain and interpret the phenomenon of his reign.

Majoritarian rule untrammelled by law; the veneer of democracy minus the substance of constitutionalism; economic freedom without political or individual liberty; the constant undermining of minorities, particularly Muslims; the impunity for Hindu right-wing rioters as opposed to the harsh treatment, including unjustified arrests and imprisonment, meted out to those deemed to be on the opposing ideological side; the persecution of activists and human rights organisations; the misuse and abuse of institutional and judicial processes to target political opponents and dissidents—the systematic manner in which Modi exploits the power of the state to crush any opposition, the sheer scale of state persecution and the efficiency with which it is executed is without precedent in India.

As Hannah Arendt wrote in the preface to *The Origins of Totalitarianism*: 'Comprehension does not mean denying the outrageous, deducing the unprecedented from precedents, or explaining phenomena by such analogies and generalities that the impact of reality and the shock of experience are no longer felt. It means rather examining and bearing consciously the burden which our century has placed on us—neither denying its existence nor submitting meekly to its weight.'

India may very well take a different direction tomorrow. A new political movement may take shape and make inclusiveness once more fashionable among the people, and turn commitment to justice and the protection of human rights, dignity and communal harmony into an election-winning strategy. A charismatic democrat might emerge on the political landscape and turn the tide. But it will, as this book shows, take something remarkable to arrest our rapid march towards becoming an unrecognisably belligerent, intolerant, perpetually aggrieved Hindu Rashtra.

I have been seen as one of the most trenchant critics of Narendra Modi and the idea of Hindutva. Through my writings and reports, I have exposed the many wrongdoings and brutalities of the Modi regime, first in Gujarat and later at the Centre. To disregard my reports and my evidence in courts, defenders of the Modi rule have persistently tried to paint me as biased and embittered. Therefore, I must begin with an account of how I was initiated into covering Gujarat and Modi.

1
A Sting in the Tale

I came to the cities in a time of disorder
When hunger ruled.
I came among men in a time of uprising
And I revolted with them.
So the time passed away
Which on earth was given me.

I ate my food between massacres.
The shadow of murder lay upon my sleep.
And when I loved, I loved with indifference.
I looked upon nature with impatience.
So the time passed away
Which on earth was given me.

In my time streets led to the quicksand.
Speech betrayed me to the slaughterer.
There was little I could do. But without me
The rulers would have been more secure. This was my hope.
So the time passed away
Which on earth was given me.

—Bertolt Brecht, 'To Posterity'

I sort of stumbled into journalism. It was the early 2000s, and I was living in my hometown Barabanki, 25 kilometres outside Lucknow, when I wrote a few articles for an English-language newspaper on a whim. One story described how a local MP was wasting taxpayers' money on self-promotion. The MP in question, having read the story, was not pleased at being publicly embarrassed. For me, discovering how the printed word could rattle his cage, despite his access to influence and power, was revelatory and empowering. I cut the story with my byline out of the newspaper, framed it and put it up on a wall.

Many years earlier, when I was studying at a Christian missionary school, the new principal, whom we addressed as 'Father', had imposed an odd rule. Absent students were required to produce a letter from their parents when they returned to school to explain their absence. Standard stuff, except that the letter could be written in no language other than English. Neither of my parents could read or write in English, so my father and I would walk some distance to the house of the only person he knew who could. While my father's friend would write a simple letter, I would watch, marvelling at his penmanship and easy facility with the language.

Hence, writing for an English-language newspaper, only a dozen years later, filled me with pride. Looking back, I know now that vernacular journalists in general are better than their English counterparts in many ways. They are better networked, more informed and harder working.

As a cub reporter, I discovered that the district officials in my neighbourhood were very respectful when I called or visited them for a quote on a story. Growing up, I had seen my father, a shopkeeper, become apprehensive whenever the police or a local government official came by the store on some routine inspection or bureaucratic mission with the side objective of soliciting a bribe. The image of my father, submissive before these petty officials, has remained with me.

My other lasting memory is of the ennui of small-town life, of being stuck in a place where time stood still. Every day, my father would go to his shop and, while waiting for his next customer, drink endless cups of tea, read a Hindi newspaper, or puff on his Panama cigarettes. The wheel would turn and turn again, seemingly without end. The only break in the drudgery was maybe a late-night movie at a small theatre in town that regularly screened black-and-white Hindi films from the 1950s and 1960s, films like *Baiju Bawra*, *Pyaasa*, *Do Ankhen Barah Haath*, *Jahan Ara*. We had to wait a year or more before the print of a new release was cheap enough to be screened in Barabanki.

Becoming a reporter helped me to escape that life. I moved to Lucknow to work full-time for the paper. Suddenly, no day was like any other. There were things to do, places to go to, people to meet. I felt plugged into the events of the day, felt I was being given an inside, up-close view of how the country was run. Before long, I became hooked to the adrenaline rush of punishing newspaper deadlines.

In those early months as a young journalist, I was struck by how the abuse of power was so commonplace, so unremarkable. Everywhere—from universities to medical colleges to police stations to ministries to government offices—those bestowed with even a modicum of authority chose to misuse it. And, instead of angering us, this behaviour was generally seen as inevitable, an unwritten perk of a job in public service. If a traffic cop stopped you, well, you just paid up and moved along. If you wanted to get a passport made, you slipped the verifying police officer some cash and got it done. Birth certificate, death certificate, caste certificate, college marksheet, registering a police complaint—everything came for a price. If there was protest, it was over the cost of the bribe rather than the act of bribery itself.

In those early days, I wrote many stories about corruption, nepotism and apathy in government offices. One of these involved exposing a judicial magistrate who had a well-oiled system for issuing favourable orders. His strategy was to issue two kinds of orders—a 'kachcha' (raw) order and a 'pakka' (ripe) one, charging different amounts for each. If the party liked the kaccha order and wanted to turn it into a pakka one, he would pay a sum to the magistrate's clerk. The actual amount depended on the stakes in the case. To expose him, I got both kinds of orders through a lawyer. My editor was brave enough to publish the story. He also gave me the key to writing stories of an explosive or sensitive nature: 'Write plain facts, no insinuations.' I had written a measured story, every word chosen carefully.

The next day, the magistrate sent us a notice of defamation. I had become a full-time journalist only a few months earlier, so this was baptism by fire. Would one of my first stories also be my last? As I walked into the editor's office, I mentally checklisted the employment options I had in case he gave me the sack. But my editor was calm; he told me to draft a response to the magistrate's notice.

I drafted one based on the documentary evidence we had collected and faxed it across. In a few hours, the magistrate was at our door, holding out an olive branch and pleading with the editor not to print any follow-ups in the paper. With some deft handling and no assurances, the editor saw him out.

For me, this episode was proof of the power of journalism. We had managed, through careful, accurate reporting, to hold no less than a judicial magistrate to account. My editor taught me another, more pragmatic, lesson. When to let go. After the splash made by that story, he told me to begin the next, rather than circle the magistrate for a second bite: 'Remember the job of a journalist is to tell the story without getting hurt. Living to tell the tale is the name of the game.' I took his advice and moved on to write about the misuse of funds by a university official, a case of bungling in a government medical college, corruption in the works awarded by the public works department and the siphoning of public funds meant for flood relief work, among other pieces.

At that time, my salary was a modest Rs 4,500, barely enough to cover expenses, but the act of probing and uncovering facts, writing articles that someone somewhere didn't want published, gave me a sense of purpose. I remember one particular story about a serial killer who was up for execution on a court-designated date. But the state had missed the date and the convict was alive and well in prison, a fact kept from the courts. I travelled to the village where the accused once lived and where he had committed a gruesome murder, slaughtering an entire family, including women and children. I met the victims' relatives and the prison officials, and found that the state had been negligent. My editor published the story on the front page, right under the masthead. I didn't sleep that night. I waited outside for the first copies, excited to hold the paper still warm off the printing press.[1] That clip still occupies a prominent place in my personal archive of articles written at a time when fragile newsprint still mattered, before the internet ushered in the present era, where everything—good or bad, trivial or profound, truth or falsehood—is preserved online forever.

·•·

My life as a journalist in Lucknow was filled with exciting incidents but was materially sparse.

On my salary, it took a combination of careful budgeting and luck to make ends meet. When a friend offered me a room in his house in Lucknow for a rent of Rs 1,500, I nearly wrenched his hand off, so eager was I to shake on the deal. Reporting across the state, I would rack up a hundred kilometres on my bike nearly every day and Rs 2,000 in monthly fuel bills. I would have been in the red most months if it hadn't been for the generosity of a dhaba owner who said he was impressed by my work and cut me a deal in which I could pay just Rs 5 for a Rs 25 thali, an 80 per cent discount! Getting back to the dhaba in Indira Nagar meant I had to travel a fair distance for my dinner, after having chased a story all day, but it was often my only meal of the day. I still remember walking into a smart new café in Hazratganj one day, and turning around and walking straight back out again once I saw the prices. Of course, I wasn't the only journalist in town scraping by on a meagre salary. The plight of reporters working for Hindi newspapers was even worse. Photojournalists were paid less than reporters. As for stringers working in districts outside Lucknow, they often went unpaid.

Being a beat reporter required, among other things, rigour. We were expected to file three or four stories daily. A typical workday would begin with an edit meeting at 11 a.m. and end twelve hours later. The pace was relentless but exhilarating.

When I first started out as a journalist, there was a BJP government in Lucknow and a BJP-led NDA government in Delhi. Rajnath Singh was the UP chief minister, and Atal Bihari Vajpayee the prime minister. At the height of the Ram Janmabhoomi mobilisation in the early 1990s, some Hindi newspapers published in UP—owned and edited by upper-caste Hindus—ran vicious propaganda against the minorities, publishing false stories with which they whipped up communal passion and hatred despite censure from the Press Council of India.

However, by the time I started out as a journalist, such blatant communalism had largely subsided. For all the years I worked as a reporter in Lucknow, I didn't see Muslims being openly or systematically discriminated against. The English-language press was liberal in its outlook and even the more virulent sections of the Hindi press had quietened down as the Ayodhya movement slowly lost its momentum and mass appeal. After the Sabarmati train burning in Godhra in 2002, right-wing Hindu groups did try to whip up communal tension across the country but failed. The BJP government in UP gave way to a succession of Bahujan Samaj Party (BSP) and Samajwadi Party (SP) governments. Caste, not religion, was the route to power, and it remained that way until 2017, when Yogi Adityanath became the chief minister.

As early as 1993, when the two caste-based parties—the SP, led by Mulayam Singh Yadav, and the BSP, led by its founder Kanshi Ram—briefly came together to form the government in UP, their slogan ran, '*Miley Mulayam-Kanshi Ram hawa me ud gaye Jai Shri Ram*', which roughly translated to mean that the alliance of the backwards triumphed over the divisive politics of Hindutva. There were Kurmi leaders, Yadav leaders, Brahmin leaders, Thakur leaders, Jatav leaders, and so on. Every politician had a captive vote bank of the people of his own caste, on top of which he would then build electoral alliances with other castes. The SP was a party of Yadavs and other backward castes (OBCs), while the BSP was a party of the Dalits. Muslims swung between the SP and BSP, depending on which of the two had a greater chance of winning. Most upper-caste Hindus saw the BJP as their party of choice, but they too switched over to the SP or BSP for power and patronage. Briefly, Brahmins gravitated towards the BSP for the spoils of power. In short, jaati trumped religion.

Once, I was sitting with a member of legislative assembly (MLA) from a backward caste, when a farmer from his constituency walked in: 'Vidhayak-ji, my son is going to the US for studies. He has got a scholarship. Can you please put in a kind word with the local vidhayak in the US to look after him?' The MLA dictated a letter to his secretary: 'Dear George W. Bush, Greetings from Uttar Pradesh. A bright student from my constituency is coming to your country. Will be grateful if you could be his guardian.' The letter was signed and handed over to the farmer, who went away satisfied. A politician did not have the option of saying no to his constituents.

I found then that the caricature of politicians in cinema and literature was way off the mark. MLAs and ministers toiled through the day, meeting hundreds of people from their constituencies, signing letters, making phone calls, attending birthday parties, weddings, mundans, funerals, listening to complaints, trying to find solutions to seemingly intractable problems. On the other hand, I found most Indian Administrative Services (IAS) officers inaccessible, insular, indolent and imperial. After twenty years in public life, including three years spent in the Delhi government, my impression about them has not changed.

By early 2004, I had started becoming restless. Journalism, it is said, is printing what someone else does not want printed. The rest is public relations. The truth of that old aphorism, credited to George Orwell among many others, was clear to me very early on in my career. Only 5 per cent of what I saw published in Lucknow could be called journalism. Editors who had direct access to chief ministers were considered valuable by their proprietors. Newspaper owners were mostly currying favour with the government of the day, trying to secure advertising, or a parcel of public land at less than the market rate, or government contracts of all kind. Reporters were meant to fill the pages with routine stories, not rock the boat. Some bureau chiefs and editors were allotted posh government houses in the tony neighbourhoods where bureaucrats and ministers lived. It was a cosy club of mutual backscratchers. Investigative journalism meant investigating a babu, an inspector, maybe the odd MLA here or an MP there who had fallen foul of someone even more powerful. And that was it.

I found Lucknow too limiting. The papers did not have the stomach for stories that questioned and probed those occupying the highest seats. I decided to move to Delhi and set my sights on *Tehelka*—the investigative news portal that had just relaunched as a crusading weekly newspaper. I took an overnight train to Delhi, took a bus from New Delhi railway station to the South Delhi neighbourhood of Greater Kailash II and walked into the *Tehelka* office on the first floor of an undistinguished building in M-Block market. After more than an hour of waiting, I met the no-nonsense investigations editor, Harinder Baweja. She asked me to write a few stories for *Tehelka*, and if they were any good, she said, I would be offered a job. Within a month, I gave her a story on the nexus between UP politicians and the local drug mafia. I had proof to show that ministers and parliamentarians were helping drug syndicates by writing recommendation letters to the state, asking for police cases pending against them to be closed. *Tehelka* put my story on the front page, and I was offered the job of a reporter in Delhi for Rs 12,000 a month.

After I got my first pay cheque, I walked straight into the Barista in M-block Market and ordered a cappuccino.

Many of the politicians whom I had nailed in my UP drug mafia story knew me personally. As a local newspaper reporter, I used to meet them regularly. After the story was published, a few of them called me on the phone. They insisted that they were innocent, told me that in politics one had to help people and that I should have been sympathetic since I was also from UP.

As a rule, I never argued with the subjects of my reporting and investigations. I was always polite. After all, it was not personal. While most people understood that I was doing my job, some did not. Threats, intimidation and abuse were par for the course. But I realised that, once the story has broken, the journalist is safe. It was while you were working on it that you were vulnerable. Collecting facts with as little fuss as possible, not leaving a trail of who you spoke to or met, and protecting, above all, the sources who were taking a risk by giving you information was key.

I moved to Delhi on a sweltering May day, over sixteen years ago. I still remember loading my motorcycle onto the goods bogey of the train I took from Lucknow. I found a barsati to rent for Rs 3,500 in Defence Colony. Even at night, the rooftop room was a furnace, making it impossible to sleep. The small fan was helpless in the face of such an onslaught. To have any chance at sleep, I had to shower and then, without towelling myself dry, doze off under the fan.

My biggest learning from those years was that challenging circumstances and meagre resources are not a hindrance to good journalism. High salaries and big media platforms help, but are not essential for high-quality reporting.

To meet sources, or chase a lead, I would go to any length, travel any distance. At the end of the day, I would always return to the office and spend hours reading on the internet (those were 2G days, there was no internet on your mobile). I loved working at *Tehelka*. I was part of the Tehelka Investigations Team, inevitably called TIT, a source of endless amusement for the other bureaus.

Tehelka had a reputation. Whistleblowers would come to us, believing that only we had the gumption to break the big stories. Once, a source walked in with graphic pictures of torture and abuse, allegedly by personnel at the Delhi Special Cell, evidently 'inspired' by the tactics used at Abu Ghraib. He wanted a large sum of money for sharing the pictures, and though TIT had plenty of guts, we had no dosh. We missed that story.

But we did plenty of good journalism. Once, I was tracking Mani Shankar Aiyar, the petroleum minister in UPA-I, for a quote on a story that was critical of his ministry. I went up to him at a private party in a South Delhi farmhouse, just as he was taking a sip of his wine. I introduced myself, told him briefly about the story and asked for his reaction. He sneered, 'You journalists are like dogs of no worth and with nothing worthwhile to do. The whole day you roam here and there, sniffing around for a juicy story.' We published the story, without his quote, but I have not forgotten his remarks, or the look of contempt as he made them. If only he knew, it was a compliment.

An investigative journalist is a sniffer dog, a rat refusing to let go of a tasty morsel, a wasp that stings, a pest digging for dirt. That is the job description. And TIT's mandate was to do major investigations, to dive into the muck and do big undercover operations.

Tarun Tejpal, the editor, outlined a set of basic rules. We were not to bribe anybody, or to induce a person into doing something wrong. Operation Westend, in which *Tehelka* exposed the corruption that was part and parcel of defence deals and cost the then defence minister his job, had brought the website accolades and fame but also much criticism for its methods, including the use of sex workers. Not anymore, Tarun had resolved. 'We are not the moral police,' he would say, 'out to catch people in their weaker moments, checking if people are strong enough to not give in to temptations.'

Instead, Baweja said, we had to learn to be flies on the wall. To be there without being noticed, to be there so persistently that, whenever our targets let their guard down, we would be around to enable them to incriminate themselves. And then to back that up with evidence from as many documents and first-hand sources as we could muster. The stings for which Tehelka became famous, the use of spy cams and surreptitious recordings, were always intended as a last resort, when all other options to get or tell a story had been exhausted.

I did a few document-based investigative pieces, some of which were even covers. But every undercover operation I was part of proved to be a dud. Once, for instance, we got a tip-off about an oil refinery on the outskirts of Delhi, where, we were told, petrol was being adulterated on a mass scale by a cartel of truck operators. For several days, I hung around the refinery with drivers and cleaners but couldn't make any headway. Another time, the former BSP chief Kanshi Ram was admitted to Batra hospital in Delhi. There were rumours that he was not getting the right treatment; in fact, according to the grapevine, there was a conspiracy to kill him. Kanshi Ram's failing health and the future of the BSP was a huge story at the time. Posing as a party worker, I tried to get into his hospital room but failed. The idea was to use spy-cam footage from inside the room to try to ascertain whether something was amiss, but there was tight, round-the-clock security, and I was twice prevented from gaining entry.

In 2004, spy cameras, or at least the ones we used at *Tehelka*, were quite rudimentary. I was given a small Rexine bag with a shoulder strap and two tiny holes on the outside. If anyone looked closely enough at the bag, they would see the holes quite easily. Inside the bag was a Sony Handycam and a mesh of wires to capture image and sound from the lens attached to the tiny holes. Compared to the advanced technology available in the market today, that spy cam was like some home-rigged contraption.

In the August of that year, I was assigned to keep vigil on the movement of trucks outside a meat factory in the jungles of Mewat in Haryana. My editor had received a tip that this meat-producing factory had won a contract to supply frozen meat to the Indian army but was mixing goat meat with calf meat, with the calves being brought to the factory in the dead of the night. Since *Tehelka* was always strapped for cash, I could not afford to hire a taxi to travel to Mewat, about 150 kilometres south of Delhi, so I made the journey on my bike, timing it such that I would reach the factory by 1 a.m.

Potholed, narrow and desolate, the road was menacing. And then, into the black midnight, came the rain. It was the monsoon season. My bike skid and I was almost run over by a state transport bus speeding towards me from behind. Luckily, the driver braked in the nick of time. He was kind and helped me pick up my bike, which, miraculously, was intact. Even through my drenched clothes, I could feel the blood dripping onto my right arm. Eventually, I arrived at the vicinity of the factory and parked my bike in a thicket from where, unobserved, I could watch the gates. After an hour, a truck came by. I switched on my spy cam, started my bike and rode towards the factory. When I got close to the gates, I got off and walked towards the truck, hoping to record the material inside it. There were many labourers preparing to take the animals from the truck to the factory. But the animals were all goats. The labourers grew suspicious and started asking questions. In the dim light, however, they realised that I was quite badly bruised. I told them that I was from a nearby village and was on my way home when I met with an accident and that I needed some first aid. They said they had none, but that there was a government hospital about fifteen minutes away. Exhausted, I got back on my bike and drove another kilometre before I came to some flat ground where I decided to lie down for a few minutes. I woke at dawn, looked at my injured right arm, and took myself straight to the hospital where I was bandaged up and given a tetanus shot.

The next few days, I followed the traders supplying goats to the factory to Ajmer and Jaipur. I hung out at truck stops, transport depots and dhabas on the state and national highways in Haryana and Rajasthan, but found no evidence of calves being supplied to the factory. It may have been bad quality meat, but the factory was not mixing goat meat with cow meat, which was prohibited by law in Haryana.

The life of an investigative reporter is full of such fruitless pursuits and dead ends. The emotional and mental toll is considerable. After weeks and sometimes months of gruelling work, meeting all kinds of people, going over troves of documents, as many as nine out of ten leads fail to materialise into a substantial story. If you are undercover, there is the added risk of getting caught; being in the wrong place at the wrong time could mean getting hurt. Still, an investigative journalist must necessarily treat each tip from a vaguely credible source as if it could lead to a blockbuster story. Even in frustration and failure, there is something to learn, the chance to meet new people, develop new contacts and, sometimes, to experience a different part of the country.

Investigative journalists have to internalise and live by that old Nietzschean saw: 'Out of life's school of war—what doesn't kill me, makes me stronger.' The Mewat investigation may have been a wild-goose (rather than calf) chase, but I was happy that I had returned alive, and wiser.

2
Theatre of Masculinity

His [Adolf Eichmann's] shallowness was by no means identical with stupidity. He personified neither hatred or madness nor an insatiable thirst for blood, but something far worse, the faceless nature of Nazi evil itself, within a closed system run by pathological gangsters, aimed at dismantling the human personality of its victims. The Nazis had succeeded in turning the legal order on its head, making the wrong and the malevolent the foundation of a new 'righteousness'. In the Third Reich evil lost its distinctive characteristic by which most people had until then recognized it. The Nazis redefined it as a civil norm.

—Amos Elon, 'The Excommunication of Hannah Arendt'

In the last week of November 2004, my editor asked me to go down to Vadodara in Gujarat. 'Zahira Sheikh has changed her story again,' he said, 'it's not adding up.'

Eighteen-year-old Zahira, with her large, guileless eyes and thick braids, had become emblematic of the Gujarat riots. She had miraculously lived to tell the story of a murderous mob who attacked the small bread-making unit her family owned in Vadodara's slum-like Hanuman Tekri neighbourhood. The family lived on the first floor and their shop was on the ground floor—a bakery owned by poor people to serve other poor people.

Armed with the most basic of spy cams, I boarded the flight from Delhi to Vadodara. It was an ATR operated by Jet Airways. This was the first time I had boarded a flight in my life. I was excited both by the air journey and the absolute uncertainty that lay ahead.

I did not know a soul in Gujarat, but to go into unknown territory to investigate a story that the whole nation was discussing was a journalist's dream. An investigative reporter is fuelled by an unwavering commitment to the democratic principle of holding elected officials accountable, and to the idea that tenaciously uncovering uncomfortable truths is acting in the public interest.

Landing in Vadodara, I figured it would be best to start with not one but two new identities. I assumed the name 'Piyush Agarwal', a right-wing nationalist whose family had long been members of the RSS and who was happy to do what it took to further the Hindutva project. My other alias was the unassuming Pranay Lal, a research scholar. Agarwal would be responsible for talking to BJP and VHP workers, while Lal would visit the victims' families and interview anyone who could be considered neutral.

I visited the Best Bakery site. Blackened and burnt-out, the building stood there like a ghost, a scarred manifestation of the horror of that night. The massacre took place on 1 March 2002; it was 8 p.m. when the mob first began gathering outside the bakery. Sheltering inside was Zahira's family, which included her mother, her uncle and his family, two sisters, four brothers and a sister-in-law. Also present in the building were migrant labourers who worked in the ground-floor bakery during the day and slept on the terrace at night. After twelve to fourteen hours of gruelling work every day, for months, they would manage to save a few thousand rupees to send to their families back home in the backward districts of eastern UP. In addition to the family and the workers were a few local families who had sought shelter at the bakery.

Recounting the events of that night, Zahira told the police that the 'mob was violent and armed. They were carrying inflammable liquid and sharp-edged weapons and came shouting anti-Muslim slogans. We were about twenty of us inside the house. We made a run for the terrace. Some who could not make it locked themselves in a room on the first floor.' The mob first looted the sacks of flour and sugar, and tins of oil and butter from the bakery, whisking the goods away in three-wheeler carriers. This was a template the rioters followed in city after city, village after village: first rob whatever there was to be robbed—electronics, cutlery, clothes, household stuff—then sexually assault the women before hacking them to death, and then lynch and burn the men. Children too were treated with near unimaginable brutality.[1]

Once everything of value was taken from the bakery, the mob pelted the building with stones and hurled Molotov cocktails filled with petrol and diesel into it and set it on fire. Inside, the occupants were making despairing phone calls to the police and to the fire brigade. According to Zahira, 'at one point, a police van did show up. It pulled up on the main road and that gave us some hope. The mob dispersed. A few of us came running down, waving and shouting for the police. But they just drove away.' Zahira and the others ran back up to the terrace. The mob resurfaced and stayed for nearly fifteen hours, murdering and pillaging through the night. The rioters dragged down two people from the first floor, hacked at them with swords and threw them into the fire. The building was ablaze and four children, all under four years of age, and three women, trapped on the first floor, were burnt alive.

'The rooftop was hot,' said Zahira, 'and our feet were turning red. We had no option but to hide behind the parapet on the terrace the whole night. Every minute on the terrace felt like an eternity. In the morning, the mob put a ladder against the wall of the bakery and asked us to come down.' The rioters—Jayanti, Sanjay, Santosh and others whom Zahira identified to the police—assured the victims that they wouldn't hurt them. The victims and the killers knew each other. 'We would call them "chacha", "mama",' said another survivor.

'We just wanted to leave. We told the rioters that we didn't want anything, we would leave the bakery behind, to just let us go. When they swore in the name of their own children that they would let us go, we believed them,' said Zahira.[2]

First, the women climbed down from the roof, then the men. They were begging for their lives with folded hands. Two tried to make a run for it, towards an open field. They were quickly caught. With each victim, the mob took its time. They did not just want to kill their captives, they wanted to make sure their Muslim neighbours suffered.

Zahira said, 'Our hands and legs were also tied together with ropes and we were attacked with swords. Then they put wooden planks on the limbs of six males and set them on fire. The mob was threatening to rape the women who were still alive.' At around 11 a.m. the next morning, a police van finally showed up. An officer with a bullhorn asked the mob to disperse. And the mob did. No teargas. No rubber bullets. Just one bullhorn. Perhaps, by then, the mob's bloodlust had been sated. Four children and ten adults had already been killed by the time the police arrived. Zahira lost nine family members, including two of her brothers, in the attack. Nine victims survived. Along with two other brothers and her mother and sister, Zahira became a prime witness in the case. She identified several key accused, as many of them lived in the same neighbourhood and were regular customers at the family bakery.

But on 17 May 2003, in a dramatic turnaround, Zahira told the Vadodara trial court that she could not identify any of the accused because she was hiding, fearing for her life. Her brothers Nafitullah and Nasibullah, mother Sehrunnisa and sister Sahira also turned hostile. After a year and a half of naming and consistently identifying the accused, the Sheikh family went back on their statements. Faced with a case of mass killings, where all survivors and eyewitnesses had refused to identify the killers, the Vadodara trial judge acquitted the twenty-one accused about a month later.

Two weeks after the acquittal, though, on 7 July 2003, Zahira surfaced in Mumbai alongside the human rights activist Teesta Setalvad. Zahira told the press that, when she reached the court complex, she was confronted by Chandrakant Bathu Shrivastav, the brother of local BJP legislator Madhu Shrivastav. 'Bathu,' she said, 'had called on my brother's mobile and threatened that unless we retracted our statement we would also be killed. Madhu Srivastav was also threatening my brother. After seeing Bathu in court, I got frightened and turned hostile.'

There were other twists to come.

12 April 2004: The Supreme Court ordered retrial of the Best Bakery case outside Gujarat, in Maharashtra. The judges gave a blistering critique of the state government's inaction during the riots—'The modern-day Neros were looking elsewhere when innocent women and children were burning and were probably deliberating how the perpetrators of the crime can be saved or protected.'

3 November 2004: Just a day before she was to appear before the Mumbai trial court, Zahira returned to Gujarat in another stunning turnaround. This time, she claimed she had been held hostage and bribed by civil society activists to misidentify the Hindu accused. Madhu Shrivastav was outside the hotel where Zahira held her press conference and fired a shot from his revolver in celebration. The Gujarat government provided Zahira security cover and she was housed in a resort, cut off from the media.

21 December 2004: Zahira deposed in the Mumbai court saying she had not seen any of the accused at Best Bakery on that terrifying night.[3]

Each time Zahira changed her stance, the suspicion grew that she was a pawn in the hands of some dark force. If journalism could shine a light on that darkness, it would be a public service. As my editor, Tarun Tejpal, said to me, 'nothing added up'. Could I go down, he asked in the next breath, and take a look?

•••

After visiting the blackened ruin of Best Bakery, I visited the victims' families and heard how they had been abandoned by the state. I met with the mother of Sanjay and Ravi Thakkar, brothers who were among the twenty-one accused. She told me that Madhu Shrivastav was in constant touch with their advocates, an incriminating fact but nowhere near enough to establish collusion. I wanted to infiltrate the circle of right-wing Hindutva leaders to hear about their involvement straight from, if you like, the horse's mouth. But the stable door was still bolted.

One day, I decided to just show up at the house of Bathu Shrivastav. I was nervous but desperate to find some opening for my investigation. Before walking into his house, on the first floor of a two-storey building, I rang up Harinder Baweja in Delhi and told her that if she did not hear from me in the next hour she should file a missing-person report. I rang the doorbell, Bathu was there. I introduced myself as Piyush Agarwal, and told him that I had been sent from Delhi by senior Hindu leaders with a message for Madhubhai. 'The message is that Madhubhai is doing a good job but because the judiciary and media are on the case, he must lie low. And there is something else, a special message which I would like to pass on to him face to face,' I said. I asked him to arrange a meeting with Madhu.

Bathu heard me out, though he looked suspicious. It was hard to tell what was going through his mind, but he did not appear convinced by my story. At the same time, I was sitting there with such purpose, such confidence, as an emissary from Delhi eager to deliver a message to the most notorious man in Vadodara that he did not want to dismiss me either. He settled for just staring at me, taking in my clothes and the clumsy Rexine bag on my shoulder, which I had angled towards him to capture his face. He asked me a couple of probing questions. Where did I live in Delhi? What exactly did I do for the RSS? Eventually, he called his brother on his mobile phone.

'I have here with me a Piyushbhai Agarwal from Delhi, he wants to tell you something,' he said and handed me the phone.

I tried hard to persuade Madhu that I needed to meet him in person, that I could not deliver my message on the phone. Madhu took my number and said he would call. After he hung up, I sat with Bathu, blabbering nervously. As I talked, Bathu kept staring at me, saying almost nothing himself. After five or ten minutes, I took his leave.

I waited for a few days, but Madhu never called. When I called him, he didn't answer.

Madhu was a local muscleman with more than half a dozen police cases against him. His family had migrated to Vadodara from UP. After failing his SSC, Madhu joined politics, and in due course came to lead a gang of petty hoodlums, according to local reports. In 1980, he contested the Vadodara Municipal Council election and became an independent councillor from Hanuman Tekri, where Best Bakery was located. He was allegedly involved in land grabs and was the henchman for big builders. In 1995, he was elected to the state assembly from Waghodia as an independent. Two years later, the BJP fielded him from the same constituency and he was re-elected by a resounding margin. After Madhu became an MLA, Bathu become the councillor from Hanuman Tekri.

After a week, luck smiled on me. I ran into another local muscleman named Nisar Bapu, a big man in his sixties, with a deep voice. Bapu's son was in jail on riot charges. Bapu himself was out on bail, having also been charged with rioting. I introduced myself as Pranay Lal, a researcher. Though he was Muslim, Bapu was on good terms with Madhu, both of them 'colleagues' in the business of crime mixed with politics.

After many years in the trenches, this is one thing I have learnt: the only broadly secular industries in India are Bollywood and the underworld. In these fields, Hindu sharpshooters happily work for Muslim bhais and, equally happily, male Khans romance female Kapoors on screen. Religion doesn't matter. What matters is performance.

I befriended Bapu, shared a few meals with him, and went around Vadodara in his SUV. I told him that I would help get his son out of jail.

Bapu showed me that Gujarat was a place twisted by hate. 'How can old wounds heal,' the novelist Kazuo Ishiguro wrote in *The Buried Giant*, 'while maggots linger so richly?'

The 2002 riots had left not only a thousand (at least) dead but displaced tens of thousands—men, women and children permanently damaged by what they had seen, whose homes were now one-room tenements built on the outskirts of cities by mostly Muslim charities. Meanwhile, hundreds of alleged rioters, most of them poor, of course, were arrested and jailed. Their families too were struggling—failing to pay the rent, to pay school fees or buy rations. The right-wing Hindu outfits did not help any but a fortunate few. Only the politicians and a few high-ranking thugs benefitted from the hate they spread, and so they kept picking at the scab, refusing to let Gujarat heal or attempt a process of reconciliation.

Bapu wanted his son out of jail. He claimed the police had framed him. He latched on to me like a drowning man will seize a piece of driftwood, frantic for even the faintest glimmer of hope. I asked Bapu if he knew anything about the connection between Madhu Shrivastav and Zahira Sheikh. He immediately told me that Madhu had paid her Rs 18 lakh to turn hostile. I asked how he could be so sure. 'Madhu himself told me,' he replied. I told Bapu that I would like to hear it from Madhu's mouth. He was obliging: 'No problem, I will take you to Madhu's house. I will talk to him and you just sit quietly and hear him tell the story.' Over the next few days, I waited anxiously for this meeting to materialise, spending a good portion of my days with Bapu. And then one day, just like that, we were expected at Madhu's house at 9 a.m.

I was living in hotels, moving to a new one every night. Early, on the morning we were to visit Madhu, I took an auto to Bapu's house. As we drove to Madhu's house, I spread a newspaper over my Rexine bag and switched on the spy cam. I had trained myself to switch it on without looking at it. I was sitting in the back of the vehicle, while Bapu was sitting in front. I could only record forty minutes of footage on one tape, so I planned to start filming shortly before we pulled up outside Madhu's bungalow. He was waiting for Bapu on a swing chair in his front garden, and asked us to take a seat on the plastic chairs arrayed opposite the swing. Over the next thirty minutes, the spy camera captured Madhu admitting that he had bribed Zahira to turn hostile.

'What happened about the home ministry?' Nisar Bapu asked Madhu, appealing to his ego.

'Are they going to give it to me? They say no,' Madhu responded, trying to be modest.

'Who says no? You have served two terms,' Bapu said, continuing to flatter Madhu.

'It's my third term,' Madhu corrected Bapu.

'It is your third term. Why do they say no?'

'They don't even give me the post of the Corporation chairman,' Madhu replied.

'What is this? What is the Godhra incident? Just before the Godhra incident, three Assembly elections were held—one election you won, one the Congress won from Mahua, only Narendra Modi had won. The results came out on the 22nd. The incident took place on the 27th. Today it is in the papers about Zahira—she has a Sumo vehicle. I used to talk to Bathu,' Bapu veered the conversation towards Zahira.

'Bathu used to tell me—'

'Yes, you people got involved with this unnecessarily,' Bapu interrupted Madhu.

'Yes. He used to tell me not to. But she came to my house and cried. None of us had gone to call her,' Madhu said.

'If you have any work related to Zahira, tell me. Anything for me, anything at all,' Bapu said in a sympathetic tone.

'We shouldn't have got into it at all. We have been defamed for no fault of ours, for [helping] a Muslim girl,' Madhu replied.

'How much did you give? You gave around Rs 18 to 20 lakh?' Bapu cut to the chase.

'Rs 18 lakh. Even after getting her 18 lakh, she has been calling me and saying—' Madhu replied.

At this point Bapu cut him off and steered the conversation in another direction. I wanted to jump at Bapu and gag him. But what I managed to catch on camera was a strong enough self-indictment.

I wanted to further strengthen the story, and so requested Bapu to set up a meeting with Bathu. I wanted him to corroborate Madhu's version. Bapu was very cooperative, and after a few phone calls, lined up a meeting with Bathu. But there was a catch—there was every possibility that Bathu would recognise me. So I decided to shave my beard. Bapu found the sudden change in my appearance very amusing, but did not make a big deal of it. At the appointed time, we showed up at Bathu's house.[4]

'Any news of Zahira?' Bapu asked Bathu.

'No,' Bathu replied.

'During the chaos, when Madhu met me, I asked him what would he do about the girl. There has been so much violence in the area. He said, you won't believe it, I have given Rs 18 lakh to this sisterf*****.' Bapu pushed Bathu towards corroborating his brother's self-incriminating confession.

'That is the truth,' Bathu replied, nodding his head.

'Did she get the entire amount or something happened, sisterf*****?' asked Bapu.

'*Poore paise.* [The entire amount],' Bathu said emphatically.

'Then why did she turn out to be utterly useless?' Bapu asked incredulously.

'What should I say. Even I can't understand, sisterf*****. [Takes off his spectacles and places them on the table] It is out of my understanding as well. I have lost my mind, friend. You know what the reality is? I didn't want any of this. The whole family [of Zahira] would keep going to Madhu, time and again, time and again. Do this for us, do this, our bakery will get started again, this will happen. Drove us up the wall. Then finally Madhu took the decision that let us give her the money. First it started from Rs 25 lakh and got stuck at Rs 18 to 20 lakh. Then, after collecting cash from everyone, she was given Rs 18 lakh in cash,' Bathu replied.

'I came to know that the money was given at Shailesh Patel's house, this happened. Two lakh and seventy thousand was given to her, she didn't get the rest of the money, so she raised a ruckus,' Bapu pressed on.

'*Nahin. Nahin. Poore paise.* Complete,' Bathu said.

Now I had corroboration for Madhu's claims from his brother as well.

After Zahira returned to Vadodara, claiming that human rights activists had threatened her, Chief Minister Modi made a curious public remark about the case. He said, 'NGOs have assumed an extra-constitutional authority and their role should be investigated.'

I decided to probe further.

I learnt that Shailesh Patel, the lawyer defending the accused in the case, was in close contact with Madhu and Bathu. Once again, I turned to Bapu, asking him to take me to Patel. I caught Patel on camera suggesting that Zahira was bribed. In response to Bapu's assertion that Zahira did not get the full money promised to her, he said, 'No, no. It has to be at least 10 lakh ... And if she had got only this amount [Rs 2–3 lakh], her mother and two brothers would not have turned hostile.' He may not have been sure how much money had changed hands, but he knew a deal had been struck.

Investigative journalism works the way they say London buses do. Nothing for ages, and then everything comes at once. Having worked for months in drought conditions, I was now in the midst of a deluge. While I was in Vadodara, Bapu's son, Abid Hussain, was released from jail on parole for four days. I caught him on spy cam telling me that Madhu had told him he had bribed Zahira and that, while they were all in prison, Bathu used to meet with the Best Bakery accused.

There was another important link in the chain—Tushar Vyas, the advocate who ran an NGO called Jan Adhikar Samiti. It was a front, floated to pick up the costs of Zahira's press conference and stay in Ahmedabad. I met him in the Vadodara court complex, where he further corroborated that Madhu and Bathu had threatened Zahira.

'In the Best Bakery case, the Muslim witnesses, like Zahira or Nafitullah, know "I have to live in Hanuman Tekri. The 1,000 who were destined to be burnt are gone. But we still have to live here and this kind of an incident should not be repeated,"' Tushar Vyas said, seated behind his desk in the court complex.

'Hostile based on realism?' I asked.

'Realism,' Vyas replied.

'Or compromise,' I asked.

'A compromise. We still have to live in Hanuman Tekri while those who were destined to burn are gone,' said Vyas.

'So this time you feel that whatever stand Zahira Sheikh, she is taking this time, it was based on compromise?'

'It was. It was an understanding that she doesn't want to fight anymore, doesn't want to make much noise. The two wanted to compromise. The local leader calls the two sides. "Don't make a sound. I will tell this side and they won't attack the other; and I will tell the other side and they won't attack the first. Otherwise, I will break your knees."'

'So this is what Madhu did?'

'Exactly, exactly. Honestly, before you even called me, I gave you your answer. The media says, "Madhu did this, Chandrakant Batthoo did that." They played their role. But a role "I will smack you. Stay quiet now, or else I will do this, I will do that." Madhu was also there at the [Zahira's] press conference.'

Zarina Shahu, Zahira's eighty-year-old maternal grandmother, was one of nine survivors from that night of terror at Best Bakery.

Two months after the incident, she returned to her native village of Jhakiya in UP. I travelled there to interview her for the story. She had no idea that her granddaughter's ever-changing testimony had perverted the course of justice. She told me how she was unable to forget the moments leading up to the death of her son Kausar Ali, who had been thrown into the furnace by the mob. Kausar continues to be listed as missing by the police, though his wife Shahjehan later testified that Zahira had told the family that she saw her uncle Kausar being thrown into a furnace. Surprisingly, the police had not listed Zarina as a witness in the Best Bakery case, but her conversation with me established that her granddaughter Zahira had lied.

The Belarusian investigative journalist and winner of the Nobel prize in literature, Svetlana Alexievich, writes in her book *Second-Hand Time*, 'When you're part of a mob, the mob is a monster. A person in a mob is nothing like the person you sit and chat with in the kitchen.' The Zahira Sheikh story was my first peek into the randomness of the communal violence in Gujarat. Those who attacked Zahira and her family included their neighbours, the local grocer, the milkman, people who had daily transactions and interactions and deep social and economic ties to the people they so easily turned against. It only took one incident—far away from Vadodara, in which fifty-nine Hindus on a train died in a fire started by a Muslim mob—for neighbours to turn on each other, for them to kill and maim the people with whom they shared their lives.

Tehelka broke the story in 2004, just before Christmas. The investigation made headlines all over the country. After the story was published, Madhu told the press that he would pump six bullets into my chest. So I decided I had to call him on his cell phone to get his official reaction to my story.

'I'm Ashish Khetan calling from *Tehelka*—the person who visited your house.'

'*Mere ghar aaye the to saamne aana tha na jo mard ke bachche ho to* (If you were the son of a man, you should have identified yourself),' Madhu said.

'But you have threatened to pump six bullets into my chest?'

'I will drag you or any other media organisation to the court. I challenge you to prove that you have seen me paying money or doing any other thing.'

'Are you not worried that if the CBI probes the case, you could be in trouble because, if there is a CBI investigation, then all the money transactions will come out in the open?' I asked him.

'Why only the CBI, what is that agency abroad called? Tell them also to investigate. What is that agency called?'

'FBI [the US Federal Bureau of Investigation],' I filled in.

'Yes, FBI. Then you will come to know who is in trouble. I don't fear anyone except God.'

'Didn't you open celebratory fire after Zahira's press conference in Vadodara's Hotel Surya Palace on November 3rd?'

'You journalists asked if it was an authentic weapon, how to fire it, so I fired in an open field. Where is the question of another motive? It was a licenced revolver. You people operate underground and malign people, now you should come out in the open,' Madhu answered.

For Madhu, 'mardangi' (masculinity) meant threatening and silencing a young Muslim girl, barely out of adolescence, who had lost most of her family in a communal massacre. But that's what Hindu nationalists have been propagating for decades: that, for too long, Hindus have been docile and timid, that they need to prove their masculinity.

My telephonic interview with Madhu was published in *Tehelka* shortly after the new year. In the wake of our revelations from Gujarat, the Supreme Court set up an inquiry and drafted the Delhi police to aid the committee. The Central Forensic Science Laboratory (CFSL) authenticated the tapes I had recorded using the spy cam. CFSL also certified that the voice of Tushar Vyas and

Shailesh Patel recorded in the tapes matched the voice samples that the CBI had provided. Madhu and Bathu refused to give their voice samples to the CBI. All four—Bathu, Madhu, Vyas and Patel—claimed before the registrar-general that the tapes were doctored.

On 18 June 2005, I testified before the Supreme Court registrar-general, B.M. Gupta. The advocates representing Madhu, Bathu and Zahira cross-examined me, trying to prove, unsuccessfully, that my story was a lie, that I was anti-Hindu, that my story was an attempt to malign Gujarat. After the cross-examination was over, Gupta called me a 'man of truth' in open court. It was a profoundly gratifying moment.

In his report,[5] Gupta concluded that Zahira and her family were induced to turn hostile, and indicted Madhu and his brother Bathu for influencing Zahira. Based on the sting operation tapes, the report concluded that that there appeared to be a high probability that money had changed hands, and that it was this bribe that induced Zahira to change her story before the trial court in Vadodara, thus aiding the accused. And so the tortuous courtroom process began again.

24 February 2006: A Mumbai sessions court convicted and awarded life imprisonment to nine accused persons. Sessions Judge Abhay Thipsay indicted the defence lawyers of the accused for colluding with the witnesses who turned hostile during the retrial in Mumbai. The judge also noted that Zahira appeared to have been given 'monetary inducements'.[6]

12 July 2012: The Bombay High Court acquitted five of the nine convicts, upholding the life sentences awarded to the other four by the Mumbai sessions court six years previously.

However, by July 2012, the direction of the political winds had shifted decisively towards the BJP. The UPA alliance, though formally in power, had lost both prestige and legitimacy. The Bombay High Court expunged remarks made by the sessions court against the defence lawyers. Madhu and Bathu were never officially charged for subverting the course of justice. On the other hand, Zahira—

who no doubt had acted unconscionably but who was nonetheless a powerless victim, susceptible to the threats and monetary inducements of the powerful—was convicted and sentenced to prison for one year on charges of contempt of the Supreme Court and to three months for perjury by the Mumbai sessions court. She spent a year in Byculla jail (the two sentences ran concurrently) before she was released.

Teesta Setalvad, who fought the longest and hardest to get justice for the victims of Best Bakery and other Gujarat riots cases, is now facing criminal investigations in six separate FIRs (first information reports) registered by the Gujarat police. The police had originally registered nine cases against Teesta, on charges ranging from the embezzlement of funds to tutoring witnesses, filing false affidavits and, most ironically, publishing inflammatory tweets that could sow communal discord. Three of the cases were quashed, and the Bombay High Court and the Supreme Court have granted her anticipatory bail, otherwise she too would now be languishing in prison, like so many other human rights activists under the current dispensation.[7]

Madhu, legal entanglements notwithstanding, went on to win three consecutive assembly elections (2007, 2012, 2017) on a BJP ticket. He has also produced several C-grade Gujarati movies, giving himself starring roles as, variously, a police officer, a social reformer and a government minister. Neither Madhu nor his brother Bathu were ever charged with the offence of bribing a prosecution witness.

Bapu passed away a few years later. Before his death, he appeared before the Supreme Court and corroborated my findings and the story I wrote for *Tehelka*. I regret not meeting him again before his death.

In 2014, I went to Varanasi to observe the high-octane election campaign of Narendra Modi, who was expected to become prime minister and wanted to make a symbolic statement by contesting from the city of Gangamata, which writer Sunil Khilnani once described as 'Hinduism's Brahminopolis'. Before flying out of the city, Modi's cavalcade paid a visit to the local BJP office. A multitude of ecstatic supporters were waiting outside. 'Har har Modi, ghar ghar Modi,' they chanted. Both the men and the women around me were hysterical, like 1960s teenagers come face-to-face with the Beatles. My eyes fell on a mustachioed man standing just a few feet away. He had a BJP stole around his neck. He turned his head towards me. In that moment, as our eyes met, he looked quizzical, like he knew my face but could not quite place me. Luckily, I could place him—Madhu Shrivastav. Before he worked it out, I melted away into the crowd.

3
The Ten-foot-tall Officer

Somewhere there are still peoples and herds, but not with us, my brethren: here there are states.
A state? What is that? Well! Open now your ears unto me, for now will I say unto you my word concerning the death of peoples.
A state, is called the coldest of all cold monsters. Coldly lieth it also; and this lie creepeth from its mouth: 'I, the state, am the people.'
It is a lie! Creators were they who created peoples, and hung a faith and a love over them: thus they served life.
Destroyers, are they who lay snares for many, and call it the state: they hang a sword and a hundred cravings over them.
Where there is still a people, there the state is not understood, but hated as the evil eye, and as sin against laws and customs.
This sign I give unto you: every people speaketh its language of good and evil: this its neighbour understandeth not. Its language hath it devised for itself in laws and customs."

— Friedrich Nietzsche, 'Of the New Idol',
Thus Spake Zarathustra

In 2005, I pursued a story on the attempted assassination of Syed Abdul Rahman Geelani, an Arabic teacher at Delhi University who was convicted by a special court for his supposed role in the 2001 terror attack on the Indian parliament, but later acquitted by the Delhi High Court. In the court of public opinion, though, and in the view of the Indian intelligence apparatus, Geelani was still guilty as charged. On 8 February that year, some fifteen months after his conviction was overturned, a gunman on a motorcycle shot Geelani five times outside his lawyer's residence and fled. The bullets struck Geelani in his abdomen and shoulder, but he survived.

I got a lead from a source in the Intelligence Bureau (IB). He said that Indian agents who were ideologically aligned with right-wing organisations had hired criminals to murder Geelani. He suspected that his colleagues had contracted the hit to members of the Chhota Rajan gang.

Following the tip, I travelled to the jails of western UP, posing as a member of a Mumbai gang. I met members of the Chhota Rajan gang in the Etawah district jail, hoping the bluster that had worked on Bathu Shrivastava in Vadodara would come to my aid again. On reaching the jail, I found that the gangsters, who enjoyed privileges that set them apart from the other inmates, were very accessible. I had gone to meet Firoz Tayyab Tanasha and Satish Kalia, lead shooters in the Rajan gang, who were serving time for a hit they had carried out in the region. The police had had a stroke of luck when the vehicle in which the assassins were making their getaway turned turtle.

Given the frisking to which visitors were subjected by prison officials, I did not bother to take my trusty Rexine bag. I was ushered into a courtyard where I met Tanasha and Kalia. I told them that their boss had sent me with a message: very soon, he would bail them out and they should lie low in the interim. Both Tanasha and Kalia would occasionally speak to Rajan from the jail, but, they told me, they hadn't spoken to him in the last six months. They asked when I had joined the gang and where I lived. I told them I was from UP, but had moved to Mumbai. During the hour-long conversation, I slipped in the subject of Geelani's attempted murder. Tanasha said that they had worked for Indian intelligence agencies in the past and carried out a few 'jobs' for them, but they did not know about this episode.

He told me that he would find out from his sources if anyone had information on Geelani. Tanasha gave me a number on which I could call him after a few weeks. I did, but nobody answered. I went to Mumbai to meet my sources in the police, to see if they had any information. The leads soon ran dry and I gave up on the story.

Seven years later, a Hindu radical, let's call him RP, was arrested on charges of plotting terror attacks targeted against the Muslim community. During interrogation, he confessed to shooting Geelani. While RP was charged with carrying out bomb blasts and later acquitted, he was never charged with the attempted murder of Geelani. His confession was buried in a government file (of which I have a copy). For RP, Geelani was a traitor. Killing him would have been a patriotic act. Why, though, was he being protected from facing the consequences of his actions? I suspected, but could not prove, that the authorities were actually protecting those much higher up in the food chain, who had put a contract out on Geelani.

By mid-2005, after more than a year of ceaseless, often nerve-wracking work, I was exhausted. I left *Tehelka* and joined a daily newspaper in Mumbai in order to settle down and cover a beat diligently, rather than chasing after scraps and tips in the hope of transforming them into sensational exposés. I was convinced that I would be improved and enriched as a journalist by returning to the nuts and bolts of newspaper reporting and getting used to the rhythm of the daily deadline once again. When you report for a newspaper, you cannot afford to miss an important story or development in your beat. There is an urgency to your work, which is subject to daily scrutiny by both your editors and your peers. And while the news of the day has to be covered and covered well, you are also expected to steal a march over rival newspapers by picking up exclusive nuggets of information. I thought Mumbai, with its film stars, businessmen, gangsters and celebrity cops, would be a fascinating place to work as a reporter.

I left the magazine for the about-to-be-launched *Mumbai Mirror*. I borrowed money from a friend and boarded a train for the city that never sleeps. On my first day, I had alighted at Victoria Terminus, and was walking towards my office when the sole of my right shoe came apart, flapping loose like a tired puppy's lolling tongue. I stopped at one of the many cobblers lined up opposite the station and had my shoe repaired for an outlay of fifty bucks. It seemed like a sign, as if the city was only too happy to oblige. Saadat Hasan Manto once wrote of Bombay that you could 'be happy here on two pennies a day or on ten thousand rupees a day, if you wish'.

A few weeks after I started at the *Mumbai Mirror*, Ajit Doval, the retired IB director (now Prime Minister Modi's all-powerful National Security Advisor), was found in Delhi in the company of shooters from the Rajan gang.[1] A special team from the Mumbai Crime Branch had travelled to Delhi to ambush the shooters—Vicky Malhotra and Fareed Tanasha—when they made this embarrassing discovery. Doval was with the shooters in a vehicle that the police had stopped. Malhotra and Tanasha were arrested, and Doval's presence in the car was hushed up. My source in the Mumbai police tipped me off. My editor asked me to get a response from Doval. When I called him, he said that, since I am a journalist, my journalism should be guided by patriotism. When we splashed the story on the front page, for all of Mumbai to see, we made sure to include his comment.

Over the next eighteen months, I reported on the Mumbai floods, the 2006 Mumbai train blasts, the murder of politician Pramod Mahajan, the unspoken agreements between 'encounter specialists' in the Mumbai police and the city's builders, and the underworld empire of a gangster called Bhai Thakur in the Vasai Virar region, known as the 'third Mumbai'. A handful of times, I even slipped back into the habits and reflexes of an undercover reporter, wearing a spy cam as I walked the bylanes of Pydhonie, Kalbadevi, Zaveri Bazaar and Bhuleshwar, the nerve-centre of the country's hawala trade. I came back with grainy images of illegal transactions, bundles and bundles of cash, and hawala traders busy dispensing crores.

Once, posing as a potential customer for an apartment, I stung an assistant commissioner of police (ACP) who was developing three prime real-estate projects in the city. The price of a single square foot in one of these 1,000-square-foot units was equivalent to a month's salary for the average policeman. We carried the story on the front page, exposing the corrupt connections between the police and the builders. Still, compared to the risks I took while working at *Tehelka*, the story was a walk in the park. There was no danger of getting bumped off if my cover was blown. I just walked into his office, in an under-construction building in South Mumbai and asked about the flats and the prices. As the spy cam recorded our conversation, the ACP told me about the property and the rates, like any other builder or real-estate salesman, and then I took the bus back to office. After the story was published, the ACP showed up at the *Mumbai Mirror* offices. He met the editor, made some lame excuse about his involvement in the construction projects, and then he walked into my cubicle with a box of chocolates. I politely refused. He made some small talk, and as he was about to leave, he whispered in my ears: 'Do let me know if you want a flat in Mumbai.' I was surprised, I had not expected him to be this brazen. I told him I did not think I needed one, and the ACP winked, smiled and left.

In December 2006, I went back to *Tehelka*. The hunger was back; I wanted to be reporting on national issues for an India-wide audience.

Over the next few months, I undertook two major investigations: one focused on the extent of movie star Sanjay Dutt's involvement in the serial bombings that shook Mumbai on 12 March 1993; the other exposed the disproportionate wealth amassed by the then Maharashtra director general of police (DGP) P.S. Pasricha. Both stories were discussed and followed up by television news channels. And there were bigger stories to come.

In March 2007, the Gujarat police made national headlines for killing Muslims in staged encounters. The word 'encounter' is a frankly offensive euphemism for extra-judicial killings in which the police stage a supposed gun battle in order to eliminate criminals who, for whatever reason, they have deemed do not deserve their day in court. Everybody, from the courts to the public, knows that the police orchestrate these supposed shootouts. Indeed, so cynical has the whole exercise become that the police hardly bother to conceal their intentions. The encounters have become increasingly laughable as cars carrying criminals inevitably turn over, unlike every other car in the convoy, and the unhurt target of the encounter just as inevitably slips off his handcuffs and snatches a policeman's gun, forcing the other officers to open fire.

In the mid-1990s, when an internecine gang war spilt onto the streets of Mumbai, with ordinary, innocent people caught in the crossfire, the Shiv Sena–BJP government gave the police a free hand to eliminate shooters. A bullet for a bullet was the new unstated police policy. 'Our message to the bhais sitting in Bangkok and Karachi was, "you make one call to extort money and we will gun down one of your shooters",' a police officer with over a hundred encounters to his credit told me.

In Gujarat, though, the purpose of police encounters was not to tame criminal gangs but to enhance Chief Minister Modi's image as a tough Hindu nationalist with zero tolerance for alleged Muslim extremists. A select squad of Gujarat police officers carried out most of these encounters. Sameer Khan, Sadiq Jamal, Javed Ghulam Sheikh, Amjad Ali Rana, Zeeshan Johar, Sohrabuddin Sheikh—the list of Muslims killed by the police under CM Modi's watch ran long. Two of these cases, in particular, caused outrage outside Gujarat. In 2005, a few days after the police killed Sohrabuddin, they raped and throttled his wife Kausar Bi before setting her corpse on fire to dispose of the evidence.[2] The year before, a Gujarat police team shot dead four alleged terrorists, including the nineteen-year-old Ishrat Jahan, a college student from Mumbai with no past criminal history.

Relatives of both Sohrabuddin and Ishrat Jahan demanded court-monitored independent investigations into their deaths. Under the scrutiny of the Supreme Court, a Gujarat Indian Police Service (IPS) officer, Rajnish Rai, arrested three senior fellow IPS officers, including Vanzara, on charges of conspiracy. I travelled to Gujarat along with Harinder Baweja. Together we wrote a cover story about how Sohrabuddin, a criminal and gangster, and his wife were killed by the police in cold blood and how the state government attempted a cover-up. A CBI investigation would later allege that some Gujarat cops had used Sohrabuddin to extort money and, when he became a liability, plotted to pass him off as a terrorist in order to shoot him dead. Three years earlier, in 2002, another petty Muslim criminal, Sameer Khan, a thief and chain-snatcher, had been gunned down in a late-night encounter, the official excuse being that he had joined Jaish-e-Mohammed and was plotting to kill the chief minister.

Once a person was labelled a terrorist and killed in a police encounter, the accusation would never have to be proven in a court of law. The TV news networks loved stories about 'terrorists'. 'Three Pak-trained terrorists killed,' screeched one headline. 'LeT Plot to Target Modi Busted,' screamed another. The public lapped it up, applauding their chief minister for being decisive in eliminating the threat. On each occasion that the Gujarat police encountered a Muslim, a plot to assassinate Modi was revealed. The police always managed to intercept the terrorists on the Gujarat border before shooting them down in a gunfight without suffering any injuries, casualties, or even the most minor of flesh wounds in return. Modi may have been the chief minister, but he was also 'Dirty Harry', dispensing instant justice on the mean, terrorist-strewn streets of Gujarat. Sameer Khan's father, Sarfaraz, distraught and broken, called *Tehelka*. 'My son was not a terrorist,' he cried over the phone. 'He had nothing to with Pakistan or Jaish-e-Mohammed. I admit he had taken to petty crime. But he deserved another chance to make amends in life. Why did they kill him? For what?'

Sameer's was the first in a series of encounter killings of 'terrorists' in Gujarat. Nine more 'terrorists' were eliminated by D.G. Vanzara-led policemen over the next four years. If Kausar Bi and Tulsiram Prajapati, Sohrabuddin's friend, were added to the list, the tally was eleven.

On the eve of the 2002 assembly elections, when Modi was touring the state in a motorised chariot on his 'Gaurav Yatra', he targeted the Muslim community in speech after speech. He described the post-riot relief camps as 'baby-producing factories'.[3] Playing to the popular prejudice that Muslims have more children than Hindus—only partly rooted in fact, since the Hindu numerical advantage over Muslims has grown and the Muslim fertility rate is declining—Modi would say jokingly to the crowds, 'hum paanch hamaare pachchees', a joke that also referenced Muslim polygamy. Such casual cultural prejudice helped boost and underline the more serious claims that Muslims represented a security threat which Modi alone could combat; he had the requisite experience after all, having fought off so many assassination attempts.

At any rate, the police encounters certainly bolstered Modi's argument. Sameer was picked up on 27 September 2002, and killed the following month. The Gujarat assembly had been dissolved in July, nine months ahead of its term, on the recommendation of the state council of ministers. Modi continued as caretaker chief minister, and elections were slated for December. Sameer's killing gave Modi yet more campaign fodder. He was a target, he said, for 'jihadis' because he was protecting 'the pride of Gujarat'. The more Gujarat police eliminated 'terrorist threats', the more Modi's popularity surged. Newspapers, activists and liberals may have cried foul, but Modi had plenty of popular support for his actions. In December 2002, he returned as chief minister with a two-thirds majority.

The questions before me as a journalist were: had Sameer really been a terrorist? And if not, who gave the trigger-happy cops the licence to kill with such impunity?

I took my spy cam and flew down to Ahmedabad.

D.G. Vanzara, who was then deputy commissioner of police (DCP), crime, said that his squad had arrested Sameer from outside the ST bus stand on the afternoon of 27 September. For the next four days, however, the police kept him in unlawful custody, violating the right of an accused to be produced in court within twenty-four hours of arrest. On the night of 30 September, the Crime Branch finally recorded Sameer as arrested under a newly registered FIR. It was in this new FIR that Sameer was implicated in a plot to assassinate Modi, PravinTogadia and L.K. Advani, arguably the holy trinity of Hindutva.

The police also claimed to have recovered some e-mails received by Sameer from Pakistan with instructions on how to execute the plot. They added in a press release that there were seven criminal cases pending against Sameer but gave no details about these previous charges. I dug into the court archives and found that the police were lying, that the only case registered against him was his alleged involvement in the murder of a constable in 1996, since when he had supposedly been absconding. After fourteen days in police remand, Sameer was sent to judicial custody. On 21 October, the Crime Branch moved an application for a transfer warrant in court so that they could interrogate Sameer about the murder of the constable. Late that night, at about 1.30 a.m., Crime Branch detectives took Sameer to Ahmedabad's Usmanpura Garden, where they claimed Sameer had knifed the constable nearly six years previously. They apparently wanted to recreate the crime scene, and since Sameer was also a 'dreaded terrorist', they had to take him there in the dead of the night. According to police records, twenty-two policemen escorted Sameer to the park.

Once there, police said, Sameer snatched the loaded revolver of Inspector K.M. Vaghela from the holster tied loosely around his waist and fired two rounds at him and tried to run away. Inspector Vaghela ducked in time to avoid the bullets, and before Sameer could fire again, Inspectors Tarun Barot and A.A. Chauhan fired, hitting him in the head and chest. Sameer was rushed to the hospital but was declared dead on arrival. This was the archetypal encounter, a template for future extra-judicial killings, in which the Muslim terrorists were to snatch revolvers away from the police but never to actually shoot an officer, while the massed ranks of the police could never overpower the assailant but only shoot to kill.

I managed to locate a copy of forensic expert Dr Kiran Pansuria's statement. It confirmed that the police had pumped three bullets into Sameer—one in the head and two on either side of his ribs. The police had said that Sameer snatched Inspector Vaghela's revolver and fired off a shot before fleeing for his life, but the trajectory of the bullet suggested he had been shot in the head from above. How, if he was running?

The then Ahmedabad Police Commissioner Chitranjan Singh was not convinced by the Crime Branch's explanation. He wrote to P.P. Pandey, the joint commissioner of police (JCP), and asked for an independent inquiry into the encounter. A copy of the letter, numbered 3788/02, was sent to the then DGP for Gujarat. I got hold of Singh's letters. He asked some tough questions:

- What were the seven other cases pending against him?
- Why was Inspector K.M. Vaghela not wearing the service revolver belt? Why were Sameer's hands not cuffed?
- If the intention was to recreate the crime scene, then why had the police not taken two independent witnesses as mandated legally?

I got to know from my sources that inspector general of police (IGP), Human Rights, Tirth Raj, had conducted an inquiry into the killing of Sameer Khan and submitted in a report that it was a staged encounter. I tried to access the report through normal journalistic methods and channels but came up against a brick wall. I then went to Raj's office in the guise of Sameer's cousin. I requested his father Sarfaraz to come along to lend me credibility.

I had been provided with a better spy cam than during my early efforts at *Tehelka*. I clipped the button camera on and found it easy to get Tirth Raj talking.[4]

> Raj: 'Now you read the post-mortem memo then only you will be able to understand the entire case. That bullet was sustained here (he pointed to his temple) ... so either you shot him from some high position or he was lying down but the police said he was shot when he was running.'
>
> Me (as Sameer's cousin, SC from now): 'Sir, was this conspiracy hatched right at the top?'
>
> Raj: 'Yes, the CM office is directly involved. *Kuch tape wape to nahi kar rahey ho?* (Hope you are not taping this conversation?)'
>
> SC: 'No way, sir, you can frisk me if you want.'
>
> Raj: 'The papers were replaced by the Commissioner of Police. He was called into the CM office. They were told that "Vanzara and his men have done this encounter in the national interest." Vanzara and his officers were doing *deshbhakti ke kaam* and they needed to be protected.'

Tirth Raj then went on to explain how a senior bureaucrat in the chief minister's office (CMO), in collusion with two senior police officers had fabricated documents and hushed up the matter. He claimed that he knew the entire cover-up backwards because he had conducted the inquiry into the encounter: 'There was one X in the Chief Minister's Office, who called up the commissioner and pressured him to burn the papers he had written and replace them with fake ones. Everybody was involved in the cover-up from the DGP's office to the CMO.'

According to Raj, a junior officer in the commissioner's office, named Satish Verma (who would later investigate the Ishrat Jahan encounter and recover tapes carrying Amit Shah's instructions to the police to spy on a young woman) refused to burn the originals and insisted that both the originals and the fakes be kept on file.

It is a procedural requirement under Indian law to commission an executive inquiry in any case of custodial death. To comply with this formality, the investigation into the encounter was handed over to the Criminal Investigation Department's (CID's) Crime Branch.

I.K. Yadav, deputy superintendent of police (DSP), was made the investigating officer. DSP Yadav started asking for relevant documents and files, like the vehicle movement register and the attendance register, which could show where the police van carrying Sameer went before they reached Usmanpura, and how many police personnel had accompanied him. He also started recording the statements of the policemen, Sameer's family members and the doctors who performed the autopsy. Perhaps because he was too conscientious about this routine inquiry, Yadav was removed from the investigation and replaced by a less scrupulous officer.

In the course of the inquiry, Tirth Raj stumbled upon Singh's original set of letters addressed to JCP Pandey and kept them along with the trumped-up papers sent to DCP Vanzara's office. Both sets of papers carried the same dispatch number. Tirth Raj claimed he made a twenty-page report indicting everybody who had covered for Vanzara and his men, from the CMO to the DGP to JCP Pandey. He also indicted Vanzara for the murder of Sameer. But the report never saw the light of day.

When Yadav was removed from his post, the inquiry was handed over to H.K. Sharma. Tirth Raj said the volte-face began 'after Sharma took over ... he made the final report giving a clean chit to Vanzara and others ... he prepared the report sitting in Vanzara's office, something which he has mentioned in his case diary ... If the Supreme Court summons his case diary, the entire cover-up will be exposed.'

'Should we take the help of some NGO to approach the Supreme Court?' I asked, still in character.

'Again Muslims will be crushed for another five years. You will again be killed, and if not you, then some of your brothers. You should approach the Supreme Court independently.'

'Sir, if the matter gets admitted in the Supreme Court, will you tell the truth?'

'I will ask the SC to summon the file from the DG's office, the case diary of the original investigating officer Yadav and then how there was a U-turn under the new investigating officer, everything will become clear.'

'Sir, why did they kill my brother?'

'To create propaganda that Muslim extremists are trying to kill Modi and look how we have eliminated the Muslim goons. Modi gets publicity and Muslims get projected as anti-nationals,' said Tirth.

I left Tirth's office knowing I had what I needed for the story. I decided to track down DSP Yadav. He did not answer my calls, so I left a message, again pretending to be Sameer's cousin and saying I wanted to meet with him. No response. I called a source in the Mumbai Crime Branch. 'I need a favour,' I said to him. 'Please note down a mobile number. I want its current location.' Within two hours, the inspector gave me the location of Yadav's number. It was in a middle-class neighbourhood in Surat. Once again, I requested Sameer's father to accompany me and set off on the six-hour drive from Ahmedabad.

After reaching the area, I knocked on various doors, asking for DSP Yadav, until finally I got the right house. But he was not home. I left a message, and at nine that evening, Yadav called: 'Meet me outside the gates of the police station.' I wanted to record my conversation with him. But there was not enough light where we were, so I persuaded Yadav to move closer to the streetlight. What he said was deeply disturbing.

'Either the man who fired at Sameer was ten feet tall,' he began, 'or Sameer was made to kneel on the ground and then the shot was fired. The point where the bullet entered the temple was rendered black and there were some gunpowder traces, indicating that the bullet was fired from close range. Two bullets also hit Sameer on his chest—on the sixth rib on the left and seventh rib on the right.' Sameer was shot from point-blank range, Yadav argued, because the 'part of the shirt where the bullets entered from was burnt'. He said Crime Branch officers had warned him off. *'Laash gira doonga'* (I'll kill you), Yadav said a 'senior Crime Branch officer' threatened him. Just standing there under that streetlight with me, I realised, could cost this conscience-stricken officer his life.

For every Vanzara, there was also a Yadav in the Gujarat police. But the state empowered the Vanzaras and hounded the Yadavs.

Sameer came from a poor family in Jamalpur, a Muslim ghetto in Ahmedabad. His father Sarfaraz was a bus driver with the Ahmedabad Municipal Corporation-run transport service. The eldest of five siblings—two brothers and three sisters—Sameer had a Class VII education. After dropping out of school, he tried his hand at being a tailor, running a paan shop and driving trucks. In 1996, the Ahmedabad police accused Sameer and his cousin Shahista Khan of killing a constable in Usmanpura Garden while he was trying to stop them from snatching a woman's gold chain. Shahista Khan was sentenced to life imprisonment but Sameer absconded, living and working in Rajasthan and Madhya Pradesh for the next six years, until he was arrested in Gujarat in September 2002. The police took out their anger at Sameer's disappearance on Sarfaraz, torturing him so brutally that he is still an invalid. Sarfaraz also lost his government job. When I met him, he was frail, old and living in abject poverty with his ailing wife in a single room by a steaming, stinking drain.

The FIR registered on the night of 30 September 2002 against Sameer Khan reads more like a political speech than a police document. The first few pages were taken up by a disquisition on the embittered history of India and Pakistan. Slowly coming to the point, the FIR claims that 'CM Narendrabhai Modi, VHP leader Praveenbhai Togadia, DPM Advaniji, Hindu institutions and saints of Gujarat face the gravest risk'. It then takes a detour to discuss terrorist attacks on the Red Fort, parliament, the American Center in Calcutta and the Akshardham temple in Gujarat. Alighting on Godhra train-burning and the subsequent pogrom, the FIR observes: 'Anti-national elements orchestrated a massacre on the Sabarmati Express train at Godhra and, in retaliation, all of Gujarat rose up in arms.' Almost every Gujarat police FIR registered in an encounter case followed this template.

Eventually, the FIR gets around to Sameer, claiming, 'Ahmedabad Police Commissioner had received an intelligence tip-off that a JeM trained terrorist, who is also an accused in a constable murder case was headed towards Gujarat from Mumbai.' Vanzara was asked to investigate whether Sameer had participated in the 24 September attack on the Akshardham temple in Gandhinagar. On 27 September, the FIR concluded, Vanzara and his team spotted Sameer 'near a State Transport bus stand and nabbed him'.

This trained terrorist, on a mission to kill Modi, among others, and who might have taken part in an attack on a temple just days earlier, was conveniently loitering alone by a bus stand, where a lone police constable was able to spot him and arrest him without backup and transport him to the station in an autorickshaw. Sameer put up no resistance and no weapons were recovered. The rest of the FIR is based on Sameer's confession extracted by the police. It is a long-winded story about how, after fleeing Ahmedabad in 1996, he spent a few years in Madhya Pradesh and Rajasthan before escaping to Pakistan.

This convoluted fiction was demolished in the lower court and its ruling was endorsed in a scathing judgement delivered by the Gujarat High Court.

The Gujarat police roped in twelve co-accused in the case against Sameer. The case was tried posthumously, since Sameer had already been encountered. This dirty dozen were also accused of waging war against the state. The lower court was so disbelieving of the police story that it refused to frame charges and dismissed the case. But the government was bent on proving that Sameer and his hapless co-accused were terrorists. It appealed before the Gujarat High Court, which observed: '... there is no evidence that

Sameer Khan went to Pakistan on January 13, 1998, as alleged by the investigating officer, and so an adverse inference is required to be drawn against the investigating agency ... It clearly transpires that accused Sameer Khan (Nawab Khan) did not go to Pakistan for terrorist activities in January 1998 ...'

The court also dismissed the agency's claim of e-mailed instructions. It said, 'There is ample evidence to say that the alleged e-mails are false and were created by the investigative agency to support their false version and support the murder of Sameer Khan ... If there was a conspiracy to kill the present chief minister of Gujarat, then why the prosecution or the investigating agency has not produced Sameer Khan before the magistrate for recording his statement under Section 164?'

The secretly recorded admissions of the Gujarat police officers, Tirth Raj and I.K. Yadav, were played on TV news across the country. Bollywood lyricist Javed Akhtar filed a public interest litigation (PIL) in the Supreme Court on the basis of *Tehelka*'s reporting, praying that the court may sanction and monitor an independent investigation into the facts as revealed in the story. To forestall any such Supreme Court-led process, on 2 April 2011, the Modi administration set up its own SIT and a monitoring committee to look into the allegations contained in the PIL. After the Supreme Court passed a detailed order enumerating how the monitoring committee would function, including submitting a status report to the top court, the retired Supreme Court judge M.B. Shah, whom the Gujarat government appointed as head of the monitoring committee, resigned his post. The Modi government again tried to appoint a judge of its choice, a retired chief justice of the Bombay High Court, K.R. Vyas, just a day before the matter was to come up for hearing before the Supreme Court. But the top court, in an order dated 24 February 2012, blocked the move and instead brought in the retired Supreme Court judge H.S. Bedi to head the committee.

On 26 February 2018, almost six years after the SIT was set up, H.S. Bedi submitted his report. He noted that though the police claimed that Sameer was a dreaded terrorist, he had not been properly handcuffed when he was taken to the site of his previous crime. After analysing the post-mortem report and the statements of forensic experts, Bedi concluded that the police were likely lying that they shot Sameer as he was running away: 'the injuries found on the dead body could not have been caused from a distance of 5 to 6 feet, but had been caused from a closer, almost point blank range. Also the bullet had gone through the head and travelled downwards, it would mean that the police officer was standing not only very near but above the deceased. It is obvious that the police officers were towering over the deceased and he was probably sitting on the ground and perhaps begging for his life.' And, the retired judge noted, when DSP Yadav tried to investigate further, he was admonished by Vanzara. Vanzara also wrote Yadav a letter, ridiculing him and asking him to update his knowledge of the law.

At first, Tirth Raj refused to depose before Bedi. When Bedi insisted, Raj filed an affidavit denying that he had conducted any inquiry into the Sameer Khan case, despite claiming that he had in the video footage I had recorded. 'I submit,' he now swore, 'that the assertions/observations attributed to me on the basis of the *Tehelka* sting operation were my personal views, opinions and misgivings. I had made off the cuff remarks in empathising with the father of the deceased and the brother (who turned out to be an undercover reporter).' Bedi refused to allow Raj to 'simply pass off the recording as showing empathy for an aggrieved father'. The judge said he had seen 'the recording twice over, and the conviction and the confidence with which he spoke confirms my suspicion that there was something drastically amiss in the death and investigation in Sameer Khan's case. I therefore use the information contained in the recording to further support my conclusion that the killing was a fake encounter.' Bedi recommended that the Gujarat police officers who participated in the encounter be tried for murder.[5]

Till date, no case has been registered against any Gujarat police officer for Sameer's murder. Sarfaraz Khan can barely walk now and is mostly confined to his small home. Justice Bedi had recommended that the Gujarat government pay Sarfaraz a compensation of Rs 10 lakh. But the government is contesting the report and has not paid up yet. Vanzara, who was charged for his role in various high-profile encounters and has spent a number of years in judicial custody, has been acquitted of all charges. Meanwhile, the senior bureaucrat in Gujarat CMO, whom Tirth had named, is now a senior bureaucrat in the prime minister's office (PMO), and is arguably the most powerful bureaucrat in the country.

4

Painting with Fire

In July 1937, four years after it came to power, the Nazi party put on two art exhibitions in Munich. The Great German Art Exhibition was designed to show works that Hitler approved of—depicting statuesque blonde nudes along with idealised soldiers and landscapes. The second exhibition, just down the road, showed the other side of German art—modern, abstract, non-representational—or as the Nazis saw it, 'degenerate'. [...]

The [degenerate] art was divided into different rooms by category—art that was blasphemous, art by Jewish or communist artists, art that criticised German soldiers, art that offended the honour of German women. One room featured entirely abstract paintings, and was labelled 'the insanity room'. 'In the paintings and drawings of this chamber of horrors there is no telling what was in the sick brains of those who wielded the brush or the pencil,' reads the entry in the exhibition handbook.

— Lucy Burns, 'Degenerate Art: Why Hitler Hated Modernism', BBC World Service

2 February 2018: Srilamanthula Chandramohan, thirty-seven, lean and tall, dressed in a tee-shirt and jeans, reached the office of the vice chancellor (VC) of Maharaja Sayajirao University (MSU) in Vadodara between 3 and 4 p.m. He was carrying a bottle of petrol, a toy gun and a matchbox in a bag slung over one shoulder.

Chandramohan ran a small arts studio in the Chhani area of Vadodara and specialised in woodcuts and printmaking. He mainly drew naked bodies, an expression of ordinary human vulnerability and defencelessness.

But on this day, he had other plans.

Two days earlier, he had waited for four hours outside the office of the registrar on the second floor. 'I wanted to make one last attempt before taking drastic measures,' Chandramohan told me later. 'When I finally did manage to meet the registrar, he mocked me for trying to get my degree. He said, of what use would a degree be after eleven years.' The registrar then directed Chandramohan to his clerk, who in turn instructed him to write an application which the university would consider in due course. This was the stock response he had been getting for the past eleven years. He had already written thirty-four applications to university authorities in those years. He had also filed a petition in the Gujarat High Court, but stopped pursuing it when the process became too expensive. Chandramohan's patience was running thin; he was done with petitioning, writing applications in triplicate and waiting for an official response.

On 2 February, he had come prepared. He walked into the office on the ground floor and told the clerk that he wanted to meet the VC. This clerk, like the one upstairs at the registrar's office, pushed some blank papers towards Chandramohan and told him to go outside and write an application, which he would then submit to the VC.

At that point, with great care and deliberation, Chandramohan took the bottle of petrol out of his bag, emptied it over the furniture in the lobby of the VC's office and struck a match. As he set the office on fire, he shouted at the clerk to run. Within minutes, the fire spread to the whole administrative block, engulfing the building in flames and smoke. No one was hurt, but the VC's office was reduced to a blackened shell.[1]

Chandramohan explained his act of arson as a piece of performance art—the protest of a man pushed over the cliff-edge by the system. He was not being facetious.

•••

Thirteen years earlier, Chandramohan had travelled to Vadodara from Madanapalle, a small village in Mulugu district, Telangana, to join the Faculty of Fine Arts at MSU as a postgraduate student in the graphics department. He was twenty-four years old and had, just a few months ago, earned a first-class degree at the Jawaharlal Nehru Technological University (JNTU) of Hyderabad. He was the first person from his village to attend university.

Chandramohan's family belonged to the backward Vadrangi caste of carpenters. His father was a carpenter, so were his two elder brothers. Their monthly income was just Rs 1,500 and they were always pressed for money. Growing up, Chandramohan saw his father carving intricate details onto wooden furniture, and was inspired to use wood as a natural material of self-expression. He started doing carpentry work alongside his father, but his academic abilities and potential were evident to all who knew him. In 1999, he passed his Class XII exams with over 80 per cent marks from the Intermediate Government College in Mulugu and wrote an entrance test to gain admission to JNTU (he was ranked ninth in the state-wide exam). The annual fee was Rs 600 for OBCs, so Chandramohan's family could afford to send him to the university. At JNTU, he excelled at working with paint on paper and canvas. Upon graduation, he wrote the entrance exam of the prestigious MS University of Baroda and was admitted into a master's programme.

To travel to Vadodara and to pay the university's registration fees, Chandramohan borrowed money from his friends, but he was convinced that better days lay ahead. At MSU, he found himself working among nationally acclaimed artists. The discussions on art and theory were enriching. He started applying his painting skills to printmaking and, more specifically, woodcuts, which he thought allowed him to use a wider visual vocabulary than was possible on a flat canvas. His woodcut 'Remorse I' was shortlisted, picked out from among many hundreds of competing works, for the prestigious National Award at the Lalit Kala Akademi's 49th National Exhibition of Art in 2006. His larger-than-life nudes gave the viewer an insight into his inner turmoil, into the toll his struggles had taken.

In May 2007, when he was ready to show his work to an external jury for his final-year assessment, Chandramohan looked set to forge an impressive career as an artist. He had completed his coursework, met all the requirements of written and practical examinations and viva voce, and secured distinctions. His images of Hindu mythological figures and Jesus Christ, which included elements of nudity, were expected to garner high praise at the external-jury assessment. For arts students, the nude form applied to Hindu mythology was not unusual or shocking; indeed, it had been a fairly standard expression for hundreds, possibly thousands, of years.

·•·

The Faculty of Fine Arts at MSU is widely recognised as among the country's finest schools. Though the state of Gujarat had taken a decisive turn towards the Hindu right in the early 1990s, the arts faculty had remained a liberal redoubt. A rift was growing now between the department's culture of openness, experimentation and rejection of orthodoxy and the rest of the university. Whenever there were incidents of communal violence in Vadodara, professors and students of the fine arts faculty would make posters promoting communal peace and brotherhood and put them up in volatile or riot-torn areas. After the 2002 riots, they condemned the state's alleged complicity and inaction. Their willingness to express opposition and disapproval of the government was not new or sudden. Indeed, the Gujarat government had banned performances of *'Yeh Nadi Kya Kahti Hai'* (What Does the River Say), a play organised and staged by the arts faculty that was a sharp critique of the government's pet project—the beautification of the Sabarmati riverfront in Ahmedabad at the cost of displacing hundreds of poor slum dwellers living along the banks.

MSU's arts faculty had included the likes of Padma Bhushan Narayan Shridhar Bendre, a founder-member of the famous MSU-based Baroda Group, the internationally renowned modernist Sankho Chaudhuri, Padma Vibhushan K.G. Subramanyan, Padma Bhushan Gulam Mohammed Sheikh, painter and art historian Ratan Parimoo and the sculptor Mahendra Pandya. Many of these venerable artists and teachers were left-leaning and quick to support free expression. When the Akhil Bharatiya Vidyarthi Parishad (ABVP), the student wing of the RSS, burnt effigies of M.F. Husain, arguably India's most renowned painter, the MSU arts faculty were among the first to pledge solidarity. While university administrations across India were being populated by right-wing ideologues, arts faculties, more than most, remained a refuge for liberals. Conflict was inevitable.

·◆·

On 9 May 2007, the final-year arts students in the MSU master's programme were already into the third day of an exhibition of their work hosted by the department. It was not a public exhibition. But that afternoon, a group of Hindu right-wing activists stormed the campus. They went straight to the spot where Chandramohan's works were on display, ransacked the place and allegedly beat him up. The police arrived on the scene and whisked Chandramohan away to the Sayajigunj police station and booked him on the charge of hurting religious sentiments. The next day, he was sent to Vadodara Central Jail.

Artists in Delhi and Mumbai staged protests. The national media criticised the Gujarat government for allowing right-wing activists to run amuck on a university campus and for beating up a student (a foreshadowing of the vicious violence perpetrated on JNU students in Delhi in 2020). To neutral observers, Gujarat was beginning to look like an increasingly lawless state, or at least one in which laws were selectively applied. Right-wing activists had only recently ransacked local cinema halls for screening *Fanaa* and *Rang De Basanti*, both starring Aamir Khan, who had had the temerity to express support for the anti-Narmada dam activists. Early in 2007, Rahul Dholakia's *Parzania*—which was partially based on the story of a Parsi boy who went missing after the Gulbarg Society massacre—was subject to an unofficial ban, with movie theatres in Gujarat opting not to screen the film rather than provoke right-wing violence.

At MSU, though, the art students showed more spine, refusing to kowtow to thugs. They mounted an exhibition tracing the history of erotica in Hindu mythology, and the use of nudes in the long history of Indian and Western art. The acting dean, Shivaji Panikkar, the head of the department of art history and aesthetics, was openly gay, and this was manifest proof of degeneration and perversion in the eyes of the right-wing-dominated university administration. He was swiftly suspended for not stopping the students from staging the exhibition.

Though Chandramohan was released on bail after six days, his institutional ordeal was only beginning. The university held back his results and refused to confer upon him the degree he had earned. He made dozens of representations, made more than fifty visits to the offices of the VC, the registrar, numerous clerks and the examiner-in-control. Finally, he was told that if he wanted his degree, he would have to apologise for hurting people's sentiments. Chandramohan asked the university to define 'people'. No definition was proffered, and, to Chandramohan's credit, neither was an apology.

The police case against him dragged on, and because he had been accused, if not convicted, of a criminal offence, the passport office refused to issue him a passport, a necessary condition of travel to cities like Paris and Bangkok, where his works were being displayed. Chandramohan wanted to write a PhD thesis, but no institution would consider him for scholarships without a master's degree. He was forced to leave the university and rent a place in Chhani, Jakat Naka, around three kilometres from Hanuman Tekri, where Best

Bakery had been burnt down in 2002, and take up piecemeal work as a painter to make a living.

On the day he set the VC's office on fire, Chandramohan was charged with arson and attempted murder, and was imprisoned for seven months before he was granted bail. In prison, he made himself popular by painting portraits of his fellow inmates and the prison guards; in return, the subjects of his portraits would buy him biscuits, soap and toothpaste. One of his subjects, a bootlegger, even arranged a lawyer who managed to get him out on bail. A condition of Chandramohan's bail was that he could not enter Vadodara for four months.[2] So he moved to Ahmedabad until it was legal for him to move back to Chhani and start painting again.

Chandramohan's artwork has won him some admiration and a few sales from collectors in Bengaluru. But he makes ends meet mostly through local painting jobs. He says he does not visit his parents in the village any more out of shame. Chandramohan is still an undertrial, with two criminal cases pending against him. One for hurting religious sentiments and the other for arson. He no longer dreams of becoming a great artist. Every week, he shows up at a police station in Vadodara to mark his presence, as ordered by the High Court.

A week after Chandramohan was beaten up and then jailed in 2007, Tarun Tejpal called me. 'Have you heard about the incident at MSU in Vadodara?' he asked me. 'It's appalling. A young artist has been put into jail, while the right-wing goons who vandalised the faculty are at large. Find out who these people are, what they do, who is behind them, and above all, what their views are in private as opposed to their public postures.'

I went back to Gujarat. Undercover again, of course. And with my spy cams.

Chandramohan's provocative art turned out to be the catalyst for a trip deep into the darklands. It led me into the underbelly of Hindutva, a world populated by murderers and rapists, controlled by puppet masters safely ensconced in the corridors of power.

5
Alone in the Dark

> Dear reader, there are people in the world who know no misery and woe. And they take comfort in cheerful films about twittering birds and giggling elves. There are people who know that there's always a mystery to be solved. And they take comfort in researching and writing down any important evidence.
> — Lemony Snicket, *A Series of Unfortunate Events*

On the surface, Gujarat looked peaceful, happy even. Its cities appeared buoyant and prosperous. Families were everywhere in the evenings, eating at restaurants, taking walks, slurping on ice creams; you could see kids picking out balloons, women sipping colas and men chewing paan. The towns and cities were crowded with malls, multiplexes, eating joints and ice-cream parlours. The streets, lined with bungalows and multistorey apartment buildings, were clean and safe and bustling with people till late into the night. This was the face Gujarat liked to show to the rest of India—a state full of hardworking traders, shopkeepers and industrialists devoted to the creation and accumulation of wealth.

Invisible to the naked eye, dark forces swirled through the air. For instance, if you were not a trader but an investigative journalist, chasing facts and not money, Gujarat could be a foreboding place. You lived with the fear that you were probably being followed, that your phone was likely being tapped, that you were one mistake away from being caught out by the right-wing organisations you were tailing, that they might hurt you, or worse, get the police to frame you on a false charge. Every bureaucrat of significance in Gujarat carried multiple mobile phones and spoke in code. Local journalists never discussed stories over the phone, and political opponents and members of the judiciary believed they were being watched and monitored.

Unlike in December 2004, when I undertook the Zahira Sheikh investigation, I was now married and had a six-month-old daughter. After three back-to-back investigations, all of which were cover stories, I needed to spend some quiet time with my wife and daughter. We were planning to take a road trip around Maharashtra. For the next few months, I had decided I would do only non-investigative stories, basic reporting jobs that did not require me to risk life and limb. Going undercover as a radical Hindu activist was the last thing I wanted to do.

But there I was, dusting off my 'Piyush Agarwal' alias, posing once again as a researcher committed to the Hindutva cause and working on a book about the long overdue Hindu resurgence. I landed in Vadodara late at night on what was then my second trip to the city. As the autorickshaw took me from the airport to Alkapuri, where all the hotels are, I passed places I had visited the last time I was here, two and half years ago—the station, the roundabouts, the restaurants. I was in a sombre mood, thinking about my family back in Mumbai. I had said nothing to my wife about going undercover, to save her the anxiety. In any case, I was anxious enough for both of us.

Besides the two spy cams, my constant companion on this trip were to be the Benson & Hedges cigarettes I smoked. I checked into a cheap hotel, the peeling paint and murky light in that dingy room doing little to cheer me up. There, I smoked and thought about how to go about infiltrating the group of Hindu right-wing activists who had allegedly assaulted Chandramohan and trashed the artwork on display at MSU.

•─•

As an investigative journalist, my basic approach to a story was to meet as many people as I could in a day. I had discovered quite early in my career that people love a captive audience, they love to tell their story and feel that they are being heard. Cops or criminals, important or ordinary, politicians or activists, movie stars or indigent, they like a sympathetic ear. And the more people you meet, the more stories you hear. I call it the first principle of journalism—S is directly proportional to H. Where 'S' is the number of stories and 'H' is the number of hours spent in the field.

I made a few calls to human rights activists protesting against the events at MSU. Also, I got in touch with a contact from Gujarat who now lived in Mumbai and had good connections in real estate (and, therefore, with criminals, politicians and the police) in both his adopted city and Ahmedabad. I once had a story ready to go about this man's misdemeanours, but a highly placed source in the police advised me to drop the story. In return, the subject of my story would provide me with information that could lead to bigger and better stories. I complied. Sometimes, as a journalist, you have to be pragmatic. I did not want to lose my police source, and I was hoping that the man he was protecting too would become a valuable source of stories. Which he did.

He once had me over for dinner at his penthouse. Potbellied and balding, he bore a striking resemblance to Prem Nath, who played the villain in some of Hindi cinema's biggest hits. Gujarati sweets and snacks were served—khandvi, khaman, khakhra, fafda—which I thought were starters. We sat on a diwan, propped up by garish cushions. He drank peg after generous peg of whisky while regaling me with gossip about politicians, cops and Bollywood starlets. At some point during the conversation, he went to sleep, snoring as he sat cross-legged on the silk upholstery. The multiple layers of fat around his chin collapsed into his chest and his protruding belly moved to the beat of his snores. I waited for ten minutes, thinking he would wake up. But then his servant sheepishly told me that 'Saheb' had indeed retired for the night. Dinner, and the show, were over.

This builder now owed me a favour. I called him up and told him to put me in touch with people in the BJP's Vadodara unit without revealing to them that I was a reporter. 'Tell them I'm Piyush Agarwal, a member of the RSS and a research scholar from Delhi University, and that I am writing a thesis on the ascent of Hindutva in Gujarat,' I said. The next day, he gave me the names and numbers of a few BJP functionaries in Vadodara. 'I hope you've told them I'm a research scholar, and not a journalist,' I checked once again. He assured me that he had spoken of me only as an academic.

The first name on the list he gave me was Mr A, who sounded suspicious: 'What will your research conclude? Hindutava is an ideology, why are you interested in meeting local BJP and VHP leaders?'

I tried to persuade him of my earnestness: 'I want to research how dedicated the local leaders are to the ideology and how their dedication has led to the resurgence of Hinduism in Gujarat.'

I could sense he wasn't buying it, but he did agree to put me in touch with Mr B, who in turn put me in touch with a man called Dhimant Bhatt, who I was told was personal assistant to the Vadodara BJP MP, and would introduce me to the right people. From the news, I already knew the name of Niraj Jain, the local BJP and VHP leader who had led the ruckus at MSU. I called Bhatt and told him that I wanted to meet Nirajbhai Jain ('bhai' is an essential suffix to male names in Gujarat).

•◆•

I had learnt over the years that it was always better to visit the subject of your reporting in their office or home. They are most comfortable and secure, and most likely to slip up or let their guard down, on their own turf. The other trick, once you are in the lion's den, so to speak, is to look him straight in the eye, to betray no fear, hesitation or nervousness. Communicating with body language and facial cues is a vital skill for a reporter, just as it is for a conman. I had, with experience, developed a knack for remaining unfazed even under intense scrutiny. When I entered the house or office of a person I was going to sting, I left my own identity at their front door and stayed completely in character. Only Piyush Agarwal existed. If I wanted to glamourise it, I could say it is how I imagine a method actor might prepare.

At the appointed hour, I walked into the high-ceilinged room of the Vadodara BJP office. Half an hour later, Jain walked in, a short, paunchy man in his late-thirties. I introduced myself and told him about my research thesis.

Jain was a natural orator, like many RSS pracharaks are. He was fixated on Muslims, whom he considered the root of all evil. He explained his views by referring to Indian history, ancient and contemporary, Muslim culture, the clothes they wear, the food they eat, their festivals and their way of life. But Jain's Muslim fixation was not central to my story. I wanted to get to the bottom of the conspiracy and identify its main actors.

I let a day pass before going to meet Dhimant Bhatt, who, besides being a BJP man, was the chief accountant at MSU Baroda. On 19 May, at 11.30 a.m., I walked into his office on the second floor of an administrative block. Bhatt was hospitable, offering me tea and water even as he multitasked, looking at the files stacked in front of him and fielding incessant phone calls. He even showed me the way to the toilet, where I switched on my two spy cams. Switching the camera on at the right time was crucial because the battery only lasted for about an hour.

·◆·

It is best for undercover reporters to keep their conversation as vague and non-committal as possible, sharing very little about their assumed identity. The advantage of not divulging details, without appearing shady or shifty, is that you do not give your subject much information to crosscheck should they become curious. And always be from out of town. If you are in Punjab, pretend to be from Gujarat. In Gujarat, tell them you are from UP. I told Jain I was from Kanpur and had attended RSS shakhas there. Since I had studied in Kanpur, I knew the city fairly well. I gave him the names of the places I used to go to, and the names of RSS office bearers in Kanpur whom I claimed I used to meet in the 1990s. His wariness of strangers, his mistrust, was at least temporarily allayed.

The other benefit of being guarded and offering minimal conversation is that it opens up gaps that your subject will try to fill, often with quite specific details in otherwise rambling stories. Reporters should remember to keep their interventions as short as possible and let their subject talk. And never interrupt a subject who is mid-flow. Only ask questions to keep the conversation moving; if, for instance, the subject is starting to clam up or if the conversation has become too digressive and you want to return it to topics more pertinent to your investigation. Throughout the conversation, you must remain fully interested and invested in what the subject has to say. You laugh at his bad jokes, you applaud him for his humour, you agree with his views, however blinkered and paranoid.

Fifteen minutes into our chat, Bhatt was convinced that I was as fanatical a Hindu as he; love for Hinduism is easily demonstrated to Hindutvawadis by heaping abuse on Muslims. He had become comfortable enough with me to utter the words that would not only redefine my story but also, I believe, help to change the way the nation sees the Gujarat riots. 'I was involved in burning the houses of Professor Bandukwala and the bureaucrat Peerzada ... I supplied weapons to rioters in the guise of a peacekeeper during the riots ... We should keep aside the stick of RSS and instead start wielding AK-56 rifles.' As Bhatt was casually uttering these words, I struggled to compose myself, to look as if what he was saying was normal rather than utterly unhinged. I had set out to find who had vandalised the paintings at MSU, and here I was, sitting with the chief accountant and auditor of the university, who was not only a member of the BJP and the RSS but, by his own admission, a proud participant in a riot. He said he was part of a mob that had burnt the houses of his colleagues and neighbours just because they were Muslim. And five years later, he still felt no remorse, let alone shame.

·•·

Violence against Muslims in Vadodara—the second largest city in Gujarat—erupted in three bursts. The first started on 27 February 2002 and lasted until 2 March, with the worst incident taking place on 1 March, when fourteen people were burnt alive at Best Bakery in Hanuman Tekri. Muslims were targeted again between 15 March and 20 March, and then again between 25 April and 2 May, with sporadic incidents of violence in between.

Almost every major Muslim neighbourhood in the city was attacked by rampaging Hindu mobs—Kishanwadi, Sama, Asha Bibi ni Chawl, Madhavpura II, Makarpura, Avdhoot Nagar, Raghavpura, Noor Park, Karelibaug, Gotri village, Hajimiyan ka Sara, Hanuman Tekri, Roshan Nagar, Panigate, Tai Wada and Macchipith. Hundreds of Muslim homes and businesses were looted and torched. In Sama, a relatively new part of Vadodara with a predominantly Hindu population, a mob, including Bhatt, attacked the residence of J.S. Bandukwala, a professor of nuclear physics at MSU.

A distinguished figure in Vadodara, Bandukwala, who was born in a Bohra family, was known for his moderate, liberal views. He abjured both Muslim and Hindu conservatism. Indeed, he was excommunicated from the Bohra Muslim community for not following its strictures. In 1989, he disapproved of Salman Rushdie's *Satanic Verses* but condemned the fatwas and threats issued by Muslim leaders against the author. This prompted the Muslim religious leaders of Vadodara to issue a fatwa against Bandukwala, but he didn't back down. He also, controversially, recommended that Muslims practise family planning and devote their resources to educating their daughters as well as their sons.

On 26 February 2002, the RSS invited Bandukwala to address a function to celebrate Hindutva ideologue Veer Savarkar. The professor accepted the invitation and spoke of the need to bridge the gulf between the Muslims and the RSS. He ended his speech by saying that Savarkar, unlike Mahatma Gandhi, made some Indians feel like they did not belong in their own country, and that it would be better to focus on uniting rather than dividing people. The very next day, a Muslim mob set fire to a train, and in a supposed response, Hindutva activists were allowed to wreak death and havoc for days.

Bandukwala's house was destroyed. He told *Tehelka*: 'My house was attacked twice. First on 28 February and then on 1 March 2002. The first day, they burnt a car in the garage and the sad part was that they were all known faces. They actually addressed my daughter by name. After that, two armed policemen were kept at my gate for my protection. The next day, the whole thing was very well planned. They collected a crowd. Provocative slogans were raised and the mob was led by a local BJP municipal corporator. I heard the two policemen telling them they had fifteen minutes to do what they wanted. They carted gas cylinders in an autorickshaw to fuel the fire. Just as they came, I jumped out of my house and hid in the bathroom of a Brahmin family. My daughter also managed to escape. They looked for me but didn't know where I had gone. The mob looted the house. My wife had recently passed away. She had a wonderful collection of silver and crystal. The mob brought the gas cylinder, released the gas, ignited it and ran out with the stolen material.'

What happened to Bandukwala and his daughter was a tragedy. Still, unlike so many others, they felt lucky to be alive. He left for the US and stayed there for three months. After returning to MSU, he asked to be assigned staff quarters. The university allocated a flat to him in a block with three other flats. When he moved in, the other families, all Hindus, left; he stayed there for three years, alone in a block at the far end of the university campus.

Bandukwala retired from the university in 2007 and still lives in Vadodara. His daughter, as he wrote in a column in the *Indian Express* in 2017, married 'the Gujarati Hindu gentleman she loved.[1] So much for the BJP's "Love Jihad"'.

As for Bhatt, his job may have been that of a chief accountant, but he identified foremost as a Hindutva foot soldier whose purpose was to make life hell for the minorities, Muslims in particular. The destruction of artwork and the beating up of Chandramohan was, for him, an amuse-bouche compared to the main meal of 2002 when he and his fellow Hindutvawadis showed Muslims that no one messed with Hindus any more.

After that interaction with Bhatt, I told my editors that I wanted to further investigate events from five years ago and dig deeper into the story of the 2002 riots. Tarun Tejpal told me he would spare no resources, and that I could take the time I needed. 'Let your story be the last word on the Gujarat riots,' said Harinder Baweja. And with those words of encouragement and support, I began a six-month journey into the heart of Hindutva, into the events of 2002 that some extremists appeared to consider the high-water mark of militant Hindu nationalism, a victory to be savoured. My only companions were fear and hope. Hope that I could tell this story, accurately and definitively. Fear that I would be consumed by the story, by its principal actors, before I could expose its horrors.

I tried to meet as many VHP, BJP, RSS and Bajrang Dal members as I could. They were everywhere, in every walk of life. They were MLAs and ministers, obviously, but also public prosecutors and police officers. I asked Bhatt for a few introductions to members of the 'Parivar'—the RSS and the vast network of its affiliate Hindu nationalist organisations are collectively known as the Sangh Parivar—in Ahmedabad.

One of the BJP leaders I met in Vadodara was Deepak Shah, who told me that the planners of the violence at MSU had met at a farmhouse in Vadodara; he also put me in touch with other foot soldiers. Each contact put me in touch with at least one other person, and gradually I had an impressive pyramid of contacts.

The more people you meet though, the more chances there are that some of your contacts will grow suspicious, wonder about your intentions. I would draw Venn diagrams with intersecting sets of all the people I had met, trying to isolate those who had expressed doubt or mistrust. I did not want those people meeting each other to discuss their suspicions and combine their efforts to find me out and blow my cover.

Over the next six months, I would meet many men who had been charged with rioting and killing, and many who had conspired first to kill and then to cover-up their deeds and stifle investigations. Along the way, I came up against and had to overcome dead ends, spells of despair and depression, and moments when I felt genuinely scared for my life. Whenever the tension became too much to take, I would go back to Mumbai, to the arms of my wife and daughter, and take enough succour and respite and light to be able to go back to the darkness of Hindutva. For six months, I transitioned between two worlds, two entirely alien states of mind—one in which I had a Catholic wife, a daughter with a French first name who was being brought up with no fixed religion, and friends from all communities and classes; and another in which I was Piyush Agarwal, a Hindu zealot who saw no problem in associating with murderers and rapists because we shared the same hatreds.

6

Truth on Trial

> Only look about you: blood is being spilt in streams, and in the merriest way, as though it were champagne ... And what is it that civilisation softens in us? The only gain of civilisation for mankind is the greater capacity for variety of sensations—and absolutely nothing more. And through the development of this many-sidedness man may come to finding enjoyment in bloodshed. In fact, this has already happened to him ... In any case civilisation has made mankind if not more bloodthirsty, at least more vilely, more loathsomely bloodthirsty.
> —Fyodor Dostoevsky, *Notes from Underground*

As I got off the plane at Ahmedabad airport on the morning of 3 August 2010, I was greeted by a posse of Central Industrial Security Force (CISF) personnel wielding automatic assault rifles, and driven straight to the City Civil & Sessions Court. The extensive security arrangements had been ordered by the Supreme Court to protect witnesses for the prosecution in nine major legal proceedings dealing with the Gujarat riots. Clearly, the apex court suspected the possibility of foul play.[1]

At around 10.30 a.m., I walked into the packed sessions court, room number thirteen. The case on trial was sessions case number 152/02, the criminal trial into the Gulbarg Society massacre.

I was prosecution witness number 313. Sixty-six accused were on trial for killing sixty-nine people in a matter of a few hours on a single day. The accused were seated in one half of the court room, separated by a wooden banister, facing the additional sessions judge, B.U. Joshi. The lawyers for both the prosecution and the defence had their backs to the accused and were facing the judge. The witness box was perpendicular to the accused, the lawyers and the judge. While everybody—the judge, the court staff, the accused, the lawyers—is seated, the witness as a rule is supposed to stand in the box.

On 26 October 2007, *Tehelka*[2] broke a story it headlined 'The Truth: In the Words of the Men Who Did It'. It included relevant portions from the sixty hours of tape I had recorded during my sting operation. The entire issue of the magazine, all 106 pages, was dedicated to the story. And the India Today Group bought the rights to turn it into a television documentary. I was elated at what I had achieved in my six-month undercover investigation. The footage was scheduled to be aired on Aaj Tak and what was then called Headlines Today, from 7 p.m. onwards and into prime time. Anxious about how the story would be received, I couldn't sleep the night before it aired.

The Aaj Tak editor-in-chief, Qamar Waheed Naqvi, had headlined the TV version 'Operation Kalank'—kalank being the Hindi word for 'blot'. The Gujarat riots were a blot, an indelible stain on Indian democracy. Group Editor Aroon Purie himself read through the script, listened to the voiceovers and made editorial interventions, ensuring that the *Tehelka* story was unimpeachable on facts and that there was no unjustified or unnecessary editorialising. I remember Tarun Tejpal saying that our investigation was going to change the narrative of the Gujarat riots and the politics around it. In our view, what we had achieved was unprecedented in the history of Indian journalism. We had recorded murderers, rapists, conspirators, bomb-makers, public prosecutors and leaders of right-wing organisations confessing to the parts they had played in the 2002 riots and explaining how they had been shielded by the state. We did not gloss over the horrors of the communal riots. Women and children were hacked to death, a foetus was cut out of its mother's womb and impaled on a sword. Ehsan Jafri, a former Congress MP who was in his seventies, was lynched and set on fire by a mob. So many women were raped and burnt alive, along with their families.

The police had not only stood by, but in some instances actively assisted the rioters, and ministers in the state government were kept in the loop by the perpetrators.[3] As if to underline that the state was colluding with the rioters, witnesses and survivors were bought or intimidated into silence, evidence was destroyed or tampered with, and judges were transferred until pliant ones were in place to grant bail to rioters, the accused told me. A VHP leader named Babu Bajrangi, a prime accused in the riots, was allowed to escape and remain underground for months until his arrest was staged. The tapes contained worshipful acknowledgements from murderers and conspirators, from Ahmedabad to Vadodara and Sabarkantha to Aravalli, that they could kill so many Muslims only because Narendra Modi was chief minister. Three public prosecutors I had stung told me that they and many other prosecutors like them were appointed by the government, not to prosecute the Hindu accused, but to ensure the cases against them collapsed.

We had also made crucial revelations about the burning of the train in Godhra, which catalysed the riots. Star police witnesses were caught on camera detailing how police had tutored them to give false testimonies, and had manufactured evidence to misrepresent a spontaneous communal riot as a cold-blooded conspiracy hatched by Muslims from Godhra. These witnesses confessed that they were party to a police conspiracy. And that the theory of the planned burning of the train and murder of kar sevaks was manufactured by the police to justify the state government's official position that the riots were a reaction to an action.

We were convinced our story would result in a nationwide uproar; that people would demand immediate action of the authorities. That there would be resignations at the highest levels of government and bureaucracy. That the killers would be put behind bars. That the victims and survivors would see some justice done at last.

How wrong we were!

If the story were not about the massacre of a thousand Muslims but about a Rs 1,000 crore scam, the higher courts in India would have ordered thorough investigations, the public would have been outraged, ministers would have resigned, some might even have been jailed. But the killing of minorities has never elicited the same response in secular India. The actions of the superior courts often appear anaemic, bereft of the urgency, intensity and animation with which they act on such piffling matters as improper bookkeeping at the Board of Control for Cricket in India (BCCI) or staying the FIRs registered against Republic TV's Arnab Goswami for stoking communal passions.

'Genocide is an evil,' the academic Claudia Card wrote in her 2010 book *Confronting Evils: Terrorism, Torture, Genocide*. 'Premeditated murder is an evil. Petty theft and tax evasion are not.' She had not reckoned with the Indian state.

After the story was aired, spokespersons from the so-called secular parties came on TV and reeled off the usual platitudes. BJP spokespersons predictably called it a conspiracy to defame the Sangh Parivar and Narendra Modi. The next day, most newspapers carried it as a front-page story. A few foreign publications also picked up the story. The Australian Broadcasting Corporation even made a special documentary. And then the story was allowed to peter out. There was no reinvigorated clamour for justice. No resignations. No public uproar.

Instead, what followed drove me to despair. The Gujarat state elections were around the corner and people—including some Muslim community leaders—began a whisper campaign that the sting operation had been orchestrated and sponsored by Narendra Modi himself. A few Congress leaders argued that Modi had hired *Tehelka* to whip up the sentiments of Hindus because he was set to lose the election. The confessions were described as deliberately inflammatory. The BJP, of course, claimed the sting was a Congress plot. It was politics as usual, in which every issue, however vital, is subordinate to the jockeying for power between the two main national parties. The late Priya Ranjan Dasmunsi, the minister of parliamentary affairs at the time, made a statement in the Lok Sabha that the *Tehelka* sting was a conspiracy hatched by some BJP leaders sitting in Delhi. He even defended the Gujarat government's decision to ban the telecast of the sting in Ahmedabad. Dasmunsi said that Central government agencies had solid intelligence about the 'deep-rooted conspiracy', and that the truth (by which he meant what passes for the truth among political parties), would emerge soon.

As the political slanging match got uglier and uglier, I remembered the six months I had spent in Gujarat. How I would frequently change hotels, how as I got deeper into the story I rarely got a full night's sleep, plagued by fear, by visions of the police or right-wing goons bundling me into a waiting car and then setting me on fire in the middle of a jungle. There were many narrow escapes when I was certain my cover had been blown.

The tapes contained serious allegations about the Nanavati–Shah Commission set up in 2002 to inquire into both the burning of the Sabarmati Express in Godhra and the subsequent riots, which many even then described as a pogrom. The special public prosecutor for the Gujarat government, Arvind Pandya, had been filmed telling me that the commission's proceedings were compromised to help the chief minister. After the exposé, the commission issued a statement that it would summon the tapes and look into them. But that day never came—it never did ask for the tapes. Nor did the commission conduct any inquiry into its contents.

Two months later, in December 2007, Narendra Modi drubbed the Congress at the polls. It was not the first, and certainly would not be the last, time that the Congress found itself at the receiving end of a Modi-inspired thrashing. But the party, confronted with the results of our sting, chose to bury its head in the sand. Myopic, unable to see past the assembly elections, the Congress failed to stand up for justice in Gujarat, failed to stand up for its own legacy, the inclusive ideals its leaders once insisted were the foundation of independent India.

•••

Realising the evidentiary potential of the *Tehelka* sting, the activist Teesta Setalvad moved the Supreme Court to take immediate cognisance of the material contained in the tapes. At the time, the matter of the Gujarat riots had reached a stalemate in the apex court. While the court said the tapes would be examined in due course, it ultimately refused to intervene. Setalvad then took her appeal for the tapes to be examined to the National Human Rights Commission (NHRC). The NHRC advised the Modi government to consent to a CBI probe.[4] Modi, not surprisingly, declined. The Gujarat government claimed that, since the riots were already being investigated by the Nanavati–Shah Commission and criminal cases were pending in trial courts, there was no need for a further CBI probe. Overruling Modi, the full bench of the NHRC, headed by Justice Rajendra Babu, in its order dated 5 March 2008, ordered the CBI to conduct an inquiry into the authenticity of the tapes and the allegations made therein. 'The revelations bode ill for the future of human rights in the country,' the NHRC ruled.

After months of despair, I saw this as the first glimmer of hope, that perhaps the work I did would not be in vain, that justice might be possible for the victims of the riots. The Mumbai wing of the CBI registered a preliminary inquiry and took into their possession the full raw footage, the spy cameras used for the recordings and the laptop on which it was all stored. CBI sleuths recorded statements by both me and Tarun Tejpal and sent the equipment and footage for examination to a forensic science laboratory in Jaipur. Six months later, I learnt from newspaper reports that the lab had found the tapes authentic and had certified that there had been no tampering or doctoring of their content.

In March 2008, the Supreme Court constituted an SIT, headed by retired CBI director R.K. Raghavan, to reinvestigate nine cases, including the Sabaramati train carnage and the Gulbarg Society and Naroda Patiya massacres in the subsequent riots. Apart from Raghavan and a retired UP Police Director General, C.B. Satpathy, the team was drawn from serving officers of the Gujarat police. This was a kind of weak compromise between the demands of the riot victims, who wanted an investigation completely independent of the Gujarat administration, and the state, which resolutely opposed any outside interference. But can ordinary people ever share the middle ground with the mighty state? For the victims to have had any sort of chance at justice, an independent investigation insulated from the state administration was essential.

I wrote to the SIT and asked to depose before it. Soon, I received a communiqué from Raghavan's camp office and was instructed to appear before him. I appeared before the full panel of the SIT, which at the time included Geeta Johri, Shivanand Jha and Ashish Bhatia, all of who were Gujarat cadre IPS officers. I submitted before the panel the full raw footage and the transcripts, which the CFSL had authenticated. Before Raghavan, I made a passionate plea: 'If I, as an individual reporter, with no powers other than that of a common citizen, can gather so much evidence and peel off so many layers of judicial subversion and miscarriage of justice, I'm sure that your team, with full statutory powers and the mandate given by the Supreme Court, can get to the bottom of the 2002 riots.' The faces of the SIT members betrayed little. I was unaware at the time that what lay ahead was a torturous journey for both survivors and witnesses. As time went by, the high-sounding SIT was window-dressing for what was essentially a team comprising Gujarat police personnel. The field and supervisory officers who were included in it, from sub-inspectors to deputy superintendents of police to inspector generals, were all linked to the state police. Raghavan worked as SIT chief in absentia. He visited Gujarat only once or twice every month. Effectively, the Gujarat police was investigating all over again.

The probe team recorded my statement about half a dozen times. It was my first substantial engagement with a police investigation. I had reported on the selective application of law and the subversion of the criminal justice system, now I was about to experience it first-hand. The investigating officers mined me for all the evidence that I could provide against VHP leaders like Babu Bajrangi, Jaideep Patel, Bharat Teli, Atul Vaidya, the BJP leader Mayaben Kodnani and scores of other foot soldiers. Every piece of the missing puzzle, as far as the roles of these Sangh Parivar members was concerned, was carved out of the tapes, corroborated by eyewitness testimonies, and then pieced together to build a case. I was told that the extra-judicial confessions of two rioters—both mohalla-level VHP cadres—recorded on the tapes was the only piece of evidence to establish how Ehsan Jafri was murdered. The SIT told me that revelations made by two lower-rung Bajrang Dal members about the role played by Mayaben Kodnani in the Naroda Patiya riots was crucial. They also told me that what Bajrangi had said on tape had filled the critical gaps in the Naroda Patiya investigation.

But all of these accused were low enough in the political hierarchy to be considered expendable. If they were convicted and imprisoned, those in seats of genuine power had little to lose. The claims they had made about the chief minister were dismissed by the SIT as hearsay and unsubstantiated. But it was never *Tehelka's* contention that the tapes in themselves were prosecutable evidence against Modi, just that they were enough to initiate a sustained and in-depth criminal investigation into his alleged complicity. Only if the SIT could show that it had a genuine desire to get to the bottom of what had happened during the riots would witnesses have the confidence to come forward and present new evidence. But that never happened.

·◆·

I must, however, return to 3 August 2010, when I was summoned to depose as a witness in the Gulbarg Society massacre. The bodies of many victims, including that of Ehsan Jafri, were never found, they were presumed dead (Indian law presumes a person dead if she has been missing for more than seven years). The judge before whom I appeared was B.U. Joshi. Many witnesses had already approached the Gujarat High Court and petitioned for Joshi's removal, on account of his blimpish attitude towards victims. One of them, Sairaben, who had lost her only son in the massacre, was humiliated by Joshi in open court. And when Rupaben Mody—whose son, Azar, went missing in the riots, and on whose story the film *Parzania* was based—broke down in tears while recounting the events of the day, Joshi refused to allow her to take a break from her testimony for even a glass of water. Before my own testimony, I asked R.C. Kodekar, the special public prosecutor, how the judge could be allowed to get away with this sort of bullying and lack of basic courtesy. We were on our way into court, and he just mumbled something unintelligible and hurried away.

When I took the stand, Kodekar asked me to tell the court about how my sting operation began and the evidence I had collected against certain accused in the Gulbarg case.[5]

'I had come to Vadodara in the second week of May 2007 and assumed the identity of an imaginary figure, Piyush Agarwal. I infiltrated the ranks of Hindu right-wing organisations. I went to the RSS headquarters in Maninagar, Ahmedabad, called Dr Hedgewar Bhavan, and met a senior RSS leader. I told him that I wanted to do research regarding the spread of Hindutva after the riots of 2002. He told me that it was the VHP that had played the main role in the demolition of the Babri Mosque and had also taken the central role in the riots of 2002. Therefore, I should meet their leaders. He had given me the name of Jaideep Patel, the general secretary of VHP in Gujarat. Thereafter, I went to meet Jaideep Patel at Dr Vanikar Bhavan, the VHP headquarters in the Paldi area of Ahmedabad,' I told the court.

I remembered my visits to the RSS and VHP headquarters. Though I normally carried both my spy cams, on those days I only wore the one spy cam that I fixed to a button on my shirt. I was too nervous to risk a larger camera that would give me away if I was frisked or searched. A beating from Hindutva activists, or just as likely the police, would then have been the least of my worries.

I would try to look as confident as I could. By then, I had acquired the mannerisms and jargon of an RSS or VHP member. I would enter their offices and greet everybody with a 'Jai Shri Ram'. I had learnt to refer to Ahmedabad as 'Karnavati'; to the 2002 riots as 'dhamal'; to the Babri Masjid as 'dhancha' (shell); to the RSS, VHP, BJP and Bajrang Dal collectively as 'Parivar'; to an organisation secretary as 'karyavah', a general secretary as 'sarkaryavah'; to service as 'sewa', nation as 'rashtra', youth as 'navyuvak', and the involvement of right-wing Hindus in the Gujarat massacres as 'pratikar' (revenge). I had also realised that it did not take much to impersonate Hindutvawadis. You needed no real knowledge of the Hindu scriptures nor to be well-versed in Hindu religious practice. Hindutva, for the right-wing extremists I interacted with, was a political, rather than religious, commitment; the only devotion necessary was to hate and violence. Spew some abuse in the direction of Muslims and you were most of the way to being welcomed into the fold.

The VHP general secretary at the time, Jaideep Patel, made me wait for a long time outside his office before he found the time to meet me. It gave me plenty of leisure to take in the photographs displayed on the wall: of the fifty-nine Hindus, including kar sevaks, who were burnt alive on the Sabarmati Express at the hands of Muslim rioters. A model of the burning S-6 coach was also on display. Because of Patel's tardiness, I had to switch on and switch off the spy cam several times in anticipation.

Eventually, I was able, on camera, to ask Patel about his role in the Naroda Patiya and Naroda Gam killings. He told me, as if discussing a successful infrastructure project, that the scale of the murder was possible only because of years of groundwork and grassroots mobilisation by the VHP in the area. After indulging in this boast, and in the pride he still felt at having engineered the deaths of dozens of innocent people, Patel said he should not say more because he was battling accusations that he had been personally involved in the two massacres. Until then, however, the Gujarat police had shielded him from being arrayed as an accused. He asked me to meet Arvind Pandya, the special prosecutor, and BJP MLA Haresh Bhatt from Godhra. He gave me the telephone numbers of both, and told me that I could arrange a meeting with them by using his name as reference.

My meeting with Patel lasted an hour. I never met him again. Instead, I pursued a meeting with Bhatt, using Patel's reference, as well as that of other Parivar leaders I had met. Bhatt agreed to see me at his Ahmedabad apartment. He was the Bajrang Dal national co-convenor in 2002, and had mobilised large groups of kar sevaks to travel to Ayodhya. He had also helped execute the 'trishul diksha' programme, in which the VHP distributed tridents through much of north, central and west India. Many young Hindus from conservative, Hindutva-friendly families were given little trishuls to carry on their person, in the manner of a Sikh kirpan; though rather than representative of self-defence, these trishuls are triumphalist symbols of Hindutva militarism, of the weaponisation of Hinduism.

Bhatt was a typically bellicose Bajrang Dal leader. He reminisced fondly of the time in 1986 when he and a bunch of other Bajrang Dal hooligans had smashed up an Ahmedabad mosque. As for his five-year term as an MLA, the only achievement he mentioned to me was that he had not helped a single Muslim in his constituency, 'not even in getting a birth or death certificate'. Half an hour into our conversation, he signalled to me to draw closer and said, 'I'm going to tell you a few things which you must promise you won't mention in your PhD thesis on Hindutava nor tell anyone.'

'You can trust me,' I said, as I turned to give the spy cam a better angle to capture the expression on his face.

'I had my own gun factory,' he said. 'I used to make firecrackers. We made all the bombs there. Diesel bombs, pipe bombs, we made them there and we used to distribute them from there as well. We ordered two truckloads of swords from Punjab; right here, in a village called Dhariya, we readied everything there and then we distributed the arms,' he whispered.

'Where did you get the arms from,' I asked.

'We got many country-made pistols from MP, from UP. We got pistols from everywhere and I distributed them from here. We distributed so many weapons that people were shocked to see how many we had stockpiled. We would make them here and then test them. We made a complete launcher inside a pipe, right here in the factory. We filled it with shrapnel and nails and beneath that placed a 595 bomb. We'd set it off and it would go through a wall nine inches thick,' Bhatt said with what can only be described as unalloyed joy.

Seeing that Bhatt was in the mood to talk, I slipped in a question on Narendra Modi.

Bhatt responded with a knowing grin: 'Narendra Modi's anger was palpable after the Godhra incident; he vowed revenge. He told us to do whatever we wanted for the next three days. When he asked us to stop, everything came to a halt.' A few days after our chat, Bhatt asked me to accompany him to Godhra. I travelled in his car from Ahmedabad to Godhra. It was an extremely hot day. I was wearing the button spy cam, which had become hot under the sun and was burning the skin on my chest. To keep the button camera firmly focused on the person I was trying to capture, I used to stick it on my chest using double-sided tape. Midway into our drive, Bhatt received a phone call. He looked grave. After he hung up, he turned to me and said he had been cautioned that a journalist from Delhi might be working on a sting operation about the Sabarmati Express burning. Just a day earlier, the news channel NDTV had telecast a 'sting' operation exposing a collusion between the prosecution and the defence in the high-profile BMW hit-and-run case in which Sanjeev Nanda, grandson of a former Navy chief, was accused of running over and killing six persons while driving a BMW car. The NDTV sting showed a defence lawyer in the case influencing a prosecution witness about his testimony. Perhaps the telephone call to Bhatt was triggered by the NDTV sting, which had become a talking point. 'We've been told to be careful,' he said, as his driver pulled off the main road into a narrow, deserted side street.

As the car stopped outside a desolate, one-storey house, another car pulled up and two men got out. Bhatt followed these men into the house, telling me peremptorily to wait in the car. I had both of my spy cams on me, and all of a sudden it seemed impossible that no one would notice. My heart was in my mouth, I was sweating bullets, I was trying to prepare myself for the worst. I got out of the car and lit a cigarette. Twenty minutes later, Bhatt returned and we set out wordlessly on the road to Godhra. The other men drove off in a different direction. Bhatt said he had some monetary matter to settle with them. My face suggested indifference, but I felt sure he could hear my heart pounding. Still, my cover, it appeared, was intact.

It was Bhatt who put me in touch with Babu Bajrangi, a cult figure among Hindutvawadis for the 'very good work' he had done in the 'dhamal'.

After that trip to Godhra, I escaped for a few days to Mumbai. Upon my return to Ahmedabad, I met Arvind Pandya, the state government's special counsel in the Nanavati–Shah Commission's inquiry. Jaideep Patel had recommend me to him too. By now, I had become an authority on the various leading figures in the Gujarat branches of the Parivar. I was able to drop enough names to convince Pandya within minutes that I was the 'right' guy, that is, connected, a 'made man' in mafia parlance. It was Pandya's job to demonstrate to the inquiry commission that the Gujarat government had done everything it could to prevent the riots, and that there was no collusion between the state machinery and the mobs. Interesting then that I should have been given his reference by a Parivar leader who was in the very thick of the riots. Presuming that he was speaking to a Hindu hardliner like himself, Pandya said quite matter-of-factly that 'practically everybody on the field was from the Bajrang Dal and the VHP'. By field, of course, he meant the killing fields that ordinary Muslim neighbourhoods in Gujarat had been turned into by the Hindu right.

I asked him whether the commission's report would go against the Parivar. 'Nanavati is a clever man,' Pandya said. 'He wants money. Of the two judges, K.G. Shah is intelligent, he is our man. He is sympathetic to us.' This was on 8 June 2007.

As Pandya had predicted, the commission dragged on for seven increasingly futile years. The Nanavati–Shah Commission later became the Nanavati–Mehta Commission, after Shah died and a new judge named Akshay Mehta replaced him. The commission submitted its report to the Gujarat government in 2015, after Narendra Modi became the prime minister.[6] It was made public by the state government in November 2019, and lo and behold, the Gujarat government, and by extension Modi, had been given a clean chit (a delicious Indianism commonly used in the media and political world to imply that those charged with wrongdoing had been cleared without the slightest stain on their character). The report only found fault with the Gujarat police for being 'ineffective in controlling the mob [either] because of their inadequate numbers or because they were not properly armed', and blamed the local members of the VHP and Bajrang Dal for 'taking part in the incidents which happened in their localities'. This too had been predicted by the extraordinarily prescient Pandya.

I met Pandya again, and this time he was more expansive about what he believed had happened during the riots. 'The Muslims,' he said, 'thought they could get away with it because the Gujarati is mild by nature. In the past, they had beaten the Gujarati, they have even beaten the entire world, and nobody has shown any courage. Nobody had ever resisted them. They thought they'd get away with it just like they always do. They used to get away with it because there was Congress rule here earlier. To get their votes, the Congress would suppress Gujaratis and Hindus. But this time, they were thrashed. It is Hindu rule now. All of Gujarat is ruled by Hindus, and that too by the VHP and the BJP.

'They miscalculated. In this instance, there was a Hindu-based government and so people were ready and the state was also ready. This is a good connivance [he meant coincidence].'

'This was the good fortune of the Hindu community, the entire Hindu samaj,' I said for emphasis.

'And let us say the ruler was also strong in nature ... The hero by the name of Narendra Modi came and he gave oral instructions to the police to remain with the Hindus, because the entire kingdom is with the Hindus,' said Pandya.

I met Pandya for the third time on 8 June 2007. I wanted to probe deeper into what he knew about how Modi had handled the riots.

'Sir,' I asked, 'is it true that when Modi went to Godhra on 27 February that VHP workers verbally attacked him?'

'No, they didn't. It's like this. There are fifty-nine bodies and it's evening, people are bound to say, "What have you done?" Modi's been of our line for a long time. But he's occupying a post, so naturally there are more limitations, and he has quite a few. But it is he who gave all the signals in favour of the Hindus. If the ruler is tough, then things can start happening.'

'Did you meet Narendra Modi on the 27th,' I asked Pandya, pushing him further, 'after he returned from Godhra?'

'No,' he said, suddenly careful. 'I will not answer queries on this. I shouldn't.'

'Sir, please, I want to know what his first reaction was,' I persisted.

'When Narendra Modi first heard it [news of the killing of fifty-nine kar sevaks on the Sabarmati Express] over the phone, his blood was boiling. If he were not a chief minister, he would have detonated a few bombs in Juhapura [a Muslim-dominated locality in Ahmedabad],' Pandya said, his chest heaving with emotion.

During our conversation, Pandya became very agitated over the criticism Modi had faced in the national media and from human rights organisations around the world. And then, in a sudden turn, he began bragging about his own hardliner credentials: 'A Hindu leader gets involved then it is dangerous, but if Arvind Pandya gets involved, it is two thousand times more dangerous.'

'Has there been any inquiry against you?' I asked.

'One was *Tehelka*-related. I had threatened the police officer, R.B. Sreekumar [a police officer who had given evidence against the Modi administration]. That leaked out and it ran on TV all day. But that was the last "tehelka".'

At this point, he reached into his drawer and pulled out his licenced revolver and put it on the table. 'I always keep this revolver loaded,' he said. 'If ever a *Tehelka* undercover reporter comes in front of me, I will shoot him dead.'

I nodded vigorously in agreement and wrapped up the meeting as soon as I could. That was the last I saw of him. I did not want to be looking down the barrel of his gun a second time.

•—•

As I told the court how the sting operation was planned, how I met one right-wing leader after another, there was palpable hostility in the room. The judge, his stenographer, the court staff, the lawyers, had all been listening, their faces set, expressions stern. There was no doubt that I was in unfriendly territory; that, if I thought my testimony would be interpreted as a quest for justice, I would have been wrong. Justice means different things to different people. I told the court about two more VHP leaders I had met in Ahmedabad, the city president Rajendra Vyas and Ramesh Dave, a mid-level functionary. Both men had told me that they had attacked Muslims in Kalupur and Dariyapur, two of Ahmedabad's most communally sensitive areas. Vyas, who had led the party of kar sevaks to Ayodhya and was with them on the way back when fifty-nine Hindus were killed in Godhra, said he had told some VHP cadres after the fire that 'the Muslims had played a one-day match and given us a target of sixty runs. We will now play a Test match and we won't stop until we score six hundred.' He told me that he himself shot dead five Muslims and burnt down nine Muslim homes.

At his house, in a narrow lane in Kalupur, I asked Vyas—like I asked others who had participated in the riots—about the role played by Narendra Modi in the 'dhamal'.

'As chief minister,' Vyas said, 'Narendrabhai couldn't say "kill all the Muslims". I could say it publicly because I was from the VHP. Pravinbhai Togadia can say it. But he [Modi] can't say it. But it's like how we say in Gujarati, "aa khada kaan khada" [to turn a blind eye], meaning, he gave us a free run to do whatever we wanted to since we were already fed up of the Muslims. The police were on our side, and so was the entire Hindu samaj. Bhai [Modi] was careful about that or else the police would have been on the other side. The police didn't go to the rescue of the Muslims.'

Ramesh Dave was the VHP's Kalupur 'zila mantri'. He said he and his fellow VHP members had targeted and killed Muslims who had been in their sights for over twenty years—or in his words, *'chun-chun ke maara is baar'* (We picked them off one by one). According to Dave, 'The police were very helpful, they were Hindus. S.K. Gadvi saheb was a new DCP here. Curfew was on and he was patrolling about. He said he wanted to set some Muslims straight. I said, if you want to set them straight, then there's a spot I can take you to. But you have to promise me that you'll kill at least four or five of them there. He promised. We went to the terrace. He started firing from the terrace, and before we knew it, he'd killed five people. All the policemen helped us, one shouldn't say it, but they even gave us cartridges.'

From my conversations, it was clear that, while Indian liberals may have thought of Modi as a wannabe fascist who demonised Muslims and failed to prevent the riots, for a majority of Gujarati Hindus, their chief minister was a hero, especially after the riots. As the liberal media and civil society kept pressing for Modi to be held accountable for the slaughter of nearly a thousand people, as human rights activists and riot survivors kept petitioning the courts for investigations and for justice, as legal scholars argued that Gujarat was not being governed as per constitutional norms, Modi's legions of supporters stood firmly behind him, sweeping him to power in election after election. For them, the Gujarat riots of 2002 were to be numbered among his accomplishments, a source of pride, not shame. For them, this was no blot on India's copybook, it was a Hindu awakening.

7

Conspirators and Rioters

> And yet identity can also kill—and kill with abandon ... Within-group solidarity can help to feed between-group discord ... Violence is fomented by the imposition of singular and belligerent identities on gullible people, championed by proficient artisans of terror.
> —Amartya Sen, *Identity and Violence: The Illusion of Destiny*

From Ahmedabad, I moved on to other districts in Gujarat, among them, Sabarkantha. According to official records, 1,545 houses and 1,237 business belonging to Muslims were torched and 549 shops were ransacked in this district during the 2002 riots. I was told by the VHP rank and file that Anil Patel, the 'vibhag pramukh' (departmental chief), was among the key planners of the carnage in the area.

I met Patel at his house in the village of Dhansura. He told me that 'after seeing the bodies of the kar sevaks at the Sola Civil hospital, we vowed that if we couldn't organise a reaction to this, I would quit the Vishwa Hindu Parishad. If I didn't kill at least 500 Muslims, I would quit this position. And since they had burnt our people alive, I would burn them alive.' It was no idle threat. Over a hundred Muslim houses were reduced to ashes in Dhansura, Patel revealed, glowing with pride in what he had done to fellow villagers. 'Our war cry was "Lock the door from outside and burn the Muslims inside."' Other men who were part of the VHP cadre told me that it was a deliberate tactic: setting Muslim-owned houses, businesses, shops, and indeed individual Muslims, on fire as a symbol of direct retribution for the deaths of the kar sevaks who been burnt alive in Godhra. Not, Patel was quick to reassure me, that other methods were infra dig: 'We brought down one mosque and killed a maulvi, killed him with an axe.'

'So how many houses did you burn in Dhansura?' I asked.

'We razed to the ground 126 properties of the Muslims,' Patel said. 'It is the only village in this whole district where 75 per cent Muslims have still not returned to their homes. Let me tell you about this district, Sabarkantha. The maximum number of FIRs were filed here, after Godhra. I know, because I handled all the cases on behalf of the VHP. There were more than forty murders here in Sabarkantha. Not even one Muslim home was spared in the entire district. Our activists had taken an oath at the main square that they would give a befitting reply.'

'In Ahmedabad,' I asked Patel, 'bombs were made at Hareshbhai's [VHP leader Haresh Bhatt] own factory; how did it happen here?'

'There are a lot of boring industries here, because of which dynamite is available. Then, we also had some [explosives] experts, they also made them [bombs] and supplied them to Ahmedabad. See, there were some areas where we were very concerned about our safety ... Kalupur, Dariyapur. Hindus live along the edges of these places. For their safety, we sent some weapons from here.'

Patel went on to explain that the police themselves had helped with logistics: 'The police would come and take the weapons and deliver them safely to the places they were supposed to go.' He added that, while there was no single, unified strategy, the broad objective was to inflict maximum casualties and economic damage on Muslims. He also said that Pravin Togadia, by then a figure of national prominence in the VHP, had been involved enough in the riots to be coordinating matters at the district level. Togadia had told Patel to plan in such a way that important VHP workers could not be booked and sent behind bars, however temporarily. What Patel described was a textbook example of ethnic cleansing: the VHP's sole objective, as he stated it, was not revenge for Godhra so much as to kill as many Muslims as they could, to burn their homes and businesses, and to ensure that those who fled did not return.

As was standard operating procedure for me, before ending my meeting with Anil Patel, I asked him to introduce me to other important VHP functionaries who had played a significant role in the 'dhamal'. I was always looking to widen my circle of contacts without arousing suspicion. Patel was obliging, calling another Patel community member, a VHP office-bearer named Dhawal Jayanti Patel, and making introductions. It took just fifteen minutes to drive to Dhawal Patel's stone quarry in Badagam, a village in Sabarkantha district. He was the area's 'zilla sanyojak' (district convener) for the VHP, and his quarry was one of the main sites for the manufacture of bombs used during the riots.

—•—

'How are you feeling in Gujarat?' Dhawal Patel asked me.

'My perspective has changed. I thought we as Hindus were weak. But Gujarat has opened my eyes, and has shown that we are not weak. I had a long meeting with Anilbhai, who spoke very openly. He told me about the dynamite. Is there a mine here?'

'There is, right here,' Patel said.

'Were bombs made here?'

'Everything went from here itself,' he said. 'See, blasting stones is our work anyway. We get material for blasting, we can use it easily.'

'Dynamite?'

'Meaning, our work is to blast stones and we blast stones with that ...' Patel said vaguely.

I persisted: 'With dynamite? So how many bombs were made at that time [in 2002]?'

'Lots of bombs, lots of desi bombs were made and sent.'

'A thousand?' I asked. 'Two thousand?'

'They [the bombs],' Patel said, 'were very useful in narrow lanes, in Juhapura, Kalupur [both neighbourhoods in Ahmedabad].'

'In Ahmedabad, and here in Sabarkantha?' I asked, trying to get him to specify where the bombs they had made in his quarry were used.

'All the Mohammedans left this area,' Patel said, ignoring my question.

'They all ran?'

'They ran away. In Dhansura, a maulvi stayed back.'

'You guys killed him?'

'He was killed,' Dhawal Patel confirmed. 'In Modasa, there were some Muslims who were left. In this area, the onslaught was one-sided. Here, the motto was to burn, burn the properties, burn whatever you can, in Modasa, Bayad and Demai. Three Muslims were killed in Modasa area.'

'Were the police with you, with the Hindus?'

'The police were with us,' Patel said. 'There were 400 families of Muslims in this area. Now, only a hundred are left.'

'Didn't the police intercept the transportation of bombs from here to Ahmedabad or try to stop it?'

'We would just say "Jai Shri Ram", and the policeman would understand,' Patel claimed.

'Would you show me how bombs are made?'

Dhawal Patel spoke to some of his men in Gujarati, calling for the bomb-making material to be brought to him.

'Stones,' he told me, 'are blasted. The stones are stuffed [with dynamite] and blasted apart. The ground breaks with the impact, so imagine what it will do to human beings. This is used to drill a hole in the boulders. Then there is this white powder, then you connect a wire. Then wire the battery, press it like this and rotate it and the blast takes place. It can be triggered with a mobile battery, it needs twenty watts power. We've become systematic now. Earlier we'd just light it and throw it, it blasts everything, boxes, you know, paan masala boxes, fill them, light them and throw them.'

'Is the bomb stable right now?' I asked, a little nervous. 'Won't it explode?'

'It is stable now. Nothing will happen. This powder is like RDX, it's super explosive.'

'Super explosive. How much does it cost?'

'In Rs 40–Rs 50, a bomb gets made,' Patel said.

I asked if I could keep one of these homemade bombs. He agreed, but warned me that the explosives might go off if I kept them too close to any kind of battery.

Taking the bomb from Dhawal Patel was a mistake. In my overzealousness in collecting evidence, I had crossed a line. I thought that the explosives would be a critical piece of proof in my attempt to show how the mass killings in Gujarat were organised and executed. It did not occur to me at that moment that, as an ordinary, law-abiding citizen, investigative journalist or not, there was no way I could travel to Delhi or Bombay with a bomb on my person. After a few kilometres, I asked the driver to pull up. I took the bomb out of the car boot and dumped it by the side of the road.

Dhawal Patel spoke to Anil Patel after my visit and told him that I had asked for, and taken, an example of the crude bombs they had manufactured at the quarry. This immediately made Anil Patel suspicious. If I sympathised with their cause, like I claimed, why did I want the bomb? It was not the sort of souvenir you took home to show the family. He called on my cell and asked me, very politely, if I would go see him. There was something he wanted to discuss. Behind the politeness, I sensed a threat. I told him I had to meet some Sangh leaders in Karnavati and needed to leave immediately. But, I said breezily, I would be back to see him in a few days.

He was upset. Why, he asked, had I taken the explosives? I said I wanted to experiment, see how they worked. He said I was lying. 'Who are you?' he shouted. 'And what are you doing in Gujarat? Who has sent you?' My voice level, I kept bluffing, trying to convince him I was one of their own. I assured him I would return in a few days and go to see him. He hung up on me mid-sentence. I told the driver to take me straight to the Ahmedabad airport, a two-hour drive away, and asked the *Tehelka* office to book me on a flight to Mumbai. By 9 p.m., I was back home.

When I landed in Mumbai and switched on my phone, I saw missed calls from Anil Patel. 'Sorry,' I blustered, 'I ran out of battery. Everything okay?'

He wasn't buying any of it. 'I trusted you,' he said to me, 'but I don't think you are telling me the truth.'

I told him I understood his concern but that I would 'never betray the Hindu cause'. 'You have my word,' I parried desperately.

He wanted to know when I would be back in Sabarkantha. A couple of days, I told him. Maybe.

After that day, I stayed away from people I knew in Anil Patel's circles. However, I did fly back to Ahmedabad the next day. I needed to meet the public prosecutors who were bringing to trial Hindus accused of rioting and murder, but who were, according to the victims I had spoken to, actually helping to weaken the case against the accused. I had to work quickly, before Anil Patel got word to enough people and made further investigation impossible. I tried to keep Anil on ice by speaking to him on the phone as often as I could and reassuring him of my bona fides, while I pressed on with other meetings. It was important for me to sting the prosecutors, to try and show that the game was rigged against the riot victims.

—•—

Since 2003, many riot victims and the human rights group Citizens for Justice and Peace had petitioned the Supreme Court to look into the conduct of law officers appointed by the government. The petitioners alleged that judicial proceedings were being compromised by prosecutors who seemed determined, through feigned incompetence, to ensure that the accused were released on bail and eventually acquitted. Indeed, many of the prosecutors were either office-bearers of the VHP and RSS or openly aligned with the Hindutva worldview. But there was not enough evidence to persuade the Supreme Court that this allegiance meant they were not doing—or could not do—the jobs they were assigned.

During my sting operation, I won the confidence of two key public prosecutors who, in essence, told me that they were protecting the accused and undermining the witnesses. They told me that almost the entire network of prosecutors in Gujarat was controlled by Hindu right-wing outfits that were working in coordination with the defence to protect the accused. On 15 June 2007, I met Dilip Trivedi, then state general secretary of the VHP and also a lead public prosecutor. In his early sixties, the grey-haired Trivedi wore vermillion on his forehead and controlled a team of about a dozen public prosecutors in Mehsana district, among the worst-affected areas during the riots. Two massacres in Mehsana—Dipda Darwaza in Visnagar town and Sardarpura—were particularly shocking for the barbarity of the violence. In Dipda Darwaza, eleven members of a single family, including four children and a sixty-five-year-old woman, were murdered, their bodies burnt by a mob allegedly led by the local BJP MLA (a Mehsana trial court sentenced twenty-one persons to life imprisonment in July 2011, while acquitting the MLA, giving him the benefit of the doubt). In Sardarpura, the police were entirely absent as a mob trapped thirty-three Muslims in a house, threw acid at them and tried to electrocute them before burning them alive.

All the accused in the Sardarpura case, prosecuted by Trivedi, were released on bail. The state government did not consider Trivedi's VHP membership a conflict of interest. In fact, as the man himself told me, it was a point in his favour, a necessary qualification even. Arvind Pandya, the state's special counsel, had recommended that I meet Trivedi and smoothed my path with an introduction. Relaxed, Trivedi did not even try to hide his complicity when we spoke in his office. 'Being a general secretary of Vishwa Hindu Parishad,' he said, 'I have coordinated all the matters in all the courts ... These cases need to be managed. I talk to public prosecutors and bring them to an understanding with the defence lawyers. This is how I have coordinated all the cases in Gujarat.'

'What has been the approach of the local judiciary towards the Hindu accused?' I asked

'It has been very good,' Trivedi said. 'There were over 4,200 complaints against the Hindus, out of which a charge sheet was filed in 1,800-plus cases. But the NGOs created a ruckus. So, the Supreme Court ordered re-scrutiny of 2,000 cases. A special team was set up to reevaluate the cases. But I am in touch with all the officers starting with the DGP and downwards.'

'What happened in the 1,800 cases which were chargesheeted?'

'More than 1,700 have been decided,' Trivedi told me. 'Only twelve have resulted in convictions. The rest have been acquitted, by God's grace.'

'How many cases were registered in Mehsana?'

Trivedi responded in detail, as if happy to be able to show me the efficiency with which he hushed up the cases: 'In Mehsana, a total of 182 complaints were filed. Eighty were chargesheeted. Only four are pending. Out of the seventy-six decided cases, seventy-four have ended in acquittals. I have filed appeals in the two cases where convictions have happened, but the accused are out on bail. Out of the 30,000 Hindus who were arrested, only 100 or 150 may still be in jail. The rest are out. In this area, there was a big case called "Sardarpura gam case". Though the Supreme Court has stayed the case, my accused are out on bail, so I'm not worried. The second big case in this area is of Dipda Darwaza, where all the dead bodies could not be found. The third significant case here was in Meda Agraj village in Kadi tehsil where everyone has been acquitted. Only one case in Ujjha tehsil resulted in some convictions. But the issue there was that the administration had to show that it was impartial.'

He then complained that after the accused in the Sardarpura riot case were granted bail by the Mehsana court, the victims made 'such a big noise' that the *Times of India* had carried a front-page story accusing him of playing a partisan role in riot-related cases. Gleefully, he said that, even though the allegations against him were true, nothing could be proved 'on paper'. Everybody knew, he said, that he had camped in every district after the riots, holding meetings with government prosecutors, his own aides and police officers.

While I was sitting in Trivedi's chambers, two people walked in to discuss a riot-related case. The men needed his help to engage a lawyer who could represent the Hindu accused. He called up a few people and tried to find his visitors a suitable lawyer. After the two men left, he said that the defence lawyer who was handling their case had fallen ill, and the responsibility of finding a new defence lawyer had again fallen on him, the prosecutor.

On 17 June, I travelled to meet Bharat Bhatt, the public prosecutor in Modasa, Aravalli district, Gujarat. He had been a prosecutor for about three years when we met outside the district court. We sat together in the back seat of my car so we could speak with some privacy. Mostly, when meeting with Hindutvawadis, I tried to appear friendly, unthreatening. With some though, and you could sense the type, you needed to stamp your authority. Bhatt was one of the latter. So, as soon as he got into my car, I started speaking as if I were the VHP president.

'How many cases have been registered against the Hindus in the district?' I said gruffly.

'In Modasa, the total number of cases are 1,400, out of which 600, or around 550, were registered in the beginning itself. The rest were reopened. When they were reopened, people were again disturbed. Due to the stand the Supreme Court has taken now, people are scared. These judges in the lower court aren't courageous enough, not daring. We are trying to fulfil our responsibility. Whatever matters I have dealt with here, I was very hard with the Muslims. They kept changing their statements, gave additional statements. I said these don't have evidentiary value. But these judges from the lower court, they also do wrong. They are scared of their seniors.'

'So what is the attitude of the police now in the cases that have reopened?'

'They help us,' Bhatt said, 'listen to us, agree with us. They also know that the Muslims are trying to get as much compensation money as they can out of us. Recently they took around [Rs] 6.5 lakh from us to settle this. A riot case. Section 436. He was asking for 20 lakh rupees.' Bhatt helped arrange money for cases that needed to be settled. 'I used to hold meetings in the villages of the accused,' he said, 'and told the rich people there that there were people in Kashmir, Punjab, Haryana and UP who had property worth crores of rupees but had lost everything once madrasas opened nearby. What is the point of having money if you can't even put it to use for the welfare of your own community? While some gave 5,000 rupees, others gave 10,000, sometimes even a lakh. This is how we collected enough to settle the case, [necessary] since it was a daylight murder and he had used his sword to cut the man to pieces.'

Bhatt's favourite tactic with witnesses who insisted on going to court was to tell them that, since they would not be emigrating to Pakistan, they would be better off compromising with Hindus, whatever the crimes the Hindus were accused of. 'Whenever I feel that there is a need to scold,' he said, 'I tell them, "You live in the village, settle the issue and keep each other's honour intact. You have all your property here, live peacefully. Whatever had to happen has happened."'

Then, as if to show me he was an equal opportunity bigot, he vented some spleen on Christian conversions. 'This is a belt which is suffering from the same problem as Assam, Nagaland and Kohima, where everyone will convert to Christianity if Hindus like us don't pay attention,' he said, and he then digressed into a lecture on how he sent food, money and gifts to tribals so that they would not become Christian.

Both Bhatt and Trivedi admitted that the petitions before the higher courts were true, that the prosecutors were deliberately sabotaging their cases so that the Hindus would be let off for the crimes they had been accused of, crimes that amounted to genocide in the eyes of many observers, both Indian and foreign. Towards the end of our conversation, Bhatt started to insist that I accompany him to his office to look at all the records he had kept. By then, though,

I was both weary and wary, and claimed I had another meeting. A few hours later, Bhatt called and said he did not think I was who I claimed to be. 'If you are truly an RSS man, come to my office.' I promised I would and, of course, never did. Bhatt saw himself on TV when my sting broke, and I was told he went into hiding for months. He probably did not need to, though; no investigation team or court took any action against the three government counsels—Trivedi, Pandya and Bhatt—who, our tapes showed, had been compromised in their duties.

Pandya only had to step down as special counsel before the Nanavati–Shah Commission because his indiscreet comments, suggesting that Modi had laid the ground for and enabled the Gujarat riots, made his position untenable.[1]

In one of its reports submitted to the Supreme Court, the SIT confirmed the fact that the Gujarat government had appointed VHP- and RSS-affiliated advocates as public prosecutors in sensitive riot cases. The SIT concluded that 'the political affiliation of the advocates did weigh with the government for the appointment of public prosecutors'. But it pressed no charges.

'The modern-day Neros were looking elsewhere when Best Bakery and innocent children and helpless women were burning and were probably deliberating how the perpetrators of the crime can be saved or protected. When fences start to swallow the crops, no scope will be left for survival of law and order or truth and justice.' With these scathing comments, the Supreme Court on 12 April 2004 had observed with anguish that 'when the investigating agency helps the accused, the witnesses are threatened to depose falsely and prosecutor acts in a manner as if he was defending the accused, and the Court was acting merely as an onlooker and there is no fair trial at all, justice becomes the victim'.[2]

In the Best Bakery case, the then public prosecutor Raghuvir Pandya had deliberately dropped key prosecution witnesses during the trial;[3] had exhibited the wrong document as the FIR; did not take any steps to protect star eyewitnesses; did not ask for an in-camera trial even as a majority of prosecution witnesses turned hostile; and as for those key witnesses who did not turn hostile, he chose not to examine them. Of the 120 witnesses listed by the prosecution in the Best Bakery case, more than a third did not depose.[4] Of the seventy-three who did depose, forty-one turned hostile. Among the hostile witnesses were Zahira Sheikh and her family, and other survivors of the carnage. Raghuvir Pandya's name became synonymous with a deceitful and dishonest prosecution.

My investigation had shown that he was not an exception. Though my evidence against Bhatt, Arvind Pandya and Trivedi was recorded by the court as part of my testimony, since they were not the accused in the case at hand (the Gulbarg Society trial), the damaging confessions of these three prosecutors have only remained a part of the court's records.

More recently, the Modi government at the Centre, in a move out of the Gujarat playbook, bypassed the elected Delhi government while appointing public prosecutors in criminal cases pertaining to the 2020 northeast Delhi riots.[5] These appointments were made even as the courts and civil society alike questioned the fairness of the police investigations, arrests and charge sheets. Justice Suresh Kumar Kait of the Delhi High Court, while dismissing a petition filed by the Delhi police in one riot case, had commented that the police was 'misusing the judicial system' and taking the 'system for a ride'.[6] In early July 2020, Justice Vibhu Bakhru had reprimanded the Delhi police for making 'unwarranted' allegations in its affidavit against a JNU student who was accused by the police of instigating the riots.[7] On 28 May 2020, a Delhi sessions court hearing the riot cases had remarked that the investigation was targeting one community and 'rival factions' were not being investigated properly.[8] There is a genuine fear that, just like in Gujarat, the government (the Centre, this time, rather than the state) will try to use the offices of public prosecutors to subvert the justice system.

8

The Gulbarg Massacre

[Men] are not gentle creatures, who want to be loved, and who at the most can defend themselves if they are attacked; they are, on the contrary, creatures among whose instinctual endowments is to be reckoned a powerful share of aggressiveness. As a result, their neighbour is for them not only a potential helper or sexual object, but also someone who tempts them to satisfy their aggressiveness on him, to exploit his capacity for work without compensation, to use him sexually without his consent, to seize his possessions, to humiliate him, to cause him pain, to torture and to kill him. *Homo homini lupus* (man is a wolf to man). Who in the face of all his experience of life and of history, will have the courage to dispute this assertion?

— Sigmund Freud, *Civilization and Its Discontents*

After I gave evidence, the court took a recess for lunch. Then it was time for me to testify about the footage I had recorded that was specific to the Gulbarg Society massacre. The prosecutor asked me to identify the accused whose confessions I had caught on my spy cams. I pointed to the accused (numbers 25, 28 and 30): Mangilal Jain, Prahlad Raju, Madanlal Chawal.

Back in September 2007, I had been undercover for almost five months. By then, I had on tape several rioters admitting to murder and conspiracy to murder. But I wanted to record more evidence in one of the most horrifying episodes of the Gujarat riot: the burning alive of families in their housing society, including an elderly former Congress MP, Ehsan Jafri, who for hours tried to persuade the police to come to their rescue as the nightmare unfolded. Located in the eastern part of Ahmedabad, the Gulbarg Society was a smart, plush Muslim enclave comprising stand-alone houses and apartment buildings in a largely Hindu area. In it was located the home of Jafri, who was a qualified lawyer and eminent Congressman, one of the few who managed to make it to parliament (from Ahmedabad, no less) when Indira Gandhi was swept out of power in a crushing post-Emergency electoral defeat. On the morning of 28 February 2002, despite the presence of a police contingent, a Hindu mob had laid siege to Muslim homes. Many sought refuge with Jafri, imagining he might still have the political and administrative influence to protect them. For over five hours, Jafri made concerned and finally frenzied appeals for help through phone calls to the police and to politicians and leaders in Delhi.

The lives of about thirty Muslim families hung in the balance. Alongside these families were a number of poorer Muslims from the nearby slums, who imagined that an upper-middle-class residential complex with its high walls and gates would be protection, an unassailable refuge from a murderous mob.

Sensing trouble after hearing about the murder of kar sevaks on the Sabarmati Express, Jafri had written a letter to the local police station on 27 February, asking for reinforcements and protection. He told other members of his housing society that the police had assured them that they would be kept safe.[1] Jafri belonged to an era when the words of people in power had value—the office of the police commissioner, or district officials, or even the local police inspector could be trusted. Sadly, that time was past.

The mob that had surrounded Gulbarg Society first set the property of poor Muslims in the surrounding area on fire: the handcarts and auto rickshaws of those who provided services to the rich, and the cheap and flimsy housing in the nearby chawls and bastis where they lived. They assaulted any Muslim they could find, many of who ran into the society. Armed with blades, sharp-edged makeshift weapons and flammable liquid, they patrolled the streets, chanting 'Jai Shri Ram' and 'kill the Muslims, burn the Muslims'.[2] A few shops owned by Hindus were forcibly shut down, their owners and workers told to leave. The police personnel present at the spot merely stood by, watching the violent mob without making any attempts to disperse them.[3]

The mob was led by leaders from right-wing Hindu organisations and was made up of their members from all over the city, as well as local people cheerfully participating in the butchery of their neighbours. By noon, just a couple of hours later, the initial mob of about a dozen people had grown to several hundred, perhaps even a thousand people.

Many of the survivors later identified local acquaintances and neighbours they may even have thought of as friends among the mob; they had played cricket together, sold to and bought from each other, exchanged greetings when they passed each other in the street. At some point in the chaos, the area's JCP, M.K. Tandon, arrived with significant backup (a fact corroborated by police witnesses in court). Witnesses also testified to the commissioner of police, P.C. Pande, coming to the society and leaving at around 10.30 a.m. But Pande's cell phone records show his presence in the society later in the evening; whether he had visited in the morning as well has not been conclusively proved.

While the mob was still controllable, Jafri left his house to meet the policemen present on the street and was assured that more police would be sent to calm the situation, the public prosecutor told the court. But the promised reinforcements never came. Tandon, who had come with sufficient men, did not disperse the mob and left the spot. The mob outside the society's gates kept growing larger, angrier and more violent, emboldened by the police inaction. They started throwing stones and burning rags into the Gulbarg Society complex. Hiding in Jafri's bungalow were many women and children from the neighbourhood, including Rupaben and her two children, knowing perhaps that their deaths were upon them.

At around 1.30 p.m., several hours after the mob had first begun to amass outside the complex, they tore down a wall and blew the front gates open by exploding a gas cylinder. They poured into the complex from the front and the back, killing anyone in their path. In an orgy of bloodlust, the Hindu fanatics bludgeoned victims to death, hacked others to pieces with swords and poured petrol on their bodies and set them alight. Their savagery knew no bounds. One witness deposed that he saw his sister-in-law being raped by an accused, and also another woman whom he could not identify. After the women were raped, they were hacked to death. The official death toll numbered sixty-nine. Jafri himself was killed, though his remains were never found. Two brothers, Imtiyaz and Firoz Khan Pathan, lost ten members of their family, including their mother, aunts, uncles and grandmother. The Pathan family lived in Bungalow No. 18, right next to Jafri in No. 19. As with Jafri, the bodies of many of the Pathan family members were not found.

Jafri reportedly came out of his house and begged the mob to take him and leave the others alone. He was dragged off like a trophy, with the mob shouting in delight, 'We have Jafri, we have Jafri!' The mob soon broke into the house, setting it on fire, breaking down doors and dragging people out into the street. When the mob set Jafri's house on fire, the women and children who had taken shelter there began to scream. Firdosbanu ran out of the house, alongside two other women, Sahejadali and Zebunben. The mob fell upon them almost instantly, as they did upon Kherunnisa, Akhtarkhan, Jamilaben, Sajedabanu, Sadabkhan and many others. Rupaben and her young daughter survived, but her son Azar perished.

As it was with so many victims in the riots, the bodies of those who perished in the Gulbarg massacre were hacked, mutilated and charred, so that it was impossible to give them individual burials. By the time the violence was over, around 4.30 p.m., the once posh residential complex was strewn with the blackened, often unrecognisable and sometimes naked bodies of men, women, small children and the elderly. When the police arrived after several hours of uninterrupted carnage, it dispersed the mob, but only after the repeated entreaties of a Muslim police inspector called Pathan,[4] and the firing of teargas shells and live bullets. By now, JCP Tandon had also reached the scene for a second time. A survivor asked Tandon to summon a fire brigade to put out the fire in Jafri's house, which was still ablaze. Tandon told the survivor that he should worry about himself and not Jafri's house, the court records show.[5] The police finally rescued the survivors and moved them to the Dariakhan Ghummat shelter, a refugee camp for people who had been displaced during the riots. The corpses that were found were buried together in a mass grave in the Musa Suhag Kabristan in the city's Shahibagh district.

⁕

At my last meeting with Babu Bajrangi on 1 September 2007, he said that many activists who had been charged in the Gulbarg Society massacre were not getting enough financial and legal support from the VHP. He told me he could arrange for me to meet with some of these disgruntled rioters, and that they might be willing to talk to me about their frustrations. On 8 September, I flew to Ahmedabad to meet the Gulbarg accused. It was the same day India was to play England in a decider at Lord's, with the one-day series poised at three each. Beside me sat Tarun Tejpal's uncle, who would be playing 'Anandji', a fictional RSS ideologue I had invented in the course of the sting operation.

I had created Anandji to bolster my bona fides and to answer a question that kept cropping up—who in the RSS did I report to about my research? I gave my fictional Delhi-based leader the suitably extravagant RSS-style title of 'Bauddhik Pracharak', an intellectual preacher and trainer of minds. There were two advantages to having Tarun's uncle play the part. He had served in the IB and knew how to operate undercover, even though he was long retired. And he also spoke in a singular manner that made him hard to understand, particularly if you were meeting him for the first time. I was hoping they would be trying so hard to figure out what he was saying that they would not have time to become suspicious about his role and his connections to the RSS.

I had pressed upon Bajrangi that Anandji would also want to meet the Gulbarg accused and help devise a legal strategy for them. We took an early flight out of Delhi. Bajrangi told me to head to his office in the Naroda area, from where one of his men would take me to meet a VHP leader named Mahesh Patel in Meghaninagar. This was the part of town where the Gulbarg Society was located. We waited for Patel on the opposite side of the street from the complex. Its desolation, in the middle of a bustling, colourful neighbourhood, was eerie. The iron gate, the walls within, the windows, the doors and the roof were still scorched black.

A steady stream of passers-by did not so much as glance at this clump of buildings, this gaping scar on an otherwise unblemished neighbourhood. We stood there for nearly twenty minutes, trying to imagine the slaughter, before Mahesh Patel and another senior VHP leader showed up. Patel took me to his house and told me he would introduce me to VHP men who had been charged for their part in the riots. He lived comfortably, his home equipped with every modern convenience. Sitting on his immaculate sofa set, we spoke of the work the VHP had done to ensure that its men in prison were looked after, with money made available to arrange legal representation and to tide their families over. They were even provided with home-cooked food in prison, Patel said.

Despite my best enactment of an RSS man, though, Patel began to grow suspicious. Questions flew like darts: who else in the RSS did I know; who all had I had met so far in Gujarat; where did I live; what did I do for a living? Meanwhile, about half a dozen VHP workers from the area began filing into the house, eager to meet a visiting RSS dignitary from Delhi. I dropped the name of every

VHP and RSS leader in Gujarat that I had either met or researched, claiming that each of them knew me personally. Mahesh then turned his inquiry towards Anandji. Now that was a problem. Anandji was not prepared for something like this, did not know any names to drop. But he held his nerve, murmuring responses that Patel had to strain to hear and strain further to comprehend. Patel was confused and frustrated. He did not know what to make of the two of us.

About forty minutes into our visit with Patel, three of those accused in the Gulbarg Society massacre—Prahlad Raju, Mangilal Jain and Madanlal Dhanraj Chawal—dropped by, distracting our host from his intent questioning. Promptly, the three men demolished Patel's claims that the VHP was taking good care of them. Their litany of complaints was long and bitter—the VHP had not paid their children's school fees while the men were in jail, and though it did offer their families a few kilos of foodgrains, it had not done this consistently every month. While they had done their duty by participating in the riots and facing the legal consequences, the VHP had failed in its duty, they argued. I took their phone numbers and left Patel's house, promising that I would ensure their complaints were addressed and that they would receive sufficient and regular support from the Sangh Parivar. From the car, I called Mangilal Jain on his cell phone and told him to meet me, along with his fellow accused, at my hotel near Ahmedabad airport, where they could tell me their concerns in greater detail, away from the eyes and ears of Mahesh Patel.

Within half an hour, all three were in my room, eager to talk, hoping I could ease their troubles. It was the chance I had been hoping for, to hear an unvarnished account of the planning and execution of the Gulbarg Society killings.

·•·

All three men were small-time shopkeepers. I could tell from their shabby shirts and worn-out rubber chappals that they were struggling to get by. Unlike Mahesh Patel, they did not have gold rings on their fingers, a gold chain around their neck or a watch on their wrist. Neither before nor after the Gulbarg massacre had they committed any serious crime. Still, on 28 February 2002, they, by their own admission, had willingly and enthusiastically participated in mass murder. Prahlad Raju told me that, in the midst of the frenzy, he took time out to collect his children from his house, which was in a neighbourhood with a mixed population of Hindus and Muslims, and drop them at a safe place, before returning to join the mob, by then engaged in murdering children younger than his own.

Five years after the massacre, none of the men expressed any remorse to me, nor did they appear to have a true understanding of the horrors that they had inflicted on innocent men, women and children. They were, however, deeply exercised about the court process, about having to serve time in jail and the effect of all this on their families. According to Raju, many of those who gathered in the morning outside Gulbarg Society, ostensibly to enforce a VHP bandh, carried tridents in their belts. Jain added that they had come equipped with weapons and canisters of petrol. Madanlal Chawal, who looked like the youngest of the three men, said the first act of violence was the setting ablaze of a shop owned by a Muslim family. Prahlad Raju said that two VHP leaders, Atul Vaidya and Bharat Teli, and a local Congress leader named Megh Singh were leading the mob.[6]

'The day this Gulbarg thing happened, were VHP people with you?' I asked, for the record.

'They were. At 8.30 a.m., they started from Meghaninagar. They were closing down shops and banding together. I joined them at 8.30. I was acquainted with Atulbhai,' Raju said.

'Atul Vaidya?' I wanted him to confirm the full name of the president of the VHP's Meghaninagar branch.

'Yes, we all moved together towards Gulbarg. We were closing down shops and people were joining us, kept multiplying.'

Initially, I met with all three in my hotel room. But in their desire to narrate the events of that day and explain their individual roles, they were constantly interrupting each other. So I told them that I wanted to speak to each of them separately.

'Who were there from the VHP?' I asked Chawal, as Raju and Jain waited downstairs in the hotel lobby for their turn.

'At that time, I didn't know all the leaders. I never had any contacts since I'm from a business background. Later, though, when I met Atulbhai, I remembered he was there too.'

'Atul Vaidya was there?' I asked again, as it was important both journalistically and legally to establish without doubt the identity of the mob leaders.

'Atul Vaidya was there, then there's one Bharatbhai Teli, he was also there. These boys, these big ones. They came to get me out of jail, it was then that I met them. And that was when I realised that they were also there in the mob. I wondered why I had been arrested while their names were dropped. I didn't give it too much importance, since these people could have helped me leave jail or do something else for me. That is why I never breathed a word anywhere about these people being there too. Nobody ever said anything about it, not even the forty boys who were in prison.'

·•·

'So how did you enter Gulbarg?' I asked.

'People [the rioters] got gas cylinders from their homes. They kept them on the outside of the society's walls, then they got pipes from a bakery and opened the cylinders with them. From afar they threw burning rags at the wall. The cylinders exploded and the wall broke. Then we got inside,' said Chawal.

'Was the wall too high?'

'It was not a two-foot wall. It must have been around fifteen to twenty feet high. On top of it, there was a barbed-wire fence too. Some tried to scale it by rope.'

'So the wall broke with just one or two cylinders?'

'Two cylinders ... The wall obviously broke with the cylinders. Cylinders are heavy and explosive,' said Chawal.

At the back end of the Gulbarg Society, there was a high concrete wall topped with broken glass to discourage potential thieves from climbing into the complex. Parallel to this wall ran a railway line. The rioters did not attempt to climb over the wall, they blasted it apart, which enabled them to flood into the residential complex. These facts were proven in court.

'So the houses inside caught fire?' I asked.

'People used the residents' own things to burn their houses, nobody needed to get anything from outside. Their own things were used to burn them.'

Jafri lived in Bungalow No. 19, located in the southwest part of the complex. Alarmed at the gathering crowd and its attempts to enter the complex, Jafri began to make a series of calls to police officers and political leaders. He was ignored. Then he tried to offer money to the rioters, asking them to leave the society's residents alone. They asked him to come out of the house with the money. Jafri did, and tried to drop a bundle of money on the street and rush back into his house, but the mob swooped on him in an instant, Chawal told me.

He then recounted the lynching: 'When those people caught him, I kicked him in the back.'

'He fell down?' I asked.

'He didn't fall, because the mob was holding him. Five or six people held him upright, then someone struck him with a sword, chopped off his hand, then his legs, then everything else. After cutting him to pieces, they put him on the wood they'd piled up and set it on fire, they burnt him alive.' Until my sting operation, there was no direct evidence or eyewitness testimony of how Jafri was killed. The confessions of Chawal and Jain provided, for the first time, gruesome accounts of Jafri's final moments.

'So did only people from the society get killed or were there other Muslims also?' I asked Mangilal Jain when he came into my room for our one-on-one.

'No, sir,' he said. 'People from outside also got killed. There are Muslims living on the streets all around the society. They are poor people, these [he meant the residents of Gulbarg Society] are rich people. These street dwellers are labourers, mechanics and factory workers. Whenever the situation would get tense, Ehsan Jafri would call everyone in. There was a masjid inside, and every year he would arrange for them to be fed. Whenever a riot broke out, all these people would take shelter inside. He was very capable. He would make just one call and the police would land up. There was always an SRP [State Reserve Police Force] post at this place. So people would feel safe there.'

'So that day, you were just one of the crowd, raising the slogan of "Jai Shri Ram"?'

'Just chanting "Jai Shri Ram" was giving people a rush,' Jain said, 'I was there with a lot of friends, sir.'

Mangilal, as his surname indicates, was a Jain. Scholars of Jainism have explained that the life force, jiva, is sacred in Jainism and can be found everywhere, in animals and plants, and even unseen souls moving through the elements. Jains believe that they must avoid causing even inadvertent harm to living things. Hindu nationalists have in the past blamed the influence of Jainism, Buddhism and shades of the Bhakti movement for the vegetarianism and non-violence that, according to them, have rendered Hinduism weak and effeminate. The militarism of the Hindu right-wing is a result of years of indoctrination that preaches violence as a manifestation of masculinity. Jain certainly had greater belief in violent Hindutva than in Jainism, his religion by birth.

'So who were our people who took part in the killing?' I asked Jain.

'Look, sir,' he said, 'there were a lot of faces whom I didn't know at all. Bharat Teli, Atul Vaidya and many other people were there. They came from faraway places like Bapu Nagar and Meghaninagar. There was a mob of 50,000 people. How could we know who was who?'

'So how did we kill these Muslims?'

'They were dragged out of their houses. Someone cut them down, another set them ablaze. Petrol was already there to set up fires.'

'So petrol was available?' I asked

'Petrol and kerosene were brought by these people. They were carted in the vehicles. [They said] "Come with us, there is a riot, our Hindu brothers are being attacked, come."'

'These were our Vishwa Hindu Parishad people?'

'Yes. They came in huge numbers, in vehicles, in whatever mode of transport they could get, they surrounded everything. There were people from the neighbourhoods near the complex. Whoever was seen was killed,' Jain said.

•—•

According to the three accused, the police not only gave the rioters a free hand, but exhorted them to kill Muslims. Jain said that K.G. Erda, the police inspector in charge of the Meghaninagar police station, told the rioters that they could have three to four uninterrupted hours to murder and rape. He made a great show of coming to the rescue of Muslims trapped in the Gulbarg Society complex only after dozens had already been killed. Even then, Chawal told me, some rioters told Erda that stopping them from killing everybody there was a mistake because there would still be some Muslims left who could testify against them.

According to Chawal, Inspector Erda told the rioters he had a plan. He said, 'When the vehicle carrying the Muslims heads this way, our constable accompanying the vehicle will get out, then you can set the vehicle on fire. The whole episode will end here itself and there will be no question of framing a case against anyone.'

But the plan could not be executed, Chawal claimed, because of the intervention of a Muslim inspector named Pathan. Chawal corroborated what many survivors later testified in court that, but for Inspector Pathan's intervention, many more Muslims would have died.

Mangilal Jain told me the same story, about the police indicating to the rioters that they could do whatever they wanted to Muslims in those few hours. It fuelled the mob's crazed urgency, their attempt to kill anyone who crossed their path.

'Erda supported us. The police kept away from the public that day,' Jain said to me without hesitation.

'Kept away from Muslims?'

'Public [the police] kept away from Hindus. They [the police] told us that everything should be finished within two–three hours.'

'That means they gave you two–three hours?'

'To finish,' Jain said.

'Finish everything?'

'This was happening across all of Ahmedabad. [It was understood] no outsider would come. Even reinforcements weren't going to come, the forces wouldn't get there till evening, so all the work should be done,' Jain said.

'He [Erda] told you to do it all in two to three hours?'

'He [Erda] said it and the mob went berserk. Some started looting. Others started killing. Someone dragged a man out and hacked him down and burnt him. A lot of this kind of stuff happened,' Jain said, almost casually.

Prahlad Raju told me that the police personnel deployed in the area not only stood back, but signalled to the rioters to go for the kill.

'How did the police behave with you on the day of the Gulbarg incident?' I asked Raju.

'The police did nothing except watch us …'

'They let you do whatever you wanted to?'

'They did not arrest a single person that day. Nobody was touched,' Raju said.

'They didn't stop anyone?' I asked.

'They dispersed us after 4.30 [in the afternoon].'

'Till then, nobody was stopped?'

'When orders came from the higher-ups, we were told to leave.'

Raju and Jain said that they were treated very well by the police even after they were arrested. No tough questions were asked, no weapons recovered, no statements were recorded and home-cooked food was served. The police made sure they were comfortable until they were bailed out by the VHP.

I read out the essential parts of the confessions made by Jain, Chawal and Raju in court. I also requested the court to play the video footage I had shot on my spy cams. But the court did not feel it was necessary, which surprised me. I thought my testimony had gone smoothly, that I had narrated exactly what I knew, but once again, I was aware of the hostile atmosphere that prevailed, even in the body language of the courtroom staff.

The hostility manifested openly in the cross-examination, which lasted for over six hours. I felt vulnerable and increasingly helpless as the defence lawyer and the presiding judge picked at me like a committee of starving vultures.

·•·

The defence first insisted that it would cross-examine me in the Gujarati language. I told the court that it would be in the interest of justice if I could be asked questions in either Hindi or English, the two languages in which I was comfortable. After much protest, the defence agreed to question me in Hindi, but not before establishing that I was a non-Gujarati, an outsider.

In its first line of attack, the defence asserted that my tapes were doctored.

'The tapes have been forensically examined by the FSL and it's the FSL that has certified them to be authentic,' I replied.

'You were in the habit of recording only those parts of the conversation that suited you, and deleting the rest,' argued the defence.

'All the recordings are complete. In each recording you will find that the recording begins much before the conversation starts and it continues uninterrupted much after a meeting ends. There is no way I could delete and chop as I wished.'

Every time the defence did not like my answer, the defence lawyer would start shouting, insisting that I reply 'only "yes" or "no"'.

At one point, the defence posed this question: 'If you are shooting a beauty contest on your camera and you inadvertently record a scene which you don't need, then do you have the facility to delete it?' The lawyer demanded that I reply with just a 'yes' or a 'no'. It was obvious the defence was trying to trap me with mischievous, even silly, questions. I replied that the lawyer's question was unclear, as I needed to know which camera the defence was referring to. Upon hearing this, the judge snapped at me that everybody else in the courtroom could understand the question.

'But sir,' I said to the judge, 'one can't tamper with a spy camera. And since it is my spy camera footage that is in question, this is not a question I can reply to with just a "yes" or "no" without a detailed answer.'

At this, the judge flew off the handle: 'You are a journalist outside, not here. Answer the court in a straightforward manner. How dare you to suggest that the defence is asking vague questions. Don't think this is some spectacle. This is my court.'

For over five minutes, he continued to harangue me. The defence lawyer joined in the bullying with relish. 'My Lord,' he screamed, 'you have just seen this man's mentality. I'm going to further expose his motives.' After ten minutes of theatrical umbrage taken by the judge and snide insults from both the judge and the defence lawyer, the court finally recorded my reply. Seeing that the defence wanted to drag the proceedings out, I asked the court if my cross-examination could be expedited so that I could catch my evening flight to Delhi.

'Why,' the defence lawyer taunted me, 'don't you like Gujarat? Spend a few days in Gujarat, why don't you.'

The accused, seated in court, were thoroughly entertained, laughing along with the defence.

I told the court that I loved Gujarat as much as anybody else, but that the people present in that courtroom were not the true representatives of the state.

The defence counsel then asked me about my salary. I replied to his question, upon which he made the accusation that the whole sting operation was a strategy to make money.

'I didn't get a single penny more than my salary.'

'You had made a fabricated identity card of Delhi University in the name of Piyush Agarwal?' he asked.

'Yes,' I said, 'but I didn't use it for any wrong purpose. I just used it to check in at the hotels because I wanted to protect my real identity.'

The judge again became angry and told me to 'only reply in "yes" or "no"'. I said, 'Sir, it's important that I give a small explanation.' The judge started shouting again. Each time he screamed at me, the accused present in the courtroom would laugh out loud.

I was taken aback by the judge's temper, which he seemed entirely unable to control. I kept telling myself that, no matter the provocation, I would not lose my cool.

'Do you know,' the defence said, going with the absurd line that the tapes were doctored, 'there is a software by the name of Audio Adding and Deleting Mixture Software?'

'I don't know about any such software,' I said.

'Why have you not produced the full transcripts?'

'I have produced the transcripts that we had prepared. Besides, I have produced the full video footage. If the court has any doubt, it must play the footage now in open court,' I said.

But the judge refused and the defence kept on about the transcripts I had produced, how there were gaps, imaginary conversations and falsifications.

I insisted that the court must play the video footage to ascertain the truth of these allegations.

Seeing that their efforts to rattle me were unsuccessful, the judge and the defence lawyer became personal. The defence asked me why I had stung Hindu rioters, but not the Muslims who were accused in the Godhra train burning. I replied that, since the accused were all behind bars, I would not have been able to sting them. The judge refused to allow my answer, and once again demanded that I say only 'yes' or 'no' in response. It was clear that the defence wanted to paint me as biased. Judge Joshi then remarked that people like me could reach anywhere: *'Tum log to kahin bhi ja sakte ho,'* implying that if I wished to sting the Sabarmati Express accused, who were all Muslims, I could have done so even inside the jail in which they were held. The defence added: 'Who knows if you are secretly recording the proceedings of this court also. Maybe you should record it as it will come to your use in the future.' The judge and the defence lawyer looked at each other and chuckled.

During the cross-examination, the defence asked me the details of my address in Delhi and whether I lived in rented accommodation. They wanted to know how long I had been living at that address. There were dozens of accused present in the court. To question me at length about my home in their presence was nothing but intimidation.

As my cross-examination progressed, the atmosphere became increasingly tense. At 5 p.m., the defence asked that I be present the next day for further cross-examination. The SIT booked me into a hotel, stationed a posse of CISF personnel to guard my room the whole night and escorted me back to court the next morning. It took a few more hours of aggressive questioning before the defence finally said it had nothing more to ask.

Months before I took the stand, the special public prosecutor R.K. Shah, who was appointed by the Supreme Court to handle the Gulbarg Society trial, resigned, hinting that the SIT was trying to protect the guilty police officers. In a letter to the SIT chief, R.K. Raghavan, Shah wrote about the conduct of B.U. Joshi: 'The attitude of the learned judge towards the witnesses, particularly victim eye-witnesses, has by and large remained hostile and unsympathetic. He browbeats them, threatens them, or taunts them. He denies the witnesses their rights.'[7]

After my testimony, I wrote a fervent complaint to Raghavan. I said the SIT should be doing more to protect its witnesses. He replied that he was sorry that I had a bad experience in court, but assured me that his officers and the prosecution were putting in their best efforts.

Joshi was later transferred out of Ahmedabad[8] and another judge, B.J. Dhandha, took over the trial. But he retired from judicial service without pronouncing a verdict. After Dhandha, another judge, K.K. Bhatt, was entrusted with the matter. But then the Supreme Court stayed the proceedings. The matter was then transferred to yet another judge, P.B. Desai, the principal judge of the City Civil & Sessions Court, Ahmedabad.

I was summoned by the court again to identify the voices of the three accused I had stung. Their voices matched the voices on the sting tapes, certified the FSL. The public prosecutor, Kodekar, submitted a list of twenty-four star eyewitnesses to the court, who, according to the prosecution, had testified in a manner that was truthful and believable, and the combined weight of their testimony proved the prosecution's case beyond reasonable doubt. My name was at number nineteen on that list.

The public prosecutor argued before the judge that my testimony established a conspiracy between Raju, Jain and Chawal. My sting operation, Kodekar said, also established the role of accused number 59, Atul Vaidya, accused number 54, Bharat Teli, accused number 58, Meghsing Roopsing, and accused number 57, K.G. Erda, in the offence.

Erda was arrested and arraigned by the SIT on the basis of my sting operation and a few eyewitness testimonies. The SIT at one point also pursued the possibility of charging M.K. Tandon for aiding and abetting the rioters, but in the final reckoning, only recommended departmental action against him.[9]

My testimony, the prosecution contended, 'established the elements of a pre-planned conspiracy existing between the accused which resulted in the carnage at Gulbarg Society'.

On 2 June 2016, fourteen years after sixty-nine lives were snuffed out, P.B. Desai convicted twenty-four accused and let off thirty-six. During the trial, six of the accused died before a verdict was reached. The judge refused to rely on my testimony on the grounds that I had not submitted the full transcripts of the sting operation. But the transcript should not have mattered—not when the video footage was available for all to examine. The three accused had admitted to their roles in the Gulbarg Society massacre on camera. More importantly, I had read out all the crucial parts of their on-camera confessions in court, and had repeatedly requested the court to play the tapes. In another case—the Naroda Patiya massacre—the judge herself had watched the tapes to ascertain the truth.

The Gulbarg trial court offered up another reason to reject my evidence. According to the judge, my tapes were forensically validated by the CBI, which was not the agency that had investigated the Gulbarg massacre.

The court went on to state, 'Again, if we look at the real intention and purpose of the sting operation, the same is clearly to implicate and establish the role of more accused in the alleged greater conspiracy which has been very zealously pursued by some of the victims, more particularly Zakia Jafri, widow of late Shri Ehsan Jafri.' The judge then concluded by saying that there was no material of conspiracy brought before him and therefore 'the sting operation has no much role to play'. It is shocking that the court could reach the conclusion that my purpose was to implicate more accused and allege a greater conspiracy. How could the court, without any evidence, attribute a motive to my investigation? It was important to discard my testimony because then it was easier to dispose of the charges of conspiracy.

Inevitably, the judge ended up acquitting the accused of conspiracy to commit murder in the Gulbarg Society massacre. Atul Vaidya, a VHP bigwig, was convicted of the lesser offence of rioting, rather than conspiracy or murder. Bharat Teli, also a VHP leader, was convicted of murder and Mangilal Jain of attempted murder.

But the court acquitted Madanlal Chawal, who had admitted to me on tape that he had participated in hacking Jafri to death and setting him on fire. It also acquitted BJP Counsellor Bipin Patel, Prahlad Raju and Inspector K.G. Erda of all charges levelled against them, giving them 'the benefit of doubt'.[10] The High Court of Gujarat has since then granted bail to many convicts, including VHP's Atul Vaidya, even as appeals are pending before it. In December 2019, the *Times of India* reported that as many as eight convicts who had been sentenced to life in jail were granted bail and their sentences suspended by the High Court in the year 2019 alone.

9

The Killing Fields

At Calcutta in 1946, and subsequently, the vengeance of the rioters had been wreaked deliberately on women. As the great migrations and great slaughters following partition got underway, so too did a sustained and brutal campaign of sexual persecution. The use of rape as a weapon of war was conscious and emphatic. On every side, proud tales were told of the degradation of enemy women.

— Alex von Tunzelmann, *Indian Summer: The Secret History of the End of an Empire*

Željko Ražnatović, who went by the assumed name 'Arkan', had been a career criminal in both the West and Yugoslavia when, in October 1990, he became the leader of the 'Delije', the ultras group of Belgrade's famous Red Star football club. As Alex Alvarez, a sociologist from Northern Arizona University, wrote: 'Arkan's involvement as leader of the fan club was encouraged by the Slobodan Milošević government which wanted to harness the energy, nationalism and violence of the young men who made up the club.'[1]

With funds, military training and arms provided by the Milošević government, as the International Criminal Tribunal at the Hague has established, Arkan set up his own paramilitary group called 'Arkan's

Tigers', recruiting members among the ultras and promoting the group as an instrument for the defence of Serbs living outside Serbia and for the protection of Serbian interests throughout Yugoslavia.[2]

A ragtag collection of petty criminals, unemployed youth, and racist, nationalist football fans who liked to fight was turned into a military-style organisation. When violence broke out in Bosnia after its declaration of independence from Yugoslavia, this group was at the forefront of what they chillingly described as 'ethnic cleansing'. On 2 April 1992, Arkan's Tigers entered the northeastern border town of Bijeljina, in Bosnia. 'Dressed in camouflage uniforms with ski masks and armed with automatic weapons,' wrote Alvarez, 'this paramilitary group rampaged through the town. Rushing from home to home, they booted in the doors of many of Bijeljina's Muslim population. They targeted the educated, influential, wealthy, and prominent Muslims and dragged them out into the street where they were summarily beaten and shot.'

State-supported and financed paramilitary groups have carried out genocides in Armenia, Liberia, Rwanda and Bosnia. According to Alvarez:

> These paramilitary organizations, often referred to as militias or sometimes as death squads, are frequently implicated in the worst excesses of the regimes which they serve, including mass murder, genocide, rape, torture, and various other human rights violations. Trained in violence, yet not bound by formal codes of conduct, these groups are a particularly deadly form of social organization. The reliance of many states upon paramilitary style units poses some potentially important questions about the nature of genocide and other human rights violations as well as the governments that create and unleash them.

On 28 February 2002, Ahmedabad witnessed meticulously planned, ethnically targeted killings of the kind that the world had seen in places like Bosnia and Rwanda. The killers in Ahmedabad were not soldiers or military forces but Hindutva activists who had organised themselves to kill Muslims in large numbers as supposed revenge for the attack on kar sevaks in Godhra. Wearing saffron-coloured headbands and chanting 'Jai Shri Ram', they roamed the streets, looting, raping, burning and killing Muslims at will. The death toll on one day in Ahmedabad was over 180, more than the number of people killed by Arkan's Tigers in Bijeljina. The neighbourhood that bled the most was working-class Naroda Patiya, with a mixed population of Hindus and Muslims. The official death toll at Patiya and nearby Naroda Gam was put at 108, with ninety-six people killed in Patiya and twelve in Gam.

About fifteen kilometres from the Ahmedabad city centre, Naroda Gam and Naroda Patiya were typical urban slums. Both were dense, closely packed settlements that had grown to their present size over seventy years and were nominally under the jurisdiction of the Ahmedabad Municipal Corporation—not that many municipal services were available here. The distance between the two was about a kilometre, with Gam being relatively compact while Patiya was a labyrinth of narrow lanes flanked by unsightly concrete structures, few of them higher than two storeys.

Both Gam and Patiya were home to around 2,000 Muslims. A majority of them were daily-wage labourers, migrants from Karnataka, Maharashtra, UP and Rajasthan. They were extremely poor, subsisting on the bare minimum and sending the substantial part of their meagre wages back to their hometowns. Many struggled to understand or speak Gujarati. They were, at best, eking out a life on the margins of society. Across the road from Patiya was the State Transport warehouse and nearby were the Hindu-dominated Gopinath and Gangotri housing societies. Also across the road from Naroda Patiya was Chhota Chharanagar, a ghetto mostly occupied by Chharas, a denotified tribe once designated as criminal under the colonial-era Criminal Tribes Act of 1871. They are now classified by the Gujarat government as OBC. The community has had a long-running problem with the police, which occasionally spilt over into violent confrontation. Many residents of Chhota Chharanagar engaged in illicit activity, including bootlegging, gambling and petty robbery.

On 28 February, in response to the deaths of kar sevaks on the Sabarmati Express, the VHP called for a Gujarat bandh. The gist of the 120 complaints filed by the survivors, as well as the testimonies of eyewitnesses before the Naroda Patiya trial court was 'that the call for the bandh was given by Vishwa Hindu Parishad and the riotous mobs were of the volunteers of Vishwa Hindu Parishad, RSS, Bajrang Dal, led by leaders of BJP', as the trial court noted in its judgement dated 31 August 2012.[3] The court noted again,[4] 'It is almost undisputed that all the eyewitnesses including the police witness have stated as their first reaction on 28/2/2002 itself that in the communal riot took place at Naroda, the Hindu leaders of the riots were of BJP, Vishwa Hindu Parishad, RSS and Bajrang Dal.'

Cold and calculated, the Hindutva hordes were not so much rioters as an execution squad that carried out a pogrom from 10 a.m. until well after dark. Apart from firearms, tridents and swords, anything the mobs got their hands on was used as a weapon—bricks, gas cylinders, kerosene stoves, diesel tankers—and unleashed on an entire neighbourhood of Muslims in Naroda Patiya. Most of the victims were burnt alive. And before being set alight, many were raped, beaten and had their limbs hacked off in an orgy of brutality.

As vicious slogans rent the air, the killers seemed almost joyous, as if they were at a particularly unbridled festival. Many of those I spoke to during the sting operation told me that phones were buzzing constantly as Hindutva activists congratulated each other on the mounting death toll. By sunset, the Muslim neighbourhoods in Naroda Patiya had been reduced to a wasteland of corpses, many of which were mutilated and burnt, their remains testimony to the mad savagery of the slaughter.

Naroda was just five kilometres from the local police control room (PCR) and less than four kilometres from Shahibaug, the Ahmedabad police headquarters. Yet no one responded and no effort was made to disperse the mob. In our conversations, the accused, not aware that they were being taped, said openly that the scale of the killing would have been impossible without tacit help from the police, who chose to simply look away as people they were sworn to protect were butchered.

Survivors from Naroda Patiya identified several Sangh Parivar members as their attackers, but those most prominently and repeatedly invoked as the leaders of the mob were BJP MLA Mayaben Kodnani and Bajrang Dal leader Babu Bajrangi. When filing the charges, though, the Gujarat police refused to indict Kodnani, citing lack of evidence. Bajrangi was chargesheeted along with a few other BJP and VHP workers and a couple of dozen people from the Chhara community. In all, the Gujarat police implicated forty-nine people in the Naroda Patiya massacre and a similar number for the killings in neighbouring Naroda Gam. Bajrangi, the accused with the highest profile, was named on both charge sheets. After playing cat-and-mouse with the Gujarat police for over three months, he was arrested on 28 May 2002 amidst much drama. Five months after his arrest, the Gujarat High Court granted him bail.

...

Bajrang Dal, the paramilitary youth wing of the VHP, was founded in 1984 to mobilise youth for the Ram Mandir movement. Members of the Dal played a prominent role in tearing down the Babri Masjid in Ayodhya in December 1992, after which it was banned by the then Congress government. But the ban was lifted one scant year later. As the word 'secular' became increasingly tainted, the Dal found a rich vein to tap among angry, young Hindu working-class men who believed that so-called minority appeasement and reservations had denied them their rightful place in Indian society and their just rewards.

Under the aegis of the Bajrang Dal, these disaffected men had a renewed purpose. They began to be put to work on the organisation's signature causes—the protection of cows, for instance. Bajrang Dal vigilantes would routinely 'monitor' the highways and administer beatings to Muslim cattle traders whom they accused of transporting cows for illegal slaughter. Another pet project was to protect Hindu girls from 'love jihad', from the 'sin' of inter-faith marriage. Such unions, according to Dal activists, could never be legitimate and were the result of a dastardly plot by Muslim men to convert Hindu women. Dal vigilantes would take it upon themselves to break up such relationships, to beat up the man, or to sometimes 'restore' the girl, against her will, to her family. Dal members loved publicity, especially having TV cameras capture the terror they sowed and the havoc they wreaked on innocent people. A particular favourite activity of Dal thugs was beating up young couples on Valentine's Day, with girls too on the receiving end of slaps and kicks. Another was to find an artist who the Dal deemed had offended the sanctity of Indian deities, or who had somehow transgressed by offering a cosmopolitan, pluralistic, secular perspective on the world.

On 2 May 1998, a Bajrang Dal mob stormed and ransacked the Mumbai home of M.F. Husain, among India's most eminent and revered painters. They accused him of the non-existent crime, in Hinduism at least, of blaspheming deities. Years later, the organisation threatened writer Arundhati Roy with similar violence if she continued down the 'anti-national' path, misusing her right to freedom of speech, as the Bajrang Dal saw it. Beyond the primetime posturing, though, the Bajrang Dal was a genuinely dangerous and profoundly violent organisation. In the late 1990s, it also began to target Christian missionaries engaged in humanitarian and welfare activities in the tribal regions of Odisha, Madhya Pradesh and Gujarat.[5]

Under the leadership of Haresh Bhatt, the Dal launched a vilification campaign against Christian missionary organisations in the Dang, Valsad and Bharuch districts of Gujarat. As a direct fallout of this campaign, churches were vandalised, copies of the Bible were burnt, and Christian functions and congregations violently disrupted.[6] Among the most vicious crimes of the decade was the Bajrang Dal-led 1999 lynching of Australian missionary Graham Staines. A group of hard-line Dal thugs, led by Dara Singh, set Staines and his two sons, Philip, nine, and Timothy, six, alight as they slept in their car in Manoharpur village in Keonjhar district, Orissa.[7] Later that same year, Dara Singh and his gang of bullies accosted a Muslim trader named Sheikh Rehman. It started as a beating but became something dark and deranged, as Singh chopped Rehman's arms off and then set him on fire before an audience of 400 people.[8]

After the Naroda Patiya massacre, Bajrangi became more notorious than Dara Singh. A survivor, Jannatbanu Kallubhai Shaikh, described a scene that became emblematic of the depravity of the Gujarat riots. She said in her police complaint that Bajrangi had cut open a pregnant woman's womb and impaled the foetus on his sword, holding it aloft and proclaiming that 'before the child comes, the child is killed'.

It was early in June 2007. I had already met Haresh Bhatt, the national vice-president of the Bajrang Dal. He had recommended that I meet Babu Bajrangi who, in Bhatt's words, was the 'chief architect of the dhamal' in Naroda Patiya.

I decided I wanted to sting Bajrangi in his den.

So, I rang him and introduced myself as an RSS man, and gave him Haresh Bhatt's reference. He agreed to a meeting in his office in the Naroda area. I must admit to feeling a journalist's thrill at the prospect. Bajrangi was arguably the most notorious face in the country. His office was on a high floor in a commercial complex near a cinema. It was a slick, air-conditioned room, busy with traffic—Bajrangi had a retinue that waited on him hand and foot, and there was a gurgling stream of visitors and sycophants eddying in and out, seeking blessings and orders.

After a few minutes in the reception, I was shown into Bajrangi's chamber. I told him that I was writing a book about the long overdue Hindu resurgence, and that I hoped I could influence and inspire the youth with stories of the bravery and strength shown in 2002 by the

Hindu community in Gujarat. He was fizzing, brimming over with energy. Just minutes into our conversation, he began a passionate rant about the number of Hindu girls he had rescued from the love jihad being waged by the Muslim community. He gestured at a young woman sitting in the reception area.

'You must have seen the young woman outside,' Bajrangi said. 'She had eloped with a Muslim boy called Javed. I abducted her and brought her back. Even as we speak, there are sixteen Hindu girls at my house. This is what I do on a regular basis. Rescue the girls and bring them home, then mindwash them and hand them over to their parents. The parents routinely come to my door, I tell them, "Don't worry, your girl will be back." If you are a parent and you go to the police station to register a complaint that "my girl has eloped with a Muslim man", they will direct you to my office.' After a few minutes, he said, unprompted—'Look, I am a tough man. And I just can't tolerate Muslims. I have only two enemies: Muslims and Christians.' Bajrangi had a foul mouth, and every few minutes he would unleash a volley of curses directed at Muslims. He seemed to be working himself up into a jittery rage. 'If I just step out of my office,' he said, 'and give out a loud call that we have to fix a Muslim, 4,000 people will come out on the roads. This is how much the people here love me, I work for the people and give work to the people.'

Part of Bajrangi's humming aggression was explained by his annoyance with the VHP leadership, who he believed had pocketed a lot of money raised in the name of Hindus. But his respect for Modi was unadulterated. 'Narendrabhai is God for me,' he said. 'The fact that I am still alive, sitting here, is because of him. He got me out on bail. For Modi, I would cut my body into pieces.' Towards the end of this first meeting, Bajrangi let slip, as if it were the most minor of details, that he had vowed to avenge Godhra, and on the night of 27 February, he had arranged for twenty-three revolvers to be delivered to him so that he could arm his supporters.

Right through our first meeting, Bajrangi was cagey. He talked about the killings in Naroda Patiya, but was very careful not to say anything that might directly incriminate him. As a journalist, one learns to read one's interview subjects. Some people tended to be reticent, cautious and tentative, like the VHP general secretary Jaideep Patel. There were others I spoke to, who were instantly suspicious and on their guard, the worst kind of interviewee for an undercover journalist with a spy cam. But Bajrangi was different. He was so sure of himself, so supremely confident that the state would not harm him or allow any harm to come to him, that he felt indestructible. To be fair, he had good reason to be cocky. After being named as one of the prime accused in the Naroda Patiya massacre, in which nearly a hundred Muslims had been murdered in what was the worst single incident during the Gujarat riots, Bajrangi was released on bail. It was as if he had never been away, quickly resuming his perch in his office from where he planned fresh ways to antagonise and terrorise minorities. He had, for instance, around the time we spoke, been leading groups of vandals around theatres in Gujarat to violently disrupt any screenings of the Hindi movie *Parzania*, which was set in the time of the riots. Most theatre-owners, in any case, were too scared to screen the film because they knew their theatres would be ransacked by Hindutva activists while the state watched impassively.

Though I was impatient to meet him again, I was careful not to appear too eager. A full fifty-five days passed before we met for a second time, on 10 August, when he asked me over for lunch. Again, he began our conversation with a self-congratulatory disquisition on the number of Hindu girls he had saved from the clutches of Muslim men. He told me he had 'rescued' 956 women, which meant he had prevented the birth of around 5,000 Muslim children. It is commonplace among Hindutvawadis to imply that one Muslim man produces five children per wife ('*hum paanch, hamare pachchees*', as Modi himself had said). He reiterated that, after returning from Godhra, he had openly declared that he would take revenge for the

Hindus killed on the train, that he then collected guns to give rioters and told the police in Naroda Patiya to stand down and let what was happening happen.

I asked Bajrangi, 'Narendrabhai, that day, did Narendrabhai extend support on the day Naroda Patiya happened?'

'*Usne to sab Ram nam kar diya na yaar, nahi to kiski taqat thi, sab uska hi hath hai bhai, nahi to police ko instruction dewe to gad phad dewe police* (It was his hand which was behind this, otherwise if he had instructed the police, the police would have torn the rioters apart).'

He added, 'A witness has alleged that Babu Bajrangi slit open a womb with a sword, *bachcha bahar nikala talwar pe ghumaya* … She was watching from the bathroom … *kahan se bhosdi ki dekh rahi thi* …'

'Is she making the right allegation,' I asked Bajrangi with a wink.

'She says she was watching from the bathroom. Who knows? That day we turned it into a "Battle of Haldighati". Not possible now,' he said.

Bajrangi was referring to a battle fought in 1576 between the outnumbered forces of Maharana Pratap of Mewar and the mighty army of the Mughal emperor, Akbar. After initial success, the Rajput army was losing ground and the Mughals seemed poised for a decisive victory. But a late burst of sacrifice and bravery enabled Maharana Pratap to escape and fight again. This 'defeat' has become legend for Hindu nationalists, a story of Hindu guts and glory that serves as inspiration to their cadres.

'Did you kill a few with your hands,' I asked Bajrangi, my tone almost gleeful.

'What should I say,' Bajrangi demurred, 'whether I killed or not killed. *Aisa ek khadda tha khadda* (there was a big ditch), they were hiding in there. Then a mob came …'

'Did they pour petrol in that khadda?' I prodded him.

'Yes, a very big khadda (he gestured with his hands) … They entered the khadda from one side, then whoever tried to come out of the khadda, we cut them. When the commissioner came in the evening and saw the bloodshed, he said "behenchod!".'

Bajrangi was referring to a specific incident in which at least fifty-eight Muslims were killed while they were hiding in a U-shaped depression in the ground between two Hindu residential complexes, the Gangotri Society and Gopinath Society, in Patiya. A survivor, Harun Mohammadbhai Shaikh, described what happened in court:

> The Hindu mob was wearing saffron bands on their foreheads and had swords, pipes, tridents in their hands. I saw Mayaben [Kodnani] and Babu Bajrangi leading the mob. They were pelting stones, torching the carts, cabins, houses, anything anywhere that belonged to Muslims was set on fire ... Along with my family we ran to the Police Post, but the police fired at the fleeing Muslims, so we then ran towards a khancha near the Water Tank at Gopinath Nagar Society. We entered in that khancha thinking we could hide there. But the mob came and continued killing us. Some people were burnt, others were hacked. By 5.00 p.m. my mother, my wife, my only son, my maternal aunt, niece and my neighbours had perished in the khancha. While the massacre was on I remembered it was the time of Maghrib Namaz.

After the killing stopped, Bajrangi told me, he was asked by the police to leave the area, and even the state's home minister told him to go into hiding. Bajrangi stayed underground for months while the police supposedly sought him out.

'Narendra Modi,' he said, 'was under immense pressure to get me arrested. So a drama to arrest me was staged. P.P. Pandey, the then JCP, crime, set up the entire drama. Twelve or thirteen vehicles came to arrest me ... Everything was decided in advance, that I would be passing that road at a particular time. They arrested me, handcuffed me, all drama.'

While he was in hiding, Bajrangi claimed, he spoke with Modi more than a couple of times on the phone. He told me he was still in touch with Modi, though he could not meet him openly because of the media. He said his respect for Modi was such that if the chief minister asked him to become a suicide bomber and kill people, he would not bat an eyelid. '*Marad aadmi hai* Narendrabhai (He is a real man),' Bajrangi said admiringly. He then called out to an attendant and instructed him to bring before us eight women he had recently rescued, as he liked to put it. They were paraded before us, and Bajrangi addressed these embarrassed, downcast women by the names of the Muslim men with whom they had eloped.

The heat from the button lens glued to my chest was beginning to bother me, so I asked Bajrangi if he could show me to the washroom. I changed the battery and memory card, switched the camera back on, and went back into the room, where we sat down to a Gujarati thali. During lunch, I asked him if he would introduce me to some of his men who had been involved in the Naroda Patiya killings. He gave me the names and numbers of Suresh Chhara, who also went by the nicknames Richard and Suresh Langdo (in honour of his distinctive limp), and Prakash Rathod. Both men were Chharas and lived in Chharanagar.

On 18 August, I met Bajrangi for the third time. The conversation veered towards Narendra Modi.

'Narendrabhai had come,' Bajrangi said. 'He didn't come inside Patiya. But he had a firm grip on what was happening [on the day of the massacre]. The police didn't make a sound, and that was because of Narendrabhai ... Otherwise you won't believe how many policemen were present on the scene. If they wanted, they could have killed us.'

'So you took the help of the police?' I asked.

'We entered from here,' Bajrangi said, drawing a map of Naroda Patiya for my benefit, 'chased them down till they reached an open ground, and then we caught them.' As he said this, he laughed.

•••

Some years later, on 19 December 2011, I was summoned to the special court set up to conduct speedy trials of riot cases. It was located in Navrangpura, at the old High Court building in a smart part of Ahmedabad. On that day, the court was hearing sessions case number 235/09 with numbers 236/09, 241/09, 242/09, 243/09,

245/09, 246/09 and 270/09, all clubbed together into one common trial dubbed the 'Naroda Patiya massacre'. I was slated to depose as a prosecution witness (number 322).

There was heavy police presence. Bajrangi was outside the court room when I got to the complex. He stared in my direction, ground his teeth and took a few steps towards me before he stopped, as if making a great effort to control his rage.

The presiding judge was Jyotsna Yagnik. The special public prosecutor, Gaurang Vyas, asked me to tell the story of my sting operation. I gave the court the full account of how I went undercover, and how one meeting had led to another, and what Bajrangi told me during our first three meetings in his office. I told the court that, after meeting Bajrangi on 10 August, I went to meet Prakash Rathod and Suresh 'Richard' in Chharanagar, or more specifically Chhota Chharanagar, a squalid urban slum across from the equally deprived Muslim slums of Naroda Patiya in the far northeastern corner of Ahmedabad. Bajrangi had told me that he had great influence in Chharanagar and commanded a substantial following among the Chharas. He praised them for what he said were their criminal tendencies. Bajrangi said he liked to call the Chharas his weapons, and that they were there to 'just kill, nothing else'. I handed over to the court the transcripts of my conversations with Rathod and Suresh Langdo, whom I had met twice on consecutive days, on 11 and 12 August, immediately after Bajrangi gave me their contact details.

On the day of the Naroda Patiya massacre, both accused told me, the BJP MLA Mayaben Kodnani was a conspicuous presence. 'Mayaben was moving around all day in an open jeep,' they said, '... she kept raising slogans. She said, "Carry on with your work, I'm here [to protect you]." She was wearing a white sari and had on a saffron band.' The conversations I had with Rathod and Suresh Langdo were used by the judge to convict Kodnani.

I had quizzed Rathod about the involvement of other BJP leaders. I was trying to be subtle, gentle in my questioning, as I did not want to set them off. This was a place where violence, even extreme violence, was routine. Had they become suspicious of my question or, worse, discovered I was wearing a spy cam, there was no telling what they might have done to me.

'Bipin Panchal was here that time?' I asked Rathod. Panchal was Kodnani's trusted lieutenant and, according to the accounts of survivors, was present on the day of the massacre with his own small band of followers.

'He was,' said Rathod. 'All the boys were with him—he came in a van full of samaan [weapons] and was distributing them. Swords, etc.'

'Where was Bipin that day?' I asked again, hoping to elicit more details.

'We were all scattered at first. Then came Bipin Panchal. There were lots of people with him. They all entered saying "Jai Shri Ram, Jai Shri Ram", shouting "they have killed our brothers and now we have to teach them a lesson". Then the setting [of Muslims] on fire started. At first, the Muslims resisted. Then we beat them and made them run. One or two of them were thrown into [the fire]. Suresh Richard fought very well, so did Gudda and Naresh Chhara. They were tireless. The Muslims are scared of Richard. He has forcibly married a Muslim girl. Even the police is scared of him. We [the Chharas] went first. The VHP followed us. Nobody could have done what we did ... We filled well after well ... we burnt enough [people] to fill tractors.'

Rathod had then walked me over to the house of another accused from the Chhara community, Rajesh Kantilal. I made some small talk with him, and he told me he had spent about nine months in jail before being bailed out. He too, Rathod said, had killed Muslims. From Kantilal's house, we went to meet Suresh Langdo.

'Jai Shri Ram,' I greeted him as he motioned at a small boy to bring me a chair. He spoke of how the police had alerted them about Muslims hiding in a ditch.

'I swear by my children,' Richard said, 'I swear by the Mata [he pointed towards the portrait of a Hindu goddess kept against a wall], today is my fast, that if we had not been there, at least thirty to thirty-five Hindus would have been killed. We'd finished with killing, burning everything and had returned. That was when the police called us. They said some Muslims were hiding in the chaali. When we went there, we saw their houses had been completely burnt down, but seven or eight of them had hidden in the gutter. We shut the lid on it. If we'd gone inside the gutter after them, we might have got stuck. We closed the lid and weighted it down with big boulders. Later, they found eight or ten corpses in there. They'd gone in there to save their lives, but they died of the gases down there. This happened in the evening, the dhamal went on till about 8.30 p.m.'

'So you went in again?' I asked.

'We were inside. By evening, things had cooled down ... After all, a man gets tired. Hurling stones, beating with pipes, stabbing, all this ... That day the police was with us, it was fun. The police were shooting at the Muslims, must have shot 70–80 Muslims, they didn't even spare the women. Bottles [filled with flammable liquids] were exploding. Gas cylinders were burning. Some pigs were lying under a truck. We killed a pig. Then we hung the pig from the mosque and raised a saffron flag. Eight or ten of us climbed on top. We broke the minaret ... One of our Hindu brothers brought a tanker, from Thakkar Nagar crossroad. He'd killed Muslims and brought the tanker. It was put in reverse and the mosque was broken. Petrol was thrown and then it was burnt.'

'It is being said the Chharas also committed rapes,' I said.

'Now look, one thing is true, Piyushbhai,' he told me, *'bhookhe ghuse to koi na koi to phal khayega na* [when hungry men go in, they will eat some fruit or the other]. *Aise bhi, phal ko kuchal ke phek denge* [In any case, the fruits are going to be crushed and thrown away]. Look, I'm not telling lies. Mata is before me. Many Muslim girls were being killed and burnt to death anyway, some people must have helped themselves to the fruit.'

'There must have been a couple of rapes,' I pressed.

'Might even have been more, then there were the rest of our brothers, our Hindu brothers, VHP people. Anyone could have helped themselves. Who wouldn't, when there's fruit ... Look, my wife is sitting here but let me say, the fruit was there, so it had to be eaten. I also ate. I also ate. I ate once.'

'Just once?'

'Just once, then I had to go killing again [turns to Prakash Rathod and talks about the girl he had raped and killed]. That scrap-dealer's girl, Naseemo, Naseemo, that juicy plump one. I got on top.'

'You got on top of her?' I asked.

'Yes, properly.'

'She didn't survive, did she?'

'No,' he said, 'then I pulped her. Made her into a pickle. Today, I will say something. If you have a child and I put him into the fire, your soul will burn, won't it? Those who survived have called me the cripple who burnt their children, some were hiding in a hut, they saw me killing their children, some survived by putting a tika on their foreheads.

'[They were] trying to pass off as Hindus?' I asked him.

'A crowd came saying "Jai Shri Ram", but we knew who was from which community. We live here. So then we killed the Muslims—ask the RSS and Bajrang Dal people. They will tell you that the Chharas were picking out the Muslims and killing them, marking them down one by one.'

The judge kept a straight face and didn't betray any emotion as I testified to what Richard had told me. I felt shame as I read from the transcript, particularly those parts where I expressed approval of what he had done. And though I was not asked, I told the judge—as much to reassure myself as her—that I was playing a part, that I had to show Richard that I was an ally if I was to get his confession on tape.

I wanted one last meeting with Bajrangi, I wanted him to talk more specifically about his part in the Naroda Patiya killings. Luck was on my side. Bajrangi called me to say that he had some work to do in Delhi and wanted to meet Anandji, the fictional senior RSS functionary to whom I reported. Once again, Tarun Tejpal's uncle prepared for his role. We put up large, framed pictures of Hindutva lodestars such as Golwalkar, Hedgewar and Savarkar on the walls of his house. I picked Bajrangi up in a cab, so I would not have to give him the address, and we made our way to Anandji's house.

We had prepared a list of questions for Bajrangi, I told the court. And he walked straight into our trap.

'My role was as follows,' Bajrangi told Anandji, no doubt hoping to impress a supposed RSS higher-up. 'I was the first to start the [Naroda] Patiya operation ... We and the local residents were all together. Patiya is just half a kilometre away from my home. I had gone to Godhra after the Sabarmati Express fire. I could not bear what I saw. The next day, we gave them a fitting reply.'

'What were you unable to tolerate in Godhra?' asked Anandji.

'Any person who saw the Godhra kaand [massacre] would have felt like just killing them [Muslims] at once, hacking them apart, that's how it was.'

'How could you organise it all in such a short time?' Anandji egged Bajrangi on.

'We organised everything that night itself,' Bajrangi said, eager to show off his efficiency. 'We mobilised a team of twenty-nine or thirty people. Those who had guns, we went to them that night itself, and told them to give us their guns. If anyone refused, I told them I would shoot them the next day, even if they were Hindu. So people agreed to part with whatever cartridges and guns they had. In this way, we collected twenty-three guns. But nobody died of gunshots. What happened was this: we chased them and were able to scare them into a huge khadda [pit]. There we surrounded them and finished everything off. Then, at 7 o'clock, we announced—'

'This was in Patiya? That's what it's called, isn't it?' Anandji asked.

'Yes, yes, Patiya.'

'Please describe the area,' I intervened.

'In Patiya, there is an ST [State Transport] workshop with a huge wall beside it; next to this wall, Patiya begins. Opposite Patiya, there is a masjid and beside it is a sprawling khadda ... That's where we killed them all. At 7 o'clock, I called the home minister [Gordhan Zadafia] and also Jaideepbhai [VHP general secretary, Jaideep Patel] and told them how many people had been killed, and said that things were now in their hands. I don't know if they did anything, though. At 2.30 in the morning, an FIR was lodged against me. The FIR said I was there, the police commissioner even issued orders to shoot me at sight ...'

'Who, Narendrabhai?' Anandji asked, meaning Modi.

'The commissioner ordered. We and the Chharas carried out the Patiya massacre. After that, we all went to jail ... People gave us a lot of money after we were jailed. I am rich, so I have no worries, but the Vishwa Hindu Parishad leaders didn't care for those who were poor and had no money. Even from jail I was telling them [the VHP] to look after their families, do something for the accused. They provided for them for some four to six months, after that all help was stopped. They had promised to fight our cases in court but till today, nobody has done a thing. Pravinbhai [Togadia, VHP international general secretary] had promised this openly and he had also said that if there were any problems at their home or any loss [he would take care of them], but no one knows where they put all the money they collected. Nobody was given any money. For five to seven months, they gave rations, but nothing apart from that—'

'You were in touch only with Jaideepbhai?'

'Only Jaideep was talking to me from the VHP,' Bajrangi complained. 'I spoke to Jaideepbhai eleven or twelve times. And we killed at will, turned the place into Haldighati. And I am proud of it, if I get another chance, I will kill even more.'

'Where was Jaideepbhai camping then?' asked Anandji.

'Jaideepbhai was sitting at Dhanvantri, which is Pravinbhai's dispensary [Pravin Togadia is a doctor by profession and runs a hospital in Ahmedabad]. He was there, in Bapunagar. There he was and I didn't even tell him that we were going to do this. In Naroda and Naroda Patiya, we didn't spare a single Muslim shop, we set everything on fire, we set them on fire and killed them. That's what we did. Up till then, they didn't know what was happening; when they got to hear how many had been killed, they got scared. There is a distance of about half a kilometre between Naroda [Patiya] and Naroda Gam. We did a lot at both places. Must have butchered not less than ... Then we dumped the corpses into a well. At first, I didn't talk [Bajrangi was referring to his first couple of meetings with me], I thought many journalists and all kinds of people come and ask me if I was in the Patiya incident. I tell them I was not involved, I was quite far away, admitted in a hospital.'

'During the Patiya massacre,' Anandji asked, 'what did Gordhan Zadafia say when you spoke to him?'

'I spoke to Gordhan Zadafia. I told him everything that had happened. He told me to leave Gujarat and go into hiding. I asked what he meant, but he told me to run away and to not ever say that we had talked.'

'Tell us how it was all done, revolvers, cylinders ...' I said.

'The cylinders were theirs [the Muslims'],' Bajrangi said. 'Whichever house we entered, we just grabbed the cylinder and fired at it, and, dhadak, they exploded. We had guns in any case. I can't tell you what a good time it was.'

'At the pit, those people had gathered there,' I interrupted. I wanted Bajrangi to elaborate on the khancha killings.

'It was a huge pit. You could enter it from one side, but you couldn't climb out at the other end. They were all there together. They started clinging to each other. Even while they were dying, they told each other, "you die too, what are you going to be saved for, you die too", so the number of deaths increased.'

'Then people poured oil in?'

'Oil and burning tyres,' Bajrangi confirmed.

'Where did the oil come from?' Anandji asked.

'Oh that,' Bajrangi said, as if marvelling at our naivety. 'We had lots of material with us. We had filled lots of jerry cans in advance. From the petrol pump, the night before. Petrol pump owners gave us petrol and diesel for free.'

'Muslims were hacked to pieces?' I asked.

'Hacked, burnt, set on fire, many things were done. We believe in setting them on fire because these bastards say they don't want to be cremated, they're afraid of it, they say this and that will happen to them. I have just one wish, one last wish. Let me be sentenced to death. I don't want to be incarcerated, I don't care if I'm hanged. Give me two days before my hanging and I will go and have a field day in Juhapura [a Muslim ghetto in Ahmedabad], where seven or eight lakhs of these people stay. I will finish them off. Let a few more of them die, at least 25,000–50,000 should die.'

'How many witnesses have testified against you?' I asked.

'Fourteen Muslims and sixteen policemen. Out of the fourteen Muslims, some have moved to Juhapura. They've left Patiya, they don't have the guts to stay there, defying us. The rest have gone to Karnataka.'

'In other words, the way [you] have killed will go down in history.'

'It has been written in my FIR. There was this pregnant woman, I slit her open, behenchod sala. Showed them what's what, what kind of revenge we can take if our people are killed. *Hum khichdi kadhi wale nahin hai,* I am no feeble rice-eater. They shouldn't even be allowed to breed, I say that even today. Whoever they are, women, children, whoever. Nothing to be done with them but cut them down. Thrash them, slash them, burn the bastards. Many [Hindus] wasted time looting. Arrey [the idea is], don't keep them alive at all, after that everything is ours. That day, it was like what happened between Pakistan and India. There were bodies everywhere, it was a sight to be seen. I felt like Rana Pratap, that I had done something like Maharana Pratap.'

Then Bajrangi told us again that, without Modi's consent, the slaughter at Naroda Patiya, and by extension elsewhere, would not have been possible.

'Nobody can do what Narendrabhai has done in Gujarat,' Bajrangi said. 'If I didn't have Narendrabhai's support, we would not have been able to avenge Godhra because the police were standing right in front of us, seeing all that was happening, but they had shut their eyes and mouths. If they wanted to stop us, there were fifty of them there, they could have stopped us. We had good support from the police because of Narendrabhai and that is because whatever happened in Gujarat happened for the best. We got some relief from these people [the Muslims], they had got so high and daring. The Muslims kept making calls to the police, kept running to the police. They had one man called Saleem, supposed to be a sort of Naroda Patiya dada. He got into a police jeep. I myself caught him and dragged him out. The cops said, "Kill him, if he's left alive, he'll testify against us." He was taken a little way away and finished off right there.'

My testimony took four days to record and ran into more than 150 pages.

During the cross-examination, the defence tried to humiliate me and level all kinds of allegations. Judge Yagnik, unlike the judge in the Gulbarg Society case, stamped out these tactics. At one point, she told the defence lawyers: 'Witnesses are the eyes and ears of my court. They come at my invitation and are the guests of this court. You may ask him whatever is relevant to your case, but I will not allow you to insult him or make wild remarks about his character.'

The defence tried to prove that I had bribed the accused to say what they said, that I had told them that it was a play and they had to act out their roles by reading from a script. They also tried to argue that, after the sting operation was aired on news channels in 2007, the subsequent SIT had based its investigation on the revelations made in the sting, and so the prosecution was relying on a made-up story, on fiction. In response, the judge took it upon herself to watch each tape from start to finish. She concluded that it was self-evident from the videos that I, as an undercover reporter, had managed to win the trust of the accused and that their statements were voluntary in nature. There was, she said, no hint of any inducement. The judge dismissed as unfounded the claim that the accused were reading from a script.

On 29 August 2012,[9] Judge Yagnik convicted Babu Bajrangi and Maya Kodnani, among others, of murder and rioting. Both Bajrangi and Kodnani were sentenced to life imprisonment. Suresh Langdo was sentenced to thirty-one years behind bars. The Naroda Patiya verdict was historic, especially in the context of the judicial performance in other cases related to the Gujarat riots. For six years, between 2002 and 2008, as all major riot cases were stayed by the Supreme Court, the rioters roamed the streets of Gujarat, threatening and buying off witnesses. In 2007, when I first met Babu Bajrangi in his Naroda stronghold, he seemed invincible. Maya Kodnani was an MLA and a powerful minister (for women and child development) in Chief Minister Modi's cabinet. The Ahmedabad Crime Branch had already told the court that there was no evidence against Kodnani.

It took considerable resolve and independence for Judge Yagnik to come to the decision she did. She wrote that the *Tehelka* sting operation was genuine and credible, and referred to its findings throughout her 1,969-page judgement. Indeed, she wrote a separate chapter dedicated to the operation, in which she detailed the evidence that emerged from my video footage and my testimony, and why the court had relied on it to convict the accused. She cited several precedents to conclude that 'if the extra-judicial confession passes the test of credibility, it can be the basis for conviction also'.

She concluded that, in the Naroda Patiya case, 'this extra-judicial confession considering the foregoing discussion on its own merits is found very dependable, reliable, having the contents full of probability and that it is absolutely found safe to convict the accused on this extra-judicial confession'. The court also found that the 'occurrence of slitting the stomach of one pregnant Muslim woman tallies with the extra-judicial confession of Babu Bajrangi and even it tallies with the complaint of said Safiyabanu Shaikh. The occurrence of slitting the stomach of one Muslim pregnant woman is a reality.' Most importantly, the court concluded that the Naroda Patiya massacre was a premeditated conspiracy, which was hatched soon after the Godhra train burning on 27 February 2002, and well before 9.30 the next morning, when the conspirators met to embark upon their long day of rape, pillage and murder.

10

The Salient Feature of a Genocidal Ideology

When the murder of a five-year-old Bosnian Muslim child is legitimized by reference to harm Muslims allegedly did to Serbs some six hundred years ago, the logic employed is one according to which an individual's destiny is predetermined: it makes no difference what a particular individual (be it a child) says, feels, or means; what makes a difference—in terms of categories such as friend or enemy, fit for life or not so—is purely collective, extra-individual factors wholly extrinsic to the individual in question. When human agency is thoroughly collectivized, in-group differences evaporate and inter-group differences are polarized in the extreme ... The guilt of one group and the victimhood of the other are both eternalized. Such eternalization of victimhood goes hand in hand with the essentialization of identity that is a salient feature of genocidal ideologies.

— Arne Johan Vetlesen, *Evil and Human Agency: Understanding Collective Evildoing*

In January 2004, a crack team of forensic experts and doctors put together by the CBI, had pitched tents in a jungle in Dahod, Gujarat, and set up camp. The CBI is a federal agency that investigates crimes of national significance. This particular team's task was to find the bodies of fourteen people who had been killed and buried somewhere deep within the jungle in March 2002. They had been assigned this task by the Supreme Court of India because the Gujarat police had closed the case, stating that it had reached a dead end in its investigation. It had been four days since members of the CBI team began their search, and all they had found, despite combing the area with the full extent of their substantial resources, were the remains of glass bangles and rubber chappals.

It took an anonymous tip from a local for the investigators to find the mass grave on 31 January 2004. Divert a small stream flowing through the jungle, a villager told them, because the bodies are at the bottom. The CBI team hired an industrial excavator from Godhra, the nearest town, and dug a ditch parallel to the rivulet, and into that the water was diverted. In the middle of the river bed was a boulder that must have weighed at least fifty kilograms. Using the excavator, the team removed the boulder and dug up the ground. Not long after digging had begun, a foul smell rose out of the pit; the team exhumed the remains of five corpses, each bearing signs of torture, mutilation and burning. The female bodies were marked by cigarette burns on their breasts and bottoms. Their genitalia had been cut open and disfigured, and sharp objects had been thrust inside. A young boy, it was clear, had been sodomised before he was killed. The bodies had been almost uniformly decapitated. The skull and cervical vertebra of the bodies were not found. The murderers had strewn bags of salt into the graves to increase the speed of decomposition and stem the stench of rotting bodies.[1]

One of the accused later told the CBI that, after burying the bodies in a pit, they had rolled a boulder down from a nearby hillock and covered the grave with it. They then diverted a nearby rivulet to flow over the grave. After all this gruesome cover-up, the murderers felt certain their victims' bodies would never be found.

Incredibly, there were three survivors of the massacre. Bilkis Bano was just twenty, and five months pregnant, when she was gang-raped, beaten and left for dead. For some time, she pleaded with the Gujarat police to investigate the murders of fourteen of her relatives, including her three-year-old daughter and her cousin's one-day-old baby. She was a victim and an eyewitness through whom the investigators could have built a case. She had named the accused who raped her and two of her female relatives. Bilkis had also named the men who killed her fourteen relatives. She located for the Gujarat police the place of the massacre.

But the Gujarat police tampered with and destroyed evidence, forged case papers and falsified Bilkis Bano's statement.[2] They threatened and intimidated her, and tried to stop her from naming names. The police even helped to dispose of the bodies before filing a summary report and closing the case. A pair of government doctors, a couple who were hand in glove with the police, wrote a tailored post-mortem that failed to include any record of the signs of trauma, injury, gang rape and mutilation.[3]

In *Modernity and the Holocaust*, the sociologist and philosopher Zygmunt Bauman, a Polish exile, argued that the Holocaust was a natural extension of the dehumanising bureaucracy of modern society in which otherwise normal individuals become capable of committing astounding atrocities against others once a sense of personal responsibility has been removed. The ideology of Hindutva had similarly dehumanised large parts of the Gujarat administration. For many in the state machinery, if the killers were Hindus and the victims were Muslims, it did not appear to amount to a crime. For some it was about 'gaurav', a matter of Hindu pride.

Vivek Dubey, at the time the CBI joint director (Special Crime) who was leading the investigation into the killings, said that when some of his team 'reached the village [Devgad Baria village in district Dahod], Bilkis and her family from a distance began gesturing with folded hands, pleading with them to go away'. The victims had no faith in the agency, another officer who was part of the investigating team told me. As Dubey later said to me, 'Out of the group of seventeen, Bilkis was the only adult survivor. The two other survivors were small boys who were just four and seven years of age. It was important for us to record her statement.'

Bilkis and her family refused to meet the CBI team. They were traumatised and fearful. It had been two years since the massacre, but the horror was still raw. The accused were still at large, confident that the authorities were on their side. Some had grabbed and occupied lands in the village that belonged to Muslims. The offenders were card-carrying Hindutvawadis who knew they called the shots in the area. It was they who decided who would be the local police inspector, the mamlatdar, the local deputy superintendent. And, indeed, the police officers who had helped the accused cover up the killings had been promoted. For the likes of Bilkis, survival was all they could hope for; justice was too big and distant a dream.

The CBI team knew they had their work cut out; they had to instil confidence in Bilkis and her surviving family, and the Muslim community at large. They converted a local government building into their temporary headquarters, turning a few of the rooms into a police lock-up. The team consisted of more than a dozen personnel. They cooked their own meals, because such was the resentment in the village over the murders being re-investigated that they had been warned the villagers might poison any food served to the officers. If they left the building, they did so in groups and carried their firearms. The CBI investigators said they often noticed they were being followed, mostly by people in private vehicles but sometimes even the local police. The hostility was thick, palpable, a hairy beast squatting on the team's shoulders. Not that they had much more support from their superiors either. At the time, there was a BJP-led NDA government at the Centre, to which the CBI bosses reported. One senior officer (who was part of the CBI team) told me anonymously that his own boss 'was determined that nothing should come of the investigation. He was a major stumbling block. When we hired the digger to excavate the river bed, he said we were wasting public money.'[4]

Bilkis had given the NHRC the name of twelve men who had been involved in her rape and the gang rape and murder of much of her family. But the CBI team knew if they questioned any of these twelve men, they would abscond with the help of their community and political backers. A CBI inspector then decided to pose as a Hindutva sympathiser. He made friends with local members of right-wing Hindu organisations, breaking bread with them and even cadging the occasional drink. (Gujarat is a dry state, but you can get your hands on liquor if you are persistent and resourceful.)

Speaking to me anonymously, as he was still in service, the officer told me what he said to his new friends. 'There is no difference,' he would say, 'between the local police and the CBI. Both are the same. In fact, many from the local police go on to be posted in the CBI. Just as the suspects have settled the case with the local police, they could do it with the CBI. Tell them to give the CBI the same amount of money they have given to the local police, and the matter will be hushed up.'[5]

On 22 January 2004, the twelve men Bilkis had named to the NHRC emerged from their hiding place and turned up to see the CBI team in their makeshift village office. The CBI officer, who by now had become thick friends with the local Hindu leaders, had insisted that all twelve should come together and meet his seniors at the camp office. The twelve accused walked into a carefully laid trap.

Dubey described them to me as 'the VHP kind. They walked into the CBI camp office with a lot of swagger, wearing vermillion tikka on their foreheads. They were confident that nothing would happen to them.' All the accused, who were eventually charged with rape, murder and rioting, admitted, as the court noted in its judgement dated 19 April 2008, 'to be either active members of the Vishwa Hindu Parishad or Bharatiya Janata Party or their sympathisers'. But on the night they visited the CBI investigators, they seemed to have no inkling that they might one day have to face up to their crimes. Instead, they seemed to think the officers would arrange dinner, a few drinks and name their price. And that would be the end of the story.

Dubey said, when the twelve men appeared before his deputy in Dahod, 'the officer called me and said he wanted permission to arrest them'. My officers knew, Dubey said, 'that the Gujarat police would not assist us in nabbing them if they went missing, so I gave my deputy permission without getting bogged down in the CBI bureaucracy.' On that same night, the CBI took all twelve men into police custody. One of the accused said as he was being taken into custody: 'I made a mistake. I should have not buried the bodies but burnt them to ashes. That way you would have never found them.' When the CBI higher-ups learnt of the arrests, they were livid. Fortunately, the Supreme Court praised the CBI team for its quick action, saving it from possibly being disbanded.

But there was no Supreme Court in Dahod to monitor proceedings. When the twelve men were produced before the local court the next morning, a crowd of 5,000 people, presumably all right-wing Hindu activists, descended on the premises. The numbers were so overwhelming that the accused must have believed they would soon be freed, and that the state would protect them just as it had done for the last two years. The arrests, though, instilled confidence in Bilkis and her family. They now came forward to record their statements before the CBI, after which seventy more Muslim witnesses came forward to give evidence. The CBI had started building a case.

•—•

Bilkis Bano was a resident of Randhikpur village in Limkheda tehsil, Dahod, Gujarat. Her father, Abdul Issak Ghanchi, used to sell milk in the village to support his family. Bilkis had two sisters and three brothers. When she was just fifteen, she was married to Yakub Rasool from Devgadh Baria village, also in Dahod. Yakub's home was only about twenty-five kilometres away from Bilkis's village, which in turn is about 160 kilometres from Ahmedabad.

On 27 February 2002, Bilkis, Yakub and Saleha, their three-and-a-half-year-old daughter, were visiting her father's house in Randhikpur to celebrate Bakr Eid. Bilkis was five months pregnant. The VHP had called for a Gujarat bandh the very next day. In the uneasy silence of that morning, the last day of February, gangs of feral Hindus began roaming the empty streets, looking for Muslims to kill. In Randhikpur too, a Hindu mob had started burning down the shops and houses of their Muslim neighbours. Bilkis and her family decided they would be safer if they went to Yakub's village of Devgadh Baria. Yakub and Bilkis's brother left together, while Bilkis travelled in a group comprising fifteen relatives. Many other Muslim families in the village also fled to save their lives.

28 February 2002

Bilkis's travelling party comprised two adult males, four boys, nine women and her little daughter. They were Bilkis's mother, Halima; sisters, Mumtaz and Munni; aunts, Sugra and Amina; her cousins, Shamim, Mumtaz and Madina; her younger brothers, Aslam and Irfan; her uncles, Majid and Yusuf Musa; Hussain, just three, who was the son of Shamim; seven-year-old Saddam, the son of Amina; and Saleha, Bilkis's three-and-a-half-year-old daughter. Saleha was playful, unmindful of the danger around her, Bilkis later told me. She was wearing a green frock, anklets on her feet and pink bangles on her little wrists. For the next three days, Saleha was on the road with her mother and their extended family, as they walked from village to village, making their way through jungles and fields, hungry, thirsty, exhausted, terrified, looking for safety, for refuge.

Bilkis's cousin Shamim was heavily pregnant, almost full term. They left in such a hurry that Bilkis was barefoot when they sought shelter at the house of Kadkyabhai, the Randhikpur village sarpanch. After a few hours, they moved towards Chundadi village, on foot, and lay low in a school for a few hours. Bijalbhai Damor, a former member of the legislative assembly from the area, gave them food and water and a place to stay at night. Both Kadkyabhai and Bijalbhai did what they could to help people in obvious need; it did not matter that they were not Muslims themselves.

1 March 2002

The next morning, the group left Chundadi on foot, trekked to Kuwajar village and took refuge in a mosque. Shamim delivered a baby girl at the house of a Muslim midwife in the village. They spent the night in her house.

2 March 2002

The group of seventeen, including Shamim's now day-old baby, began to walk to another village. On the way they met Nayak, a tribal man, who took pity on the group and invited them to rest in his house. They stayed the night there, adopting tribal dress to avoid recognition.

3 March

The group left for Sarjumi, another village on the way to their destination. After walking a few kilometres, they reached a dirt track in Chapparwad village. Bilkis was dehydrated and felt dizzy. Shamim, who had given birth only the day before, was struggling to walk, clutching her newborn. To the left of the track were fields. On the right was hilly jungle. It looked sufficiently remote, the group thought, for it to be safe to rest until they regained some strength. They did not imagine that they were being tracked by people, including their neighbours, intent on 'revenge'.

An hour or so before noon, two white jeeps containing about thirty men pulled up on the kuchcha road beside the fields. They were armed with swords, sickles and sticks. At least twelve of the men were from Randhikpur, where Bilkis's father lived and where she was born and raised. Though Bilkis and her family were wearing Adivasi dress, they were identified: '*Aa rahya Musalmano, emane maro kapo,*' the men shouted. There they are, the Muslims, kill them!

Bilkis knew many of these men. They had been her neighbours for years. The house of Bipin Chandra Joshi, for instance, had faced her own. Bilkis's father often visited Bipin's father, who ran a clinic, for treatment. Radheshyam Shah, an advocate, also owned a bangle shop in the village. The bangles Bilkis wore on her wrists that morning were from his shop. Pradip Modhiya ran a small hotel, as did Naresh Modhiya; Raju Soni owned a shop. These were all men who had known Bilkis's family, had lived alongside them.

Shailesh Bhatt, who lived close to a mosque in Randhikpur, snatched Saleha from Bilkis. 'Don't hurt my daughter,' Bilkis begged. Just a few weeks earlier, Shailesh had visited Bilkis's house in the village for a cup of tea. On this day, he killed a three-and-a-half-year-old child by dashing her head against a rock. Some other middle-aged Hindu men, including Jaswant Nai, Govind Nai and Naresh Modhiya (who died during the trial) dragged Bilkis towards a tree and tore at her clothes.[6]

She turned to Jaswant: 'Chacha, I am five months pregnant, please spare me.' She told Govind and Naresh that they had been like brothers to her. Naresh held her arms down. Govind put the weight of his leg down on her chest and neck. All three men took turns to rape her. At some point during the assault, Bilkis lost consciousness. The men, believing she was dead, left her 'corpse' on the side of the unpaved road. While Bilkis was being raped, eleven other men hacked and stabbed the two adult males who were travelling with her, and raped and murdered the other women, including Shamim. And they killed her newborn.

After a few hours, Bilkis regained consciousness. All around her were the bodies of her family, the horribly mutilated and defiled corpses of the people she loved. Here was her one-day-old niece. There was her own daughter, her bangles unbroken on her little wrists. Bilkis's clothes were strewn beside her. She put her lehenga back on and crawled on all fours up a hillock.

Can a woman, assaulted, gang-raped and left to die remember how she felt when she came to, cast adrift in a sea of corpses? How does anyone find the strength to survive such horror? To have one's family murdered by one's friends and neighbours with such gratuitous, delirious savagery?

Manto tried to capture the horrors of the Partition killings in his short story 'Khol Do'. He wrote: 'The special train left Amritsar at two in the afternoon and reached Mughalpura eight hours later. Many people were killed en route, many injured; some went astray ... Ten a.m. Old Sirajuddin opened his eyes on the cold floor of the camp; seeing the swelling sea of men, women and children, he became still more confused ... His eyes struck the sun, and he awoke with a start as its sharp blaze entered him. Images assailed from all sides. Loot. Fire. Stampede. Station. Bullets. Night. And Sakina. Sirajuddin stood up immediately, and like a madman, began surveying the sea of people all round him. For three full hours he scoured the camp crying, "Sakina Sakina". But he learned nothing of the whereabouts of his only daughter.'[7]

Sunil Khilnani, writing about Manto's story, observed: 'The old man, Sirajuddin, eventually finds his daughter in a hospital—dying, barely conscious. When she hears a doctor request that a window be opened—"khol do"—she reflexively parts her legs. The doctor, understanding the implication, is left in a cold sweat.'[8]

·—·

After escaping from the scene of the crime, Bilkis spent the rest of the day and night hiding on the hillock. It was her memory of this hiding place that helped her lead the CBI investigators to the scene of the crime. Besides Bilkis, only two others survived, seven-year-old Saddam and three-year-old Hussain, both of who had also lost consciousness and were presumed dead.

Saddam was twelve when he testified in court in 2007. He was able to accurately describe the jeeps and the men who descended from them like beasts. He said he saw his mother being hacked to death and little Hussain being thrown into a bush. He lost consciousness when he was hit on the head with a stone. When he woke up, he saw Hussain weeping. They ran towards the road, where a man driving past saw the boys and stopped to help.

4 March 2002

The next morning, Bilkis was able to crawl to a nearby Adivasi village. She saw a handpump and drank her first mouthfuls of water in nearly twenty-four hours. A passing Adivasi woman gave her an old choli and odhni to cover her body. At the village, Bilkis saw a jeep and a man in a Home Guard uniform. She told him her story and he took her to the Limkheda police station. Bilkis gave the names of her assailants to Somabhai Gori alias Som Singh, the head constable on duty. She said she would be able to identify more men from the mob in a line-up. Bilkis told the policeman the men had raped her, and that she could take the police to the place where her family's bodies still lay. Som Singh waited till she had finished, then threatened to kill Bilkis for talking too much. He said he would take a syringe and inject her body with poison if she breathed a word about rape or took the names of any of the accused.

Som Singh then falsified the FIR to render any investigation meaningless. Instead of twenty-five or thirty attackers, he wrote Bilkis had been attacked by a mob of 500 people who could not be identified. Any mention of rape was omitted. Bilkis could not read or write, so Som Singh took her thumb impression on the FIR. He neither accompanied her to the scene of the crime to identify the bodies, as required by law, nor did he arrange for her to be medically examined, as also required by law.

The CBI discovered that the bodies had been moved from the actual scene of the crime—a field in Pannivel village, adjacent to a stretch of mud track—to a desolate spot in Kesharpur jungle. By moving them to a place inaccessible by vehicle, the police were trying to discredit Bilkis's account that the mob had driven up to them in two jeeps. The Limkheda police even hired a private photographer, Bhavin Patel, to document the bodies in the jungle. There were only eight bodies in the new crime scene and the photographer was told to only take pictures of five, including Saleha, Bilkis's daughter.⁹ The photographs, along with negatives, which were not made part of the police record, were recovered in 2004 by the CBI.

Section 174 of the Criminal Procedure Code (CrPC) requires that, when a police officer receives information that a person has been killed, he shall immediately give intimation thereof to the nearest executive magistrate empowered to hold inquests, and shall proceed to the place where the body of such deceased person is, and there, in the presence of two or more inhabitants of the neighbourhood, shall make an investigation, and draw up a report of the apparent cause of death, describing such wounds, fractures, bruises and other marks of injury as may be found on the body, and stating in what manner, or by what weapon or instrument such marks appear to have been inflicted. The process of inquest is crucial in a murder investigation. On 4 March, the day Bilkis was able to report the murders, the Limkheda police did not carry out an inquest. Nor were the bodies sent for post-mortem to determine the cause of death.

5 March 2002

The police took another photographer, Ramesh Soni, who was related to one of the Limkheda police personnel, to the spot to which the bodies had been moved. The new set of pictures clicked by Soni showed seven dead bodies; this time, Saleha's body was not one of them. Bilkis had told the Limkheda police that they were a group of seventeen, of whom only three had survived. But the Gujarat police made no attempt to find the missing bodies. Instead, they showed on record that they had found only seven bodies, those of four women, one teenaged girl, and two boys aged thirteen and eleven.

No effort seemed to have been made to record or collect evidence. The police did not take Bilkis to identify the bodies. Instead, they took Abdul Sattar, a Muslim man from her village and a distant relative, who immediately identified all the bodies. In the case papers, though, the Gujarat police wrote that Abdul Sattar identified just one body, that of Bilkis's mother Halima. The other six were marked as unidentified.

Again, it was the CBI in 2004 that identified the remaining bodies, with the help of the recovered pictures and the mutilated remains they exhumed from the spot. All the bodies showed signs of sexual assault. They had all been decapitated so that, even if they were recovered, identification would be complicated. The CBI never found the heads. The Limkheda police had hired a local villager called Mukesh Harijan to dispose of seven bodies. He testified in court that the police took him to a kotar (ravine) on the outskirts of Kesharpur village, where he dug a waist-deep pit and stacked seven bodies—four women, two boys and one girl—one on top of the other. He also told the court that he saw two doctors, one male and one female, at the spot. These were Arun and Sangeeta Prasad, a married couple who were both government doctors. The Prasads helped the police suppress facts by preparing a false medical report that did not record the injuries or the actual state of the dead bodies. They did not record indications of rape and sexual assault, and did not collect evidence from vaginal swabs, saliva, blood samples or the clothes worn by the deceased. They wrote in their report that the bodies had decomposed, which was a blatant lie. The couple were present when the police dumped the bodies into the pit, pouring in ninety kilograms of common salt to hurry the process of decomposition and mask the smell. A few months after hiding these seven bodies, the Gujarat police said that, despite their best efforts, they could not identify the killers, and since there was little prospect of success, they were closing their investigation.

Only when human rights activists persuaded Bilkis to approach the NHRC, which filed a motion with the Supreme Court, which then assigned the CBI to the case, did justice in this ghastly crime become possible. For the CBI, the most difficult step was the first one—recovering the bodies. The investigators knew the bodies were buried in Kesharpur jungle, but little else. Mukesh Harijan, who had dug the pit, described the location as 'lying off the kuchcha road branching off a pucca road leading from Piplod to Randhikpur village'. He said it could be reached by walking 'for two kilometres on a pagdandi (foot trail) across the hill'. The interrogation of B.R. Patel, the station house officer (SHO) at the Limkheda police station, led the CBI to the doors of the private photographer Soni who in turn indicated to the CBI the jungle where he had clicked the pictures.[10] The CBI dug up several spots in the jungle before they found the mass grave, with the help of an anonymous tipper.

Meanwhile, Bilkis and Saddam described the actual scene of the crime for the CBI: a field abutting a kuchcha road leading to the village of Pannivel.[11] On 28 January 2004, the CBI found pieces of broken bangles and slippers and clothes in the area that Bilkis identified belonged to the victims.[12] Between 31 January and 1 February, they exhumed the remains of five of the seven bodies that had been buried in the pit by Mukesh Harijan. There were still more bodies to find, including that of Saleha, Bilkis's daughter, and Shamim's newborn baby, but these could never be located. One would never know how they were disposed of. The CBI charged B.R. Patel, four other officers and Som Singh for conspiring with the alleged murderers and rapists, and for falsifying reports and tampering with and destroying evidence. 'Initially, the Limkheda policemen kept lying. But the recovery of the pictures clicked by Bhavin Patel on 4 March 2002 by one of my CBI inspectors was a big leg-up in the investigation. When we confronted the Limkheda police with the picture of Saleha's body clicked by Patel, but which was not present in the pictures taken by Soni on 5 March, they cracked,' said my source in the CBI. The CBI also charged the Prasads, the doctors who aided the police in covering up the murders.

•••

Before the riots in 2002, there had never been a major incident of communal violence in Randhikpur. Though Gujarat has had a long history of communal riots, there was no history of bloodletting and barbarism in Limkheda teshil. There were just forty or so Muslim families among the 2,000 families who lived in the village. After the demolition of the Babri Masjid in 1992, Muslims did leave the village en masse as a precautionary measure, but there was no violence, and they soon returned.

After 1992, though, political Hindutva spread its tentacles far and wide through Gujarat. The VHP, backed by the rest of the Sangh Parivar, conducted regular mass mobilisation and training programmes. Some of this activity reached Limkheda as well. There was a surge in the number of VHP, Bajrang Dal and BJP volunteers in the area. Still, there had been no discord between Bilkis's family and the accused who so brutally murdered them. Bilkis told the CBI that she addressed many of these men as 'chacha', had served them tea in her house, and knew them as friends and acquaintances of her father and uncles. The catalyst for all the violence was the Hindutva-generated frenzy of 'revenge'. Though the Muslims of Randhikpur had nothing to do with what had happened in Godhra, though they had always lived peacefully alongside their neighbours and vice versa, they were held guilty by reason of their faith. Their houses and shops were looted and burnt down, and inhuman violence was meted out to people who were suddenly Muslim first rather than old neighbours.[13] The Limkheda police never investigated who was behind the burning of Muslim houses in the village. All the cases were simply closed.

But for the doggedness of a team of CBI investigators, who themselves were deflecting heat from politically minded superiors, what happened to Bilkis Bano might never have become known.

Bilkis was a woman of very few words—her interactions with lawyers and investigators were mostly monosyllabic. But when it came time for her to testify in court, she did not flinch while identifying her assailants. At the time of her rape, and the murder of her family, she was a lactating mother. Since then, she gave birth to her baby and would go on to have four more children. 'Bilkis was an extraordinarily courageous woman,' Vivek Dubey told me. 'She was sure she wanted justice.' A fellow CBI officer who did not want to be named told me that Bilkis was 'the bravest woman I ever met'. Bilkis returned the admiration. 'Though the defence did try to intimidate me,' she told me, 'the CBI was very supportive. And it was because of their support and the help of the human rights activists that I could give my testimony in court.'

Saddam was helped by Mukhtar, a human rights activist from Gujarat who found him a place in a religious boarding school in Anjar, run by the Jamiat-ul-Ulama, an Islamic charity. But Saddam was severely traumatised, often screaming in his sleep. 'He would suddenly start laughing in the middle of a conversation,' Mukhtar told me. 'The doctors said he needed a family, so I brought him to stay with me.' Saddam lives in Ahmedabad now, a married man and father to a baby son. He is mostly better now, Mukhtar says, 'but he still sometimes screams at night. He says he still remembers scenes from the massacre.' Saddam was able to identify three of the accused in court.

In 2008, six years after Bilkis was gang-raped and left for dead, a Mumbai trial court convicted and sentenced eleven of the twelve accused to life in prison. Sangeeta Prasad, one of the doctors who faked the medical report, was declared temporarily unfit to stand trial after she was diagnosed with paranoid schizophrenia. Another accused, Naresh Modhiya, died in jail while he was being tried for rape and murder. The seven policemen and the two doctors were, however, acquitted. In 2017, the Mumbai High Court upheld the life terms and set aside the acquittals of the policemen and doctors.[14] The state of Gujarat, which had taken no action against anyone accused in the case, had to be ordered by the Supreme Court in 2019 to stop paying a full pension to the (by then retired) policemen who had tampered with the evidence.

The Gujarat government told the Supreme Court that it was willing to pay Rs 5 lakh as compensation to Bilkis. She refused the offer. On 23 April 2019, the Supreme Court ordered the state of Gujarat to pay her a sum of Rs 50 lakh as compensation, and to provide her with a government job and government accommodation.[15]

Zakia Jafri, in her petition, had demanded action against senior Gujarat police officers for the cover-up in the Bilkis Bano case. But the SIT did not act against the erring officers. Nor did the SIT believe that the cover-ups in the cases of Bilkis Bano, Zahira Sheikh, Naroda Patiya and Gulbarg Society indicated any larger conspiracy. However, the amicus curiae Raju Ramachandran vehemently disagreed with the SIT. He wrote in his report to the apex court:[16] 'The investigative agencies let off the accused in Bilkis Bano case. If the CBI had not stepped in, the accused would have gone unpunished. Similarly, in Best Bakery case, it appears that the prosecution was done in a shoddy manner to protect the accused.' Ramachandran wanted both the Best Bakery and Bilkis Bano cases to be 'examined by SIT so as to fix responsibility on the investigating and prosecuting officials'. In the end, though, the SIT might as well not have been appointed, so little did it do.

If there is something to be thankful for, it is that Bilkis continues to live with her husband and children in Gujarat. Her eldest daughter, who was in Bilkis's womb when she was gang-raped, is eighteen years old and in her last year at school.

11
The Artful Faker

More than a decade ago, when Narendra Modi was a nobody, a small-time RSS pracharak trying to make it as a small-time BJP functionary, I had the privilege of interviewing him ... Modi, it gives me no pleasure to tell the readers, met virtually all the criteria that psychiatrists, psycho-analysts and psychologists had set up after years of empirical work on the authoritarian personality. He had the same mix of puritanical rigidity, narrowing of emotional life, massive use of the ego defence of projection, denial and fear of his own passions combined with fantasies of violence—all set within the matrix of clear paranoid and obsessive personality traits. I still remember the cool, measured tone in which he elaborated a theory of cosmic conspiracy against India that painted every Muslim as a suspected traitor and a potential terrorist. I came out of the interview shaken ... for the first time, I had met a textbook case of a fascist and a prospective killer, perhaps even a future mass murderer.

— Ashis Nandy, 'Obituary of a Culture'[1]

I visited Gujarat in 2004. By then, the battle lines were clearly drawn. Modi had become a pariah. Bashing him had become a fashion. People who differed even slightly with this trend were branded communal or belonging to RSS and VHP. I decided to confront him directly ... I looked into his eyes and asked him, 'Did you do all that was in your capacity to stop these riots?' The directness of my question surprised him. After regaining his composure, he replied with moist eyes, 'Guruji, do you also believe in this propaganda?' Nothing much was spoken after that. I knew he could not have played a role in the riots. Why would a chief minister paint his face black and destroy his own reputation? It didn't make any sense. We sat in silence for few minutes. I assured him that the truth was on his side and one day the whole nation would recognize him.

— Sri Sri Ravishankar, 'My First Meeting with Narendra Modi'[2]

There is nothing to show that the CM intervened on 28.02.2002 when the riots were taking place to prevent the riots ... Neither the CM nor his personal officials have stated what he did on 28.02.2002. Neither the top police [officers] or bureaucrats have spoken about any decisive action by the CM.

—Amicus Curiae Raju Ramachandran in his report to the Supreme Court of India[3]

Zakia Jafri has always demanded that Narendra Modi's role in the 2002 Gujarat riots be subject to a fair investigation. An octogenarian now, Jafri survived the massacre by a stroke of miraculous luck. A rioter who had been part of her husband Ehsan Jafri's lynch mob told me, a little ruefully, that he was not sure how she got away. 'She may have escaped,' he said, 'by posing as a Hindu house maid.'

Frail and heartbroken, Zakia Jafri petitioned the courts for an independent investigation into what she suspected was a conspiracy—at the highest levels, including the chief minister— to permit, even actively aid, the killing of Muslims in the Gujarat riots.[4] Though Jafri's efforts have not led to charges that have stuck against Modi, her persistent legal battles for accountability have had a notable impact.

On 27 April 2009, the Supreme Court responded to a petition she filed by directing the SIT to 'look into the matter'.[5] It was an ambiguous, even offhand order. The SIT read it as an instruction to carry out an inquiry, that is, a preliminary step before a criminal investigation is contemplated. Two retired CBI officers, Paramvir Singh and A.K. Malhotra, were assigned the job.[6] After a few months, Singh left the SIT, and Malhotra carried out the probe by himself.

Malhotra's expertise lay in investigating corruption cases, the Bofors scandal being the most famous of these. His efforts, many believe, prevented Malhotra's promotion to the rank of joint director, as the UPA, led by a grudge-bearing Congress, did not give its assent. However, an inquiry into a sitting chief minister's role in an alleged state-sanctioned mass murder was of an order greater than anything he had ever dealt with. How many layers would Malhotra have to peel back to get to the core of any conspiracy? Would he be given the necessary support and resources?

There was obvious circumstantial evidence against Modi—after all, for three days, as Gujarat burnt, the state government was missing in action. How could the riots have gone on as long as they did without the government intervening with all the resources available at its disposal, including asking for the Centre's support in getting the army involved if the police force was proving to be insufficient?

Subsequent scrutiny by the Supreme Court, the CBI and the amicus curiae revealed that police investigations into some of the grisliest, most disturbing murders during the riots—Best Bakery, Bilkis Bano,[7] Naroda Patiya and Gulbarg Society,[8] for instance—were designed to protect the accused.[9] In case after case, the Gujarat police had booked only small-time VHP and Bajrang Dal hoodlums, letting off the leaders who plotted and facilitated the rioting. Even ordinary foot soldiers were the beneficiaries of what could only be described as the Gujarat police's deliberate laxness. Inevitably, loopholes would be left, the most basic investigation procedures would be ignored and evidence would disappear. Was this systematic subversion happening only at the level of local inspectors and constables? It seemed hardly credible.

The state had also protected and promoted police officers who had been accused of standing by or even encouraging violence against Muslims, while it overlooked those who had either acted or wanted to act against the rioters.[10] When Malhotra recorded my statement in his office in Gandhinagar, he specifically focused on what Babu Bajrangi and Haresh Bhatt had said about Modi. Besides the statements of Bajrangi and Bhatt, my sting operation contained indirect evidence against Modi—specifically, how his government had subverted the investigations and protected the accused. Malhotra, inexplicably, focused only on Bajrangi and Bhatt.

Besides the allegations against Modi that came up in my sting operation, there were various, more direct, charges against him. One was that Modi had himself said to those attending a high-level meeting in Gandhinagar on 27 February 2002 that Hindus should be allowed 'to vent their anger on minorities'.[11]

This allegation was levelled by two IPS officers and a citizens' group. An IPS officer named Sanjiv Bhatt, the then deputy commissioner of intelligence, claimed, almost nine years after the incident, he was present in the meeting in which Modi made this statement. Another IPS officer, R.B. Sreekumar, claimed that he was told by the then director general of police, K. Chakravarthi (who died in August 2020), that the chief minister had told the DGP to allow 'Hindus to vent their anger'. Then there was the testimony of retired Supreme Court judge P.B. Sawant and retired Mumbai High Court judge Hosbet Suresh. Both judges were from Maharashtra, but after the riots, they toured the state of Gujarat as part of a concerned citizens' group. They met various people, including Haren Pandya, a minister in the Modi government. The two retired judges said that Pandya had told them that Modi told police officers and civil servants that 'Hindu aggression should not be curtailed'. But Pandya's testimony before the judges was not recorded. He had deposed on the condition of confidentiality.

In 2003, Pandya was murdered, shot by assassins after a morning walk. Questions were asked in parliament about the low level of security cover provided to a prominent politician whose life was widely reported to have been under threat.

Narendra Modi, still Gujarat chief minister, having been emphatically re-elected in 2007, was summoned by Malhotra for questioning at the SIT office in Gandhinagar. On 28 March 2010, at nine in the morning on an already blazing Sunday, Modi arrived, a seemingly humble figure, prepared to answer questions like any ordinary citizen, without attempting to pull rank. It was the first time a sitting chief minister was being questioned on charges of conspiring in a communal massacre. A crowd of supporters had gathered outside the SIT office. A few minutes after Modi slipped into the office with little fanfare, one of his aides told television crews that Modi was observing a vrat, a fast, on that day. It became, of course, breaking news, flashed on screens around the country, reinforcing Modi's image as a pious, devout Hindu.

Soon after Malhotra took over the inquiry in June 2009, it became clear to him that he had been given a job no one else wanted. Paramvir Singh left in February 2010. Even Malhotra's boss, the former CBI chief, R.K. Raghavan, appeared less than keen. Many years later, a member of the SIT told me in confidence that 'Raghavan just dumped the whole thing on Malhotra because he himself didn't want any role in the probe'. It was an attitude shared by serving and retired police officers and senior bureaucrats who performed important administrative functions at the time of the riots. Everyone strove to put as much distance between themselves and any investigation of Modi as possible. Raghavan was in Ahmedabad on the day Modi appeared before the SIT, but he chose not to participate in the questioning. My source in the SIT told me that, on that day, 'Raghavan had parked himself in the IPS officers' mess in Ahmedabad'. Malhotra had 'requested him to at least be present for the first hour of the question-and-answer session, after which he could leave. But he just refused to be anywhere near the SIT office while Modi was there.'

In the sparely appointed room the SIT used for interviews, Modi expertly deflected questions, like an opening batsman deploying his arsenal of glances and leaves to douse the fire of a fast bowler.[12]

'Please see the text of the public speech delivered by you at Becharaji, Mehsana district on 9.9.2002, as a part of your "Gaurav Yatra",' Malhotra said, as he placed the text of one of Modi's many incendiary speeches on the table.

'What, brother,' Modi had said in a typical stump speech in September 2002, as state elections approached, 'should we run relief camps? Should I start children-producing centres? We want to achieve progress by pursuing the policy of family planning. "We are 5 and we have our 25!" On whose name is such development pursued? Can't Gujarat implement family planning? Whose inhibitions are coming in our way? Which religious sect is coming in the way? Why money is not reaching the poor? If some people go on producing children, the children will do cycle puncture repair only?'[13]

Are these references to Muslims, Malhotra asked.

Modi looked at the text and said, 'This speech does not refer to any particular community or religion. This was a political speech, in which I tried to point towards the increasing population of India.'

Malhotra persisted. 'Please refer to your interview given on 01.03.2002. In this interview you stated that *"Kriya pratikriya ki chain chal rahi hai. Hum chahte hain ki na kriya ho aur na pratikriya."* [There is a chain of action and reaction going on. I want that there be neither action nor reaction.] You also stated in the said interview that "the Godhra incident had caused a big shock in India as well as abroad. These people from the Godhra area have criminal tendencies and had earlier killed female teachers and now they have committed this heinous crime, for which a reaction is being felt." Please explain these remarks.'

'Those who have read the history of Gujarat would definitely be aware that communal violence in Gujarat has a very long history,' Modi said evasively. 'Since before my birth, Gujarat has witnessed a series of incidents of such communal violence. As per available history, from 1714 AD to up till now, in Gujarat, thousands of incidents of communal violence have been recorded.'

He had not answered the question. But Modi paused here for effect before continuing: 'As far as the Zee TV interview of 01.03.2002 is concerned, today, after a period of eight years, I do not recollect the exact words. But I have always appealed only and only for peace. I have tried to convey the message to people to shun violence in straight and simple language.'

Then Modi became lyrical. 'There is a saying in Gujarati—"*Ver thi ver same nahi*". It has been my constant opinion that violence cannot be a reply to violence and so I had appealed for peace. I had not and would never justify any action or reaction by a mob against innocents.'

To Malhotra's more direct questions, Modi gave increasingly vague responses. The interview, of course, was not an interrogation. It was merely a preliminary inquiry. No FIR had been registered against him, so if he had wanted, Modi could have ignored the SIT's summons altogether. Yet here he was, making a show of being happy to answer questions about his conduct. Despite the official nature of this inquiry, Malhotra could not press Modi beyond a point. When he asked Modi about his movements on 28 February 2002, the first and worst day of the riots, he responded, 'On that afternoon, I met the press at Circuit House. I informed them about the government's enquiry commission and also made an appeal to the general public to maintain peace and communal harmony. It may be added here that on 28.02.2002 itself, I recorded a message for the general public to maintain peace and harmony.'

When Modi assumed the chief ministership of Gujarat in October 2001, he retained the portfolio of the state's home ministry. In effect, all matters relating to law and order and intelligence were under his purview. But when the SIT asked him direct questions on issues related to intelligence inputs, and law and order pertaining to the period immediately before and after the riots, he pleaded ignorance.

For instance, when he was asked about the State Intelligence Bureau (SIB)'s inputs on the 'Ram Mahayagnas' being organised by the VHP across Gujarat in February 2002, in advance of a few thousand kar sevaks travelling up to Ayodhya to participate in another yagna calling for the building of a Ram temple on the site of the Babri Masjid, Modi offered this rambling, unfocused response:

'I would like to add that I became chief minister, Gujarat state in October 2001. Before that I was general secretary of BJP with headquarters in Delhi. It was only after the earthquake in 2001 that I was deputed by the high command to do relief as well as constructive work in Gujarat state. It may be further added here that I had contested my first election from the Rajkot assembly constituency. The by-election to this constituency was held on 24.02.2002. I was elected to the Gujarat assembly. As regards the intelligence reports about the Ram Mahayagna, these reports are normally received by the DGP and ACS Home (additional chief secretary) and as per the rules of business they only look after this issue.'

Modi had been the chief minister of Gujarat since October 2001, and had retained control of the home ministry, but claimed that inputs from the SIB in February 2002 were not his business. That these were entirely the responsibility of bureaucrats and police officers.

Were, Malhotra asked, 'the intelligence inputs received by SIB communicated to the Government? If so, when and to whom?'

'I did come to know that some of the Ram-sevaks from Gujarat were going to Ayodhya for the Ram Mahayagna,' straight-batted Modi, 'but I had no knowledge of their programme as it was the duty of the police and the home department to make the necessary bandobast in this regard.'

Malhotra then put in front of Modi a so-called demi-official letter, dated 22 April 2002, written by Gujarat Police Commissioner P.C. Pande and copied to the most senior officers of the state intelligence department about the 'undesirable activities' of Sangh Parivar activists. 'Was this letter,' Malhotra asked Modi, 'brought to your notice? If so, what was the action taken by you on the matter?'

Modi replied: 'In this connection, it is stated that I do not remember now, whether this issue was brought to my notice or not. But, it has been my and my government's approach, right from the first day, that a culprit is a culprit irrespective of his caste, creed, religion and socio-political background, as nobody is above the law.'

Modi was not biting, but Malhotra continued to fish. 'Did you ask G.C. Murmu, Secretary (law and order) Home Department and Arvind Pandya, a government advocate, to brief [DGP] R.B. Sreekumar before his deposition before the Nanavati Commission and also influence the latter to not make any deposition against the government?'

'No,' said Modi. 'This allegation is false and baseless.'

In the sting operation I had done for *Tehelka*, Pandya admitted that he had threatened Sreekumar to try to get him to falsely testify before the commission. But Malhotra did not use this part of the sting to confront Modi with Pandya's claims. He moved on to ask Modi about the VHP's call for a state-wide bandh on the day after the kar sevaks were burnt alive on the Sabarmati Express. In the light of the horrors enacted the next day, the bandh appeared to have been little more than a pretext to keep the streets clear for 'revenge'.

'Who gave the call for Gujarat Bandh on 28.02.2002 and Bharat Bandh on 01.03.2002? Were these bandhs supported by the ruling party?'

'On 27.02.2002,' Modi said, 'I remained busy throughout the day and could only go to Godhra at night. I had come to know that a bandh had been called by the VHP. However, on 28.02.2002, I came to know from newspaper reports that the bandh had been supported by the BJP.'

In other words, the party's chosen chief minister, in a state it controlled, was unaware that the BJP supported at the national level a call to shut down the state he was heading.

'Did you receive any information about an attack by a mob on Gulbarg Society,' Malhotra asked, 'and, if so, when and through whom? What action did you take in the matter?'

'To the best of my recollection,' Modi said, 'I was informed in the law and order review meeting held in the night about the attack on Gulbarg Society and Naroda Patiya.'

'Did you know the late Ehsan Jafri, ex-MP who was residing in Gulbarg Society?'

'I had not known Jafri as he was elected as MP sometime in 1970s,' Modi said, 'when I was not in politics. I was told subsequently that Jafri was residing in Gulbarg Society and had been killed during the attack on the society.'

Malhotra, though he was getting nothing from Modi, had more questions: 'Whether Jaideep Patel, Babu Bajrangi and Mayaben Kodnani were in touch with you during the riots from 28.02.2002 onwards?'

'I came to know Babu Bajrangi through media reports and he is not known to me. Dr Mayaben Kodnani is an MLA from BJP and used to meet me. Jaideep Patel is a VHP leader, who is also known to me. As far as I recollect, they never contacted me over phone during the riots.'

'Please see the statements given by Haresh Bhatt, the then MLA, Babu Bajrangi, Rajendra Vyas, VHP president, Ahmedabad City to Ashish Khetan, Special Correspondent, *Tehelka* and published in the special issue of *Tehelka* dated 2.11.2007 and confirm the contents.'

Modi was unfazed. 'The allegations levelled against me by any of the aforesaid persons are false and incorrect. It may be added here that this particular issue was raised in November 2007, through *Tehelka* magazine, about six years after the incident and that too at a time when elections were held in December 2007. These issues were again raked up when SIT was appointed by the Supreme Court in April 2008. This issue was again raised in this week on 22.03.2010, when I was to appear before the SIT for my examination. In view of all these factors, I would say that the whole episode is motivated and stage-managed. I have no personal knowledge about the authenticity of the said CD.'

'It has been alleged that after the riots the public servants who connived with those responsible for carnage were doubly rewarded,' said Malhotra, 'and those who tried to uphold the law were punished in various ways through transfers and supersessions in promotion and this sent a message to government functionaries to be committed to the political agenda of the CM rather than their constitutional obligations ... What do you have to say?'

Again, Modi appeared unfazed. 'The allegation is vague, false and without any basis. Postings and transfers are the prerogative of the administrative ministry and a routine affair.'

'It has been alleged in the complaint,' Malhotra tried again, 'that the public prosecutors appointed in Gujarat to handle the riot cases were either members or supporters and sympathisers of the ruling party or the Sangh Parivar widely believed to be involved in the carnage and that there was deliberate attempt to scuttle most of these cases. What do you have to say?'

'The procedures,' Modi said, 'with regard to selection of the public prosecutor is quite transparent in as much as the district judge writes to the district collector regarding the vacancy and the district collector advertises the post. The applicants who apply for the vacancy are interviewed by a committee ... On the basis of the interview held, a panel of three advocates for each post is forwarded to the government. It is binding upon the government to appoint an advocate out of that panel only. It may thus be seen that the government has no role to play in the selection of a public prosecutor. This procedure is in vogue since 1960.'

Modi was questioned till one in the morning, with only two short breaks. At 8 p.m., he went back to his chief ministerial residence to break his fast. Characteristically sarcastic and bullish, Modi said he 'wanted to give the SIT a break so that they could do their homework'. He returned to the SIT office an hour later.

On his blog, after he was released from the attentions of the SIT, Modi thanked his supporters 'from the bottom of my heart for your good feelings ... during the difficult moments of yesterday. May God, after this event, instil further strength in me.'

During all the hours he spent being questioned, Modi projected himself as an apostle of communal harmony. Yet, his public utterances, at rallies in particular, are there for all to see.[14] Can demagoguery, insults and dog whistles to Hindu hardliners be explained away as political rhetoric? Can a riot that continued unchecked for days and, was of such violence and fury that it could justifiably be defined as a pogrom, be shrugged off as not the responsibility of the sitting chief minister? And when that chief minister refuses not only to apologise for allowing nearly a thousand people from one specific community to be brutally killed on his watch but also characterises criticisms of his failures as an attack by outsiders on the pride of the state and the character of its people, can he then present himself as representing all communities equally?

Modi, now the prime minister of India, has deliberately shrouded himself in a fog of enigma and contradictions. As a public figure at the head of the world's most populous democracy, even some of the most basic facts of his life are hard to ascertain and verify. He is everything to (nearly) everyone. He is the chaiwala who has risen to unimaginable heights and so has a special affinity for the poor and the working class. He is the ascetic devoted to his calling as leader—hardly eating, sleeping or displaying any signs of a personal life so that he can devote all his time to working for the nation. Yet, he is the dandy whose asceticism does not negate his penchant for flashy outfits, designer spectacles and monogrammed suits. Is he the uneducated man he has claimed to be in TV interviews, the man who makes up for what he lacks in book-learning with his abundance of life experience and capacity to strive (hard work, not Harvard, in his words)? Or did he actually earn undergraduate and postgraduate degrees from Delhi University and Gujarat University as he claims he has, albeit through correspondence?

A young techie by the name of Neeraj Sharma asked Delhi University to provide the names, father's names, roll numbers and results of all the students who had appeared in the Bachelor of Arts exams in 1978. 'I didn't specifically ask for Narendra Modi's degree records because that would have raised suspicions, and the application could have been rejected. So, instead, I asked for general information,' Sharma told me. Other applications under the Right to Information (RTI) Act were also filed by people asking specifically for Modi's records. Both universities, in Delhi and Gujarat, refused to disclose the information on the grounds that it was private in nature and would not serve any larger public interest.

Sharma then appealed to the Central Information Commission (CIC), a body constituted under the provisions of the RTI Act, 2005. Hearing the appeal, Information Commissioner M.S. Acharyulu, observed that Delhi University had for many years been releasing the results of exams into the public domain, including the names, marks and roll numbers of all its students. In any case, the educational records of students at universities are not private in nature, ruled the CIC, ordering the university to permit Sharma to see the relevant registers containing information for all the students who had been awarded a Bachelor of Arts degree in 1978.

Then Arvind Kejriwal, the Delhi chief minister, joined the fray. He had been an RTI activist before founding the India Against Corruption movement and later the Aam Aadmi Party. An RTI application had been filed seeking Kejriwal's academic records. When the CIC sought Kejriwal's response, he answered with his usual rhetorical vigour that, while he had no problem with his records being made public, he wondered why the CIC had failed to order that Modi's records be made public. This prompted the CIC, through an order dated 29 April 2016, to order the PMO to provide specific information pertaining to Modi's degrees. He also ordered both Delhi University and Gujarat University to find the relevant information and provide it to Kejriwal. Neither the universities nor the PMO paid heed to the order. Strangely, Gujarat University did upload a document it said was Modi's master's degree, but then took it down. Both universities also contested the CIC's order that RTI applicants be allowed to search its records.

Instead, the two universities went to the High Court in their respective states to challenge the CIC's orders. Their main argument was that they held the degrees of the prime minister in a fiduciary capacity. The CIC's argument that the degrees of public figures were not a matter of private record cut no ice. The courts in Delhi and Gujarat stayed the CIC's order until such time as they arrived at a verdict. Little has been heard about any progress these courts have made in reaching that verdict. Bizarrely, though, while the PMO and Modi's alma maters did not provide information on the degrees under RTI, Amit Shah, the then BJP president, and the late Arun Jaitley, the then finance minister, posed for photographs at a press conference while holding photocopies of Modi's degrees. The MA degree was awarded to Modi for his studies in 'Entire Political Science', a subject many have pointed out does not exist and has never been taught at Gujarat University.[15] In January 2017, Acharyulu again directed Delhi University to allow inspection of records related to all the students who had passed BA degree in 1978, the year in which Modi had supposedly cleared the examination. Two days later, he was stripped of the charge of the ministry of human resource development (now ministry of education) that enabled him to deal with RTIs pertaining to state and central universities.[16]

The point being made by the activists is not about Modi's degree or lack thereof. A university degree certainly cannot—and should not—be a requirement to becoming prime minister of India. It is the lack of transparency. Who is Modi? It is not a question he wants to answer because the banal reality can only undermine the myth.

12

The Smoking Gun

It took me nearly five to six years to realise that my belief that the killers would receive exemplary punishment for such a heinous act would remain just that—a mere belief. As time flew by, it became evident that the Indian state was just not interested in penalising the guilty ... A group of Uttar Pradesh's armed reserve police force selected forty-two youngsters, in full public view, from among a crowd of more than 500 people, loaded them into an official police truck, took them near the water canal, killed them one by one, threw them into the water, hopped on to the truck, reached their camp and went to sleep. Twenty-eight years later, the court acquitted them. Yes, it all happened, but the investigators did not have enough meat in their material to make the killers sleep in jails.

— Vibhuti Narain Rai, *Hashimpura: 22 May: The Forgotten Story of India's Biggest Custodial Killing*

What does it take to hold a chief minister legally responsible for the killing of a thousand people in his state?

A communal mindset, inflammatory speeches, destruction of crucial records, appointment of Sangh members as public prosecutors, questionable positioning of ministers in police control rooms during the riots, rewarding officers who acted unconscionably during the riots while sidelining the officers who carried out their duty, not taking action against the bandh called by the VHP on 28 February, which paved the way for the killings—this is how SIT member A.K. Malhotra summed up the findings of his preliminary inquiry into the role Narendra Modi, as chief minister, played in the Gujarat riots.[1]

Malhotra's report denounced Modi for making 'sweeping' and 'offensive' comments against the Muslim community, which 'showed a measure of thoughtlessness and irresponsibility on the part of a person holding a high public office'. He noted that the 'Chief Minister has admitted to visiting Godhra on 27 February 2002. He has further admitted to visiting Gulbarg Society, Naroda Patiya and other riot-affected parts of Ahmedabad city only on 5 March and 6 March 2002. This possibly indicates his discriminatory attitude. He went to Godhra by travelling almost 300 kilometers in a day, but failed to go to the local areas, where serious incidents of riots had taken place and a large number of Muslims were killed.'[2]

Reading the report, it is apparent that Malhotra thought Modi's conduct, given that he was the chief minister for everyone in Gujarat, not just Hindus, was reprehensible. 'In spite of the fact that ghastly and violent attacks had taken place on Muslims at Gulbarg Society and elsewhere,' he wrote, 'the reaction of the government was not the type which would have been expected by anyone. The chief minister had tried to water down the seriousness of the situation at Gulbarg Society, Naroda Patiya and other places by saying that every action has an equal and opposite reaction.'[3] He added that Modi's 'implied justification of the killings of innocent members of the minority community read together with an absence of a strong condemnation of the violence that followed Godhra suggest a partisan stance at a critical juncture when the state had been badly disturbed by communal violence'.[4] Even Malhotra's boss, R.K. Raghavan, generally reluctant to engage with Modi, acknowledged that 'accusing some elements in Godhra and the neighbourhood as possessing a criminal tendency was sweeping and offensive coming as it did from a chief minister, that too at a critical time when Hindu-Muslim tempers were running high'.[5]

It is to Malhotra's credit that he recognised Modi's speeches in the run-up to the 2002 assembly elections as being one long, continuous dog whistle. Modi had referred, during his so-called 'Gaurav Yatra' (as if pride were a legitimate response to an administrative catastrophe), to riot-relief camps being 'baby-producing centres' and taunted Muslims for following the policy of 'us five and our twenty-five'.[6] Modi told the SIT his speech did not refer to any community, that it was a political speech in which he highlighted the increasing population of India. 'The explanation given by Modi is unconvincing and it definitely hinted at the growing minority population,' Malhotra wrote.[7]

He did not stop with simply condemning Modi for his communal utterances. Malhotra also concluded that political and communal agendas 'weighed heavily' in Modi's handling of the criminal justice system, his government's abject failure in providing justice to the victims. Ultimately, though, Malhotra concluded that Modi's communal rhetoric and his seemingly partisan handling of the riot investigations were 'not sufficient to make out a case'.

In a questionable move, the Modi government had placed two senior ministers—Ashok Bhatt and I.K. Jadeja—in the Ahmedabad city PCR and Gujarat state PCR during the riots. Jadeja was minister of urban housing, while Ashok Bhatt was the health minister. Neither had any business being at the police headquarters. Was their presence a literal reminder of the political pressure being put on the Gujarat police? Raghavan, the SIT chairman, noted that the two ministers were positioned in the control rooms with 'no definite charter', fuelling speculation that they 'had been placed to interfere in police work and give wrongful decisions to the field officers ... The fact that he (Modi) was the cabinet minister for Home would heighten the suspicion that this decision had his blessings.'[8]

Analysis of Ashok Bhatt's cell phone records of the time showed that he was in touch with VHP leader Jaideep Patel, whom the SIT charged as a key conspirator in the Naroda Gam massacre, and with

Gordhan Zadafia, the then minister of state for home who was later denounced by the SIT for his partisan conduct. The SIT's report also found that police officers who took a neutral stand during the riots and prevented massacres were transferred by the Gujarat government to minor postings. SIT chairman Raghavan described these transfers as 'questionable' since 'they came immediately after incidents in which the officers concerned were known to have antagonised ruling party men'.[9]

Rahul Sharma, a 1992 batch IPS officer, was transferred to a desk job a couple of weeks after he took swift action against a 10,000-strong Hindu mob that had surrounded schoolchildren taking shelter in a madrasa by opening fire to disperse the mob. Vivek Srivastava, a 1989 batch IPS officer, who was superintendent of police of Kutch district, was shunted out to a side posting after he arrested and chargesheeted a BJP leader on charges of assaulting a Muslim family. Srivastava also told the SIT that he got a few phone calls from the office of the chief minister inquiring about the case. IPS officer Himanshu Bhatt was transferred after he initiated action against a sub-inspector who had assisted rioters. As it happened, the sub-inspector concerned had important political connections and was both reinstated and allowed to resume his duties at the very same police station. Himanshu Bhatt has since left the country and settled abroad. A senior policeman, Satish Verma, had issued a formal order to arrest a sitting BJP MLA, Shankar Chaudhary, for his suspected involvement in the killing of two Muslim persons. For his temerity, Verma was transferred soon after to the State Reserve Police Training Centre, Junagadh.

These transfers, Malhotra concluded, were 'unusual' and 'fishy'.[10] But neither he nor Raghavan took the next step and directly accused the state government of subverting the system in favour of the rioters.

Even as upright officers were shunted away to insignificant roles, derelict officers, who had made a mockery of their uniforms and the law, were rewarded.

Shortly after the riots, M.K. Tandon was made inspector general, Surat Range, a significant step up in prestige. In July 2005, he received another promotion, becoming additional director general of police at the state police headquarters, a post with statewide jurisdiction. The SIT found that Tandon deliberately did not respond to distress calls from Gulbarg Society and Naroda Gam and Naroda Patiya. Instead of intervening where it was most necessary, he had a series of fabricated complaints registered in other parts of Ahmedabad to try and justify his absence and that of his men.

By 2012, ten years after the riots, P.B. Gondia, deputy to Tandon at the time, had become an IGP, posted with the state's crime inspection department (CID). In his report, Malhotra says of Gondia's performance in the riots: 'In my view Gondia virtually ran away from Naroda Patiya at 14:20 hours when the situation was very serious and virtually uncontrollable.' The SIT also found that Tandon and Gondia were in touch by telephone with Jaideep Patel and Mayaben Kodnani—Hindutva leaders who were among the prime accused in the Naroda Gam and Naroda Patiya cases—on the day of the riots.

'It is evident that Tandon and Gondia did not visit Gulbarg Society under various pretexts,' noted Malhotra. 'Moreover, both of them were in touch with the main accused persons, namely Mayaben Kodnani and Jaideep Patel. This is suspicious.'[11] In its closure report, though, the SIT, despite the questions it had raised, exonerated both officers from any criminal liability, and only recommended departmental action or censure.

The SIT noted the asperity with which an additional sessions judge hearing the Best Bakery trial spoke of the conduct and performance of senior police officers K. Kumaraswamy and Ramjibhai Pargi in Vadodara. There seemed little doubt, in the judge's mind, that both officers had attempted to subvert justice. Despite the severity of these remarks, the state government took no notice, let alone action. Having collected all the evidence and made various remarks about the prima facie collusion between the state government and the state police to permit Hindu extremists to take 'revenge' for Godhra, the SIT still persisted with the lame excuse that transfers and postings were the prerogative of the government.

The SIT report also confirmed that the Gujarat government appointed VHP- and RSS-affiliated advocates as public prosecutors in sensitive riot cases. Even if the SIT flinched from confronting the implications of its own evidence, it is instructive to read its findings.

Chetan Shah, a VHP member, who at one point had faced trial under the Terrorist and Disruptive Activities (Prevention) Act (commonly known as TADA; the precursor to POTA) for killing nine members of a Muslim family, was appointed as a public prosecutor on 17 June 2003 for a period of three years. Before his appointment to this post, where he was leading the state's case against rioters and murderers, Shah had defended some of the alleged rioters and murderers accused in the Gulbarg Society massacre. H.M. Dhruv, who had been Chetan Shah's lawyer in the TADA case, was appointed special prosecutor in the Gulbarg Society and Naroda Patiya trials.

Piyush Gandhi, an ABVP and VHP leader, was appointed public prosecutor in Panchmahal district on 15 March 1996 and continued to hold that post for over thirteen years. Despite his evident ideological affiliation, Gandhi was allowed to conduct the prosecution in several riot cases. There was, the state government concluded, no need for him to recuse himself on the basis of those affiliations and, clearly, no conflict of interest. Then there were the appointments of the likes of Dilip Trivedi (in Mehsana district) and Bharat Bhatt (in Aravali district) as public prosecutors. The SIT chairman wrote that 'it has been found that a few of the past appointees were in fact politically connected, either to the ruling party or organisations sympathetic to it'. But, when it came to action, the SIT, led by its chairman, chose to remain silent, to do nothing about its own investigation.

The SIT noted that the Gujarat government did not take any steps to stop the illegal 28 February bandh called by the VHP. And when the bandh became a pretext to keep the streets clear for

Hindu mobs to do their worst, the police, the report noted, were inexplicably lax about the necessary imposition of curfew to contain the violence. When the curfews were eventually announced (at noon on 28 February 2002 in Naroda and 2 p.m in Meghani Nagar), the worst of the violence was already well underway.

On 28 February, the day after the Godhra tragedy, *Sandesh*, one of the largest circulating Gujarati dailies, published photographs of the burning Sabarmati Express coach with the headline 'Fifty Hindus Burnt Alive' in a large font above the masthead. Inside was a grisly colour spread of the Godhra corpses. Also on the front page of *Sandesh* that morning was a headline in smaller type that read: 'From among those abducted from the Sabarmati Express, two dead bodies of Hindu girls found near Kalol in mutilated state'.

The report below observed: 'In an act of inhumanity that would make even a devil weep, both girls had their breasts cut off. It is evident from the dead bodies that the victims had been repeatedly raped. There is speculation that the girls might have died because of gross sexual abuse.' After investigation, the police found the report to be entirely false. Another newspaper, the *Gujarat Samachar*, also published a series of communally charged, and often misleading and simply untrue reports. Such 'fake news', to borrow a phrase that came into currency much later, continued to be disseminated for weeks even as the state was in the grip of evidently one-sided violence.

Despite detailed reports recommending strict action that were submitted to Chief Minister Modi by field officers of the SIB, his government chose not to even lodge protests with editors of the newspapers responsible for publishing patently inaccurate and inflammatory stories. The SIT observed that these newspapers could be said to have been inciting communal violence and stirring base emotions, but the Gujarat government took no action.

Nearly two decades later, Modi continues to resort to Hindutva dog whistles and communal innuendoes during election campaigns (the 2020 assembly elections in Delhi, for example, in which the Indian prime minister cast aspersions on Indian citizens protesting peacefully in Shaheen Bagh[12]). His government also continues to turn a blind eye to the sensationalised and communally provocative content that masquerades as news on mainstream media aligned with the BJP agenda.[13]

The SIT report asserted that, in August 2002, in a bid to ensure an early assembly election, top officials of the Modi government misled the Central Election Commission by presenting a picture of normalcy when Gujarat was still simmering with communal tension.[14] Modi had prematurely dissolved the assembly on 19 August 2002, nine months before the expiry of its five-year term, to take electoral advantage of the consolidation of the Hindu vote bank, as communal feelings still ran high.

Whatever the other concerns, the crux of the case against Modi and the Gujarat government rested on its inaction during the riots. The SIT found that the state police had carried out patently shoddy investigations into the massacres in Naroda Patiya and Gulbarg Society. It deliberately overlooked the cell phone records of Sangh Parivar members and BJP leaders involved in the riots, prominent among whom were the VHP Gujarat President Jaideep Patel and BJP Minister Maya Kodnani.[15]

Would the police, without political sanction, have so methodically botched their own investigations? Who had vested interests in avoiding an extensive investigation into the involvement of the Sangh Parivar in the riots? Was it a random police inspector or assistant commissioner of police, or was it the leadership of the BJP and the VHP? Malhotra found that '[no] record/documentation/minutes of the crucial law and order meetings held by the government during the riots had been kept'.[16] Why were these records not kept? And if they were, who destroyed them? And on whose orders? The SIT hinted at these questions but did not pursue them.

In his concluding statements, R.K. Raghavan said: 'As many as 32 allegations were probed into during this preliminary enquiry. These related to several acts of omission and commission by the state government and its functionaries, including the chief minister.

A few of these alone were in fact substantiated.' He went on to add that 'the substantiated allegations did not throw up material that would justify further action under the law'.

•••

In almost every respect, the SIT report was exasperating. While Malhotra meticulously made note of malfeasance on the part of Modi and his government on several counts, he was unable to bring himself to recommend a further, more detailed investigation into the riots. There was, he established, a strong prima facie case that the Gujarat government, led by Modi, was uninterested in keeping the peace in the state after Godhra. It was inclined to let the violence play out, to let Hindus vent their anger. What resulted was a pogrom, the targeted ethnic cleansing of whole communities from the places they had lived in all their lives. But that, the SIT decided, was as far as it was willing to go. Something truly dreadful had happened in Gujarat, someone was responsible, but they did not want to dig any deeper.

Reading the SIT report was a strange and unsettling experience. Right through, there was a peculiar see-sawing between the report's startling findings and its weak, watered-down conclusions—a discrepancy that told its own story. Not satisfied with the preliminary report placed before it by the SIT, the Supreme Court appointed former additional solicitor general and senior Supreme Court lawyer Raju Ramachandran as amicus curiae, and asked him to examine the evidence collected by the SIT and then place his own independent recommendations before the court.

In his thirty-one page report to the Supreme Court on 25 July 2011, Ramachandran recommended that Modi could be charged with such serious offences as promoting religious enmity, acting in a manner prejudicial to national integration and the maintenance of harmony, and deliberately and wantonly disobeying the law with intent to cause injury.[17] He recommended 'the offences which can be made out against Shri Modi, at this prima facie stage, are offences inter alia' under Sections 153A(1)(a) & (b), 153B(1)(c), 166 and 505(2) of the Indian Penal Code, which call for a sentence of one to three years in prison.[18]

On the most serious allegation—that Narendra Modi, on 27 February 2002, in a meeting at his official residence, after the carnage at Godhra, had instructed senior officers to allow Hindus to give vent to their anger—Ramachandran wanted Modi to face trial. IPS officers Sanjiv Bhatt and R.B. Sreekumar had testified that such instructions were indeed given. While Sreeekumar's account was based on what he had heard from the then director general of police, K. Chakravarthi, who was a key participant in the meeting, Bhatt had claimed to be present in the meeting room—a claim denied by Modi and his senior officials.

When Malhotra questioned the seven confirmed participants of that meeting—all senior IAS or IPS officers—they either claimed loss of memory or denied outright that they had heard Modi say any such thing. Two officers are still serving, two have pleaded loss of memory, while 'three officers had been accommodated in post-retirement jobs and are therefore not obliged to speak against the chief minister or the state government', SIT chairman Raghavan wrote.[19] The pointed reference to 'post-retirement jobs' hinted at favours exchanged. In the mother of all ironies, Raghavan himself was appointed Indian high commissioner to Cyprus by the Modi government in August 2017. The appointment was political in nature, as ambassadorial posts are usually meant for serving Indian Foreign Service officers. Raghavan, a former IPS officer, was seventy-six years old at the time of his appointment. Malhotra noted the constraints of investigating Modi by specifically mentioning that officers who could have given the true picture were either retired, and therefore reluctant to 'get involved in any controversy', or 'were retired and provided with good post-retirement assignments', and thereby felt obliged to the chief minister or 'were serving public servants who had been empanelled for higher posts and did not want to come into conflict with politicians in power'.[20]

Yet, Malhotra disregarded Sreekumar's testimony as hearsay, and Bhatt's claims as ill-motivated because he thought he was being denied a promotion. In its 'closure report', the SIT argued that 'Even if such allegations [against Modi] are believed for the sake of argument, mere statement of alleged words in the four walls of a room does not constitute any offence.'

Ramachandran was not buying the SIT's argument. He said that the evidence of Sanjiv Bhatt could not be summarily discarded, particularly in the light of other circumstantial evidence. Whether the accounts of Bhatt was credible could only be determined, Ramachandran observed, through a judicial examination during trial.

He also opined that 'a case under Section 304A IPC as well as under Section 166 IPC is made out' against Tandon and Gondia. If followed up on, Ramachandran's recommendations would have had an unprecedented impact on the Indian criminal justice system, in which the powerful and the wealthy are rarely punished for their actions. Inevitably, in such cases, investigations are sloppy, evidence is unaccountably misplaced or the proceedings peter out as the decades pass. Ramachandran's report demonstrates that the course of justice is impeded not by lack of evidence or weak laws but by lack of will. Our justice system is plagued by the disturbingly selective application of laws.

The SIT's assertion that there was no prosecutable evidence to proceed against Modi was contrary to its own reported facts. 'If there is some material which supports the allegation being made by the Complainant, a case for proceeding further is made out against the accused,' said Ramachandran.[21] But the SIT dug in its heels and rejected Ramachandran's suggestions. In a closure report filed before an Ahmedabad metropolitan magistrate, it further watered down its own initial findings that indicted Modi on various charges.

On 13 September 2013, claiming the SIT's reluctance to prosecute as a clean chit for Modi, the BJP declared him its prime ministerial candidate. Teesta Setalvad and Zakia Jafri contested the SIT's closure report, but the magistrate rejected the protest petition and accepted the report. Jafri, an octogenarian now, is still fighting spiritedly, not so much for justice, but to be given the opportunity to fight for justice. By the government's own assertions, nearly a thousand Muslims were killed over several days of unimpeded rioting. The police did little. The elected executive did even less. And the chief minister, immediately after the violence, swaggered around the state, still flinging communally tinged barbs. But no one was to blame. No one was accountable.

It is a shame that Zakia Jafri has to fight so hard, so futilely and without the support of the justice system to persuade us of the truth of this most basic social compact: you cannot be allowed to get away with murder.

13

Drum Rolls of an Impending Massacre

It is so short and jumbled and jangled, Sam, because there is nothing intelligent to say about a massacre. Everybody is supposed to be dead, to never say anything or want anything ever again. Everything is supposed to be very quiet after a massacre, and it always is, except for the birds. And what do the birds say? All there is to say about a massacre, things like 'Poo-tee-weet?'

— Kurt Vonnegut, *Slaughterhouse-Five*

In 2013, I was working with the India Today Group as their editor for investigations. For the past ten years, the Gujarat government's main defence had been that the riots were an 'instantaneous reaction' to the carnage on the Sabarmati Express, and that the state machinery was overwhelmed by the sudden burst of communal violence. By February 2012, the SIT had already filed a closure report before an Ahmedabad court.

But in April, a year before Modi would become prime minister, I got access to a trove of secret documents: the Ahmedabad PCR messages and the SIB reports, which revealed that as early as the afternoon on 27 February—the Sabarmati Express coach had been burnt down that morning—top Gujarat government functionaries began receiving a steady stream of field inputs from police personnel about VHP and Bajrang Dal leaders making provocative speeches, mobilising angry mobs and inciting violence.[1] The field intelligence officers warned of the possibility that major anti-Muslim riots might break out. Anarchy and confusion were allowed to prevail, the PCR messages clearly showed. Additionally, the state's home department had also received messages between 2 February and 25 February 2002 about large-scale mobilisation of Hindu cadres for a temple ceremony in Ayodhya, with large batches of kar sevaks from Gujarat leaving for Ayodhya by train, and about their provocative and aggressive behaviour en route. Many kar sevaks were armed with trishuls and daggers, the reports said. It is relevant to note here that this mobilisation of kar sevaks was in keeping with the VHP's call to perform a ram mahayagya over several days beginning on 17 February 2002 in Ayodhya.[2] Bajrang Dal Gujarat Unit President and BJP MLA Haresh Bhatt had told me that his organisation had distributed large amounts of swords, bombs, tridents and fire arms among the Hindu activists much before the Godhra incident had occurred (see Chapter 6). The SIT in its closure report had termed Bhatt's claims as exaggeration. But the police intelligence reports and the scale of violence that followed these reports show that the Hindu right-wing outfits were prepared for large-scale riots and their cadres did use all kinds of weapons on their Muslim targets. In fact, I was given a tutorial in bomb-making by a VHP leader at his stone quarry, which I had captured on a spy camera. The VHP leader even gave me the bomb-making material to carry with me. Then how can it be termed an exaggeration?

Despite a flurry of advance warnings, the government took no pre-emptive measures or proactive steps to either prevent or quell the riots. The police did not impose a curfew in Ahmedabad till the afternoon of 28 February. The VHP leaders who were instigating the Hindu masses and making preparations to kill large numbers of Muslims were not arrested or detained. No help was sought from the army until 2 p.m. that day, by which time the worst of the massacres were already underway. In 2018, Lieutenant General (retired) Zameer Uddin Shah revealed that Modi delayed the deployment of the army, because of which it could begin its work only on 2 March.[3] Shah, who was leading the troops flown into Gujarat to stop the riots, described those portions of the SIT report that claimed that there was no delay in army deployment in Gujarat as 'a blatant lie'.[4]

The SIT had concluded in its closure report that there were no contemporaneous records to show that Modi had given any specific orders to the police and administration to go slow on the Hindu rioters, since, either records were not kept or they had been destroyed, and senior officials would not speak up. But it failed to assess evidence in the form of police wireless messages—these make it clear that the state government was fully informed of the potential for violence and thus could not claim to be taken unawares when the riots began. What did Modi, chief minister and home minister of Gujarat, do to prevent violence in the crucial hours after the burning of the Sabarmati Express coach, as mobs, urged on and equipped with weapons by Hindutva organisations, were preparing to kill? Did the chief minister have to give written orders to the administration and police to leave the rioters alone, or was it enough for the chief minister to conspicuously look the other way when reports made it clear that violence was at hand?

These were the questions that the editorial team at India Today asked in a two-hour-long show aired on the group's English-language news channel, then called Headlines Today (now India Today), on 16 April 2013.[5] Aroon Purie, besides being the proprietor of the media group, was also its editor-in-chief. When I pitched the story, based on the documents I now had access to, he vetted it and personally edited the scripts I had written, making some important adjustments and clarifications. Already, with just over a year to go before the Lok Sabha elections, an atmosphere of hype and euphoria had started building up around Modi. Top industrialists, business executives and owners of media houses were full of effusive praise for his leadership qualities and economic vision. In 2013, Modi seemed to make it a point to only speak about his government's economic achievements in Gujarat. He presented himself as a chief executive who knew how to get India Inc. moving on a steep upward trajectory of economic growth. The media was awash with admiring stories about the Gujarat model and the prosperity it had brought to the state. In this sycophantic environment, it took resolve for Purie to not only approve yet another investigation into Modi's inept handling of the Gujarat riots but also to give it two hours of prime time.

•••

The Ahmedabad police control room was located in Shahibag in the heart of the city. Gulbarg Society was just three kilometres from it, while Naroda Patiya was around six kilometres away. The SIB headquarters were located in Police Bhavan in the state capital Gandhinagar, twenty-three kilometres north of Ahmedabad.

Every report pouring into the PCR on 27 and 28 February warned of an impending massacre, which at the very least showed that the state had abdicated its constitutional responsibility to protect the lives and properties of its citizens.

Within a few hours of the carnage on the Sabarmati Express, the three most senior office-bearers of Gujarat's VHP unit—Jaideep Patel, Dilip Trivedi and Kaushik Patel—had issued a statement declaring a state-wide bandh.[6]

The SIT report noted that the BJP, which formed the government in Gujarat, had supported the bandh called by the VHP.[7] The evidence adduced in the Naroda Patiya and Gulbarg Society trials showed that the bandh called on 28 February 2002 was a pretext for Hindutva mobs to be unleashed on streets and neighbourhoods emptied of people, businesses and the routine of a typical day.[8] These police messages bolstered the evidence that the bandh had indeed paved the way for mass murder.

A field-level officer faxed this statement to the SIB headquarters in Gandhinagar at 8.38 p.m. on 27 February 2002: 'VHP General Secretary Dilip Trivedi & VHP joint secretaries Jaideep Patel & Kaushik Mehta issue a statement. VHP declares Gujarat bandh to protest killing of kar sevaks. Statement says Muslims pre-planned Godhra attack. Innocent (Hindu) ladies were molested and compartments were set on fire and Ramsevaks were burnt alive.'[9] Already, by the evening of 27 February, the SIB was flooded with reports of provocative sloganeering by the VHP and Bajrang Dal and mass gatherings of their volunteers. Right-wing activists in different parts of the state, the SIB documented, were holding public meetings, making provocative speeches and inciting revenge. 'VHP, BJP leaders gave provocative speeches at a meeting held at Sardar Chowk, Vapi Town,' read one such report dispatched from Surat. 'VHP's Dinesh Behri, Bajrang Dal's Acharya Brahmbatt, BJP's Jawahar Desai & RSS member Vinod Chowdhary ... exhorted crowds to take revenge for Godhra.'[10]

Field reports showed that already, by the afternoon of 27 February, sporadic instances of violence had broken out, including Muslims being stabbed and their properties being burnt down.

The Sabarmati Express train, after the burnt and damaged coaches were detached at Godhra, arrived in Ahmedabad at 4.30 p.m. 'Sabarmati Express reached Anand Railway Station at 1500 hrs. Karsevaks from the train stabbed 4 Muslims present at the station. One victim named Abdul Rashid aged 65 years, resident of Anand, died. Remaining were hospitalised at Anand government hospital,' read a message faxed to the SIB.[11] Another message sent to the SIB, at 6.10 p.m., warned that kar sevaks who had alighted from the Sabarmati Express in Ahmedabad at 4.13 p.m. were armed with rods and sticks and were shouting slogans such as 'khoon ka badla khoon'.[12]

Later that night, a police inspector with the CID in the city of Bhavnagar sent a fax to the SIB: 'Sadhu Samaj president Gopal Nand gave provocative speech at Junagadh Kadva Chowk between 7:30

pm-9 pm. Gopal Nand questioned lack of response from Hindus even 12 hours after burning of train. Gopal Nand questioned Muslim patriotism to India and incited mobs to attack them.'[13]

Reports of violent attacks on Muslims kept coming in from across the city of Ahmedabad on 27 February.

'A mob attacked AMTS and ST buses at Bapunagar at 15:00 hrs and broke windows of buses. Shops were shut down.'[14]

'A 100 men strong mob pelting stones and burning houses, rickshaws and damaging public property on 27.2.2002 at 17:15 hrs.'[15]

'Man critically injured after attack at Ahmedabad railway station at 5 pm.'[16]

'Juhapura resident attacked at V.F. Hospital.'[17]

'Factory [owned by a Muslim] burnt at Ambikanagar.'[18]

'A mob killed one Muslim with sharp weapons near the Express Highway at 21:45.'[19]

At least fourteen FIRs registering violence against Muslims were recorded on 27 February in Ahmedabad alone. There were desperate SOS messages from policemen on the ground seeking reinforcements.[20]

At 12.30 a.m., the SIB received a fax with a specific warning that, because the bodies of kar sevaks were being brought to Ahmedabad for funeral processions, there would be a '[h]igh possibility of riots in Ahmedabad ... take preventive action'.[21]

The motorcade carrying the bodies of kar sevaks from Godhra finally reached Sola civil hospital in Ahmedabad at around 3 a.m. Already, in the pre-dawn dark of 28 February, a mob comprising members of the VHP and RSS had gathered outside the hospital. The police personnel van positioned at Sola civil hospital sent several messages to the Ahmedabad PCR:

'Arrange for SRP Bandobast at Sola Hospital because dead bodies are to arrive from Godhra.'[22]

'Mob of 3000 RSS members gathered at Sola Hospital.'[23]

'Mob assembled at Sola Hospital. The crowds were getting restless.'[24]

'Mob set vehicle on fire, arson on highway.'[25]

'Riots have started at Sola Hospital & near High Court where bodies were brought.'[26]

'Sola Hospital staff surrounded by 500-strong mob. Please provide security at hospital urgently.'[27]

In its closure report, the SIT had cleared the Gujarat government of the specific charge that it had allowed the taking out of funeral processions of kar sevaks. But the PCR messages offer considerable evidence of both funeral processions and violence at the Sola civil hospital. 'Funeral procession of 10 bodies taken out from Ramol Jantanagar to Hatkeshwar crematorium,' read a message from the PCR van outside the Sola hospital. '6,000 people accompanied procession.'[28]

Another message was sent to the SIB in Gandhinagar on 28 February, indicating that the violence was spreading: 'Funeral procession allowed at Khedbrahma town in Sabarkantha district. Situation tense, 2 Muslims stabbed at Khedbrahma.'[29]

The next message to the SIB revealed the menacing fact that '150 Bajrang Dal members on way to Khedbrahma'.[30] In the same area, the police reported a '[f]uneral procession organised for Godhra train victim Babubhai Patel in Sabarkantha'.[31]

These messages show how mobs were allowed not only to congregate at the hospital but also to take out emotive funeral processions through the city.

The city's police commissioner, P.C. Pande, when asked by the SIT about why no curfew had been imposed in Ahmedabad, answered without compunction that the 'circumstances did not exist on 27.02.2002 or even on 28.02.2002 to warrant the imposition of a curfew and any hasty decision would have led to panic in the city. Even otherwise with limited forces available imposition of curfew becomes a serious problem and large scale breach becomes common.'[32] Pande claimed that he 'went to Sola civil Hospital around 10:00 am and found that doctors were under pressure to complete the documentation and relatives were in a hurry to take the bodies. However, I didn't find anything alarming and as such returned around 11:00 am.'

But what circumstance could possibly have been more compelling to warrant a curfew than specific field reports indicating that significant violence had already broken out, and that more was in the offing?

In the small hours of the morning on 28 February, PCR messages reported incidences of violence from Naroda and Meghani Nagar where Gulbarg Society is located.

Before the sun had risen, at 4.30 a.m., a PCR message reported '[o]ne critically injured near Kathwada Road, Naroda'.[33] Another, from two hours earlier, said: 'Mob torched buses & rickshaws, damaged public property.'[34]

How, despite all these reports of unrest, could the Ahmedabad police commissioner tell the SIT that that he did not find the 'circumstances on the 27th and 28th fit for curfew'?

Despite regular reports about VHP and Bajrang Dal mobs swelling in size at both Naroda and Gulbarg Society on 28 February, P.C. Pande admits that no curfew was called in either place until the early afternoon. By then, according to some estimates, the crowds at these places had swelled to between 10,000–15,000 people, and whatever curfew had been declared was both ignored and unenforced.

On 28 February, in the four hours between 2 p.m. and 6 p.m., more than 175 men, women and children were burnt and hacked to death at Naroda Patiya, Naroda Gam and Gulbarg Society. Just a few kilometres away, the Ahmedabad police headquarters and senior officials in Shahibag were aware of the horrific violence as it was unfolding. The SIB in Gandhinagar was also apprised of the worsening situation as these messages show:

At 12.15 p.m.: 'Muslims reside in Gulbarg Society. Mob is surrounding the place. Strict watch should be kept there,' read a message sent by Inspector C.J. Bharwad to the SIB control room in Gandhinagar.

At 2.50 p.m.: 'Mob of 3000 rioters has surrounded Gulberg Society, take immediate action,' Bharwad messaged again.

At 5 p.m.: 'Mob attacked the society from all sides. Ehsan Jafri and women and children burnt alive. Houses are ablaze. Mob is looting from homes,' Bharwad sent his final message, his despair evident even through the necessarily telegraphic prose.

The SIT admitted in its reports that Sanjiv Bhatt had sent four wireless messages on 27 February to all jurisdictional officers, asking that they take precautionary messages to prevent communal riots as the Godhra train-burning and the murder of kar sevaks was likely to have state-wide repercussions. He also faxed a message confirming the details of the Gulbarg Society massacre on 28 February to the secretary of the home department, the chief minister's personal secretary, the Ahmedabad police commissioner and the director general of the Gujarat police.[35] In the state government's defence, Pande, the police commissioner, said: 'On 28.2.2002 requests were received from different police stations seeking additional force and SRP and whatever forces were available with me, the same were dispatched. However, I found that no feedback had been received by any one of them. This led me to presumption that additional forces reached in time and they were able to control the situation.'

The SIT's unquestioning acceptance of this weak defence, this pretence that there was no way police bigwigs or the highest levels of the state government could have known the extent of the violence is in stark contrast to the urgency of the PCR messages.

In real time, updates were being sent by policemen on the ground, waiting to be given their instructions. But no instructions were forthcoming. The upper echelons of the state government and police did not provide any credible leadership or direction to the police force. Is it a surprise then that survivors from both Gulberg Society and Naroda testified in court that when they approached the policemen deployed on the ground for help, the police told them that they did not have orders to protect them?

While the worst of the violence occurred on 28 February and 1 and 2 March, incidents of killing Muslims or burning their properties continued for several weeks. Four members of the VHP—Dhawal Patel, Anil Patel, Ramesh Dave and Rajendra Vyas—had said to me how the cadres of VHP and Bajrang Dal were armed with bombs and sharp-edged weapons for several weeks after the Godhra train carnage (see Chapter 6). Violence spread to nineteen out of the state's twenty-five districts, official statistics show. As many as 326 people were killed in Ahmedabad city, ninety-three in Panchmahal, sixty-one in Mehsana, thirty-six in Vadodara city, thirty-three in Ahmedabad rural district and thirty-two in Sabarkantha—the six worst-affected districts—between 27 February and 7 August 2002.[36]

After we broke the story in Headlines Today and Aaj Tak, the Congress party questioned the genuineness of the SIT probe. But Raghavan and the Gujarat government maintained a studied silence, and refused to respond to the story.

Besides the question of criminal culpability, we must ask whether this utter failure to take any kind of decisive action—despite being in possession of intelligence and real-time field reports that could have enabled, if not complete prevention, at least a substantial reduction of the violence—can be described as good governance. Yet, Modi, despite the colossal administrative disaster of being unable to prevent a pogrom on his doorstep (if we accept the government's claim that it did not deliberately down tools) was able to sell an image of himself as the consummate executive, the man who would bring managerial competence and best practices to Delhi.

Speaking at a public forum in October 2020, the economist and Nobel laureate Joseph Stiglitz warned that Modi's politics of division would weaken India forever. He said 'the source of economic prosperity of the last 250 years is one of tolerance'. He pointed out the inherent conflict between India's desire to be economically prosperous, while at the same time becoming increasingly parochial and sectarian. 'Politics of division is an antithesis of what needs to be done,' Stiglitz said. 'Modi has tried to divide your country, Muslims against Hindus, and that is going to undermine your society and economy no matter what else happens.'[37] Modi's economic performance, as prime minister, has been mediocre at best. Prosperity and fulfilling, productive employment is available to only a fraction of Indian society.[38] For the rest, the BJP's shift right to a hard-edged Hindutva offers only anger, resentment and hatred. The language of the BJP's Delhi election campaign and the swift rise of Yogi Adityanath, so that people are actually talking of him as a possible successor to Modi, gives us a glimpse of the future. It is bleak, violent and pitch black.

14

The Godhra Conundrum

> The principle that the end justifies the means is and remains the only rule of political ethics; anything else is just a vague chatter and melts away between one's fingers.
> —Arthur Koestler, *Darkness at Noon*

The killing of fifty-nine Hindus, some of who were kar sevaks, in coach S-6 of the Sabarmati Express at Godhra on 27 February 2002 is perhaps the most challenging story I have reported. Not because the truth was difficult to find, but because almost nobody—not the state, not even the political opposition—was interested in the facts. Civil society too, by and large, decided to gloss over the tragic burning alive of fifty-nine Hindus, including women and children, at the hands of a violent Muslim mob. By the time I came to the story, the case was covered with layer upon layer of falsifications, half-truths and propaganda.

I began investigating the Godhra train carnage in the middle of June 2007—over five years after the incident. When I first started rooting around, I found there were two contesting narratives, each the other's polar opposite. One was the official story being pushed by the state, in which Godhra was a premeditated conspiracy masterminded by local Muslim religious and political leaders. The opposing theory was equally conspiratorial, except the conspirators were not Muslims but Narendra Modi himself. In this version, the fire was lit inside the train, by Hindutva hardliners, to trigger an anti-Muslim pogrom. Of course, neither narrative was true.

The first thing I did in my quest to dig deeper was to pore through volume upon volume of court documents. In these papers, the many contradictions and lies were laid bare. And it was this information that prepared me for the sting operations on the chief investigating officer and the star prosecution witnesses. Each meeting uncovered new facts and more carefully calibrated lies. My investigation showed that the Gujarat police had manufactured a false case in which well-known faces in the Muslim community's religious and political circles were falsely implicated to show that the train-burning was a planned ambush. But my reporting also indicated that several coaches of the train had been attacked by a violent Muslim mob that threw stones, burning rags and other inflammable projectiles into the coaches. Coach S-6 appears to have been set on fire by an unruly mob in mid-riot. I could not pin down the identities of anyone in the mob, but reliable eyewitness testimonies and circumstantial evidence indicated that the Muslim mob included many thugs and street toughs from the Muslim neighbourhoods near the tracks.

In 2008, the Supreme Court had set up the SIT to probe nine major riot cases—the Godhra train carnage, Naroda Patiya, Naroda Gam and Gulbarg Society were among those. In an ironic twist, the same SIT that had cited me as a star witness in a few post-Godhra riot cases forestalled all attempts to bring my evidence before the courts. An application was made by the defence to summon me as a defence witness and to place the sting operation material on record, but it was rejected by the trial judge.

Later, an application was moved before the Gujarat High Court by the accused who were on death row, requesting it to take account of my evidence, but that met with the same fate. This was in spite of the fact that three other courts in Gujarat had found my sting operation to be authentic, and a government forensic lab in Jaipur had certified it as such. The prosecution in the Naroda Patiya, Naroda Gam and Gulbarg Society trials had marshalled my evidence to strengthen their case and press the charge of conspiracy. The Naroda Patiya trial judge had used the sting operation to convict the key accused and uphold the charge of conspiracy, which was also upheld by the High Court of Gujarat. It just goes to show how unpredictable the courts are in our country. Whether evidence is accepted or not seems to rely as much on whim as it does on principles of law. Inevitably, it is the disadvantaged and the minorities who suffer the most from the dysfunctionalities in the criminal justice system.

In 2007, then again in 2008 and 2011, I pieced together the Godhra story and published, in a series of articles, a factual account of what had happened. I also told the SIT what my sting operations revealed.

Based on thirteen years of research, and after following up on every lead possible since 2007, I have attempted to put together an objective account of what happened on the railway tracks in Godhra, and subsequently in the police investigation and in the courts. Every fact here is gleaned from court records, police files and first-hand accounts of key eyewitnesses whom I secretly recorded as an undercover reporter in 2007 and which, till date, no court or investigating agency has refuted.

The Godhra case is now pending before the Supreme Court. Perhaps, before sealing the fate of the accused, it may decide to consider the evidence I have gathered.

Sabarmati Express arrives at Godhra railway station

It was around 7.40 a.m. on 27 February 2002. The Sabarmati Express, train no. 9166 UP, carrying hundreds of ordinary passengers as well as kar sevaks returning from Ayodhya, arrived at platform number one, Godhra railway station. The train from Muzaffarpur in Bihar to Ahmedabad in Gujarat was running four and a half hours behind its scheduled arrival time of 2.55 a.m. at Godhra. The train contained eighteen coaches. The S-1 to S-10 coaches were reserved, there were six general coaches and two luggage coaches. S-6 was the ninth coach from the engine in front and the eleventh from the guard's coach in the rear.

Several ordinary passengers, who were travelling in S-6 and survived the carnage, testified in court that it was packed with kar sevaks, many of who were Bajrang Dal members occupying reserved coaches without tickets. They had simply taken the seats reserved for other passengers. The kar sevaks were rude, rowdy and violent, many of their fellow passengers testified in court. One passenger told the court that when he asked a kar sevak to vacate the seat he had paid for, so that his pregnant daughter-in-law could use it, the man refused to budge.[1] The ticket inspector was physically prevented from entering the coach to do his job.

Kar sevaks clash with Muslim vendors

Soon after the train arrived at the Godhra station, kar sevaks and other passengers alighted on the platform for tea and refreshments. The kar sevaks were shouting anti-Muslim slogans, clearly spoiling for a fight. A few minutes later, a group of Muslim tea vendors began to brawl with some kar sevaks. A passenger told the court that he 'wanted to buy tea for my wife from a Muslim vendor who had come inside coach S-6 but the kar sevak did not allow him and the tea vendor was thrown out of the compartment'. Another S-6 passenger testified that '[a]fter three or four minutes, a few passengers came running inside the coach, closed the door and said a quarrel had taken place on the platform and the Muslim tea vendors were pelting stones. They told everybody to shut the windows and doors.'

A kar sevak tries to abduct a Muslim girl

There was more happening on the platform than just a fight between belligerent kar sevaks and the Muslim tea vendors they were trying to bully. An eighteen-year-old Muslim girl named Sofiya Dhantya, accompanied by her mother and sister, was standing on platform one, waiting for a train to Vadodara. When the fight broke out, the frightened Sofiya and her family tried to get out of the way. In the fracas, a kar sevak grabbed her from behind, clamped a hand over her mouth and tried to drag her towards the Sabarmati Express. When her mother shouted loudly for help, the man let her go. Sofiya says she and her family ran into the booking clerk's office and gave up on the idea of taking a train that day. Instead, they took a rickshaw back to an aunt's house in Godhra.

The attempted abduction of Sofiya aggravated the situation, both the trial and appellate courts have concluded. The trial court found that a rumour spread through the station that kar sevaks had abducted many Muslim girls, which enraged a gathering Muslim mob. Eyewitnesses told the court that the Muslims at the station began shouting for the women to be released from the coach. And then they started pelting the train with stones. The kar sevaks threw some stones back at them.

The train departs but stops again, 800 m from the platform

Though the brawl was still simmering, at around 7.45 a.m., the Sabarmati Express resumed its onward journey. 'The train had just started moving,' said its driver Rajendrarao Jadhav to the court, 'when the chain was pulled at about 7.47 a.m. The engine stopped some 800 metres from the platform. My assistant driver and guard found that the chain had been pulled from four coaches.' The evidence given by the train guard, however, shows that the emergency chain had been pulled in five coaches, which did not include S-6. But it was rectified in only four coaches, the court records show.

Several testimonies during the trial established that the train was probably stopped because a few passengers had not been able to make it back on before it pulled away from the station, which also possibly explained why passengers in four different coaches pulled the chain. The High Court accepted 'that some of the passengers were left out on the platform and thus the possibility of pulling of the chain first time to help the said passengers boarding the train, from three or four different compartments, cannot be ruled out ... the evidence of the passengers and bystanders on the platform do not cogently and conclusively establish the first chain pulling by accused as part of conspiracy'.[2]

When the train stopped because the chain had been pulled, Muslims on the platform began throwing stones at it again. Passengers in some coaches shuttered the windows and closed the doors to protect themselves, the trial court noted. By 7.55 a.m., the chain-pulling was rectified in four coaches and the Sabarmati Express began to leave the station for a second time. This sequence of events also shows that, until this moment, the riot was not of such intensity that it stopped the railway staff from setting right the chain-pulling in four coaches.

The train stops again, this time near Cabin A

A couple of minutes later, at around 7.57 a.m., the Sabarmati Express stopped again, this time near Cabin A, also known as Signal Falia, a gathering place of sorts for drivers, mechanics, tea sellers, garage owners and locals from the surrounding areas. The streets near here were dotted with repair shops and garages stocked with plenty of flammable material.

It was this second stop that was bitterly disputed in court. The prosecution claimed that it was caused by two Muslim vendors who got on the train and pulled the chain to execute a preconceived plan to burn down coach S-6. But there was also evidence that emerged during trial to suggest that the stop was caused by burst hose pipes—hose pipes run through the train and maintain the vacuum—rather than the pulling of a chain.

Staff on board the train deposed in court that the vacuum pressure had fallen to zero, which, the defence argued, could not have been a consequence of chain-pulling. Jadhav, the train driver, told the court that the lobby assistant in the carriage department at the Godhra station had told him that two hose pipes had burst.[3]

The police did not carry out any technical investigation into the cause of the second stoppage. The guard's book has an illegible entry about 'vacuum pipes' but with no mention of the relevant coach. The station master's record suggests that a vacuum issue in one of the coaches was not rectified.[4] Justice Patel of the trial court held that the 'train stopped because of dropping of vacuum, as someone turned outside Vacuum Disk or cut the hose-pipe'.

The Muslim mob strikes

Before the railway staff could find out why the train had halted a second time, the Muslim mob attacked the train using sharp-edged weapons, flammable materials, burning cloth rags, Molotov cocktails and acid bulbs. Many in that mob would have come from Signal Falia. Jadhav said he saw a thousand-strong mob throwing stones, but he could not see much more because he was separated from Cabin A by eight to ten coaches. The heavy stone-pelting had begun to shatter window panes. Survivors told the court that they downed all the iron shutters and locked the doors to save themselves.

The police had not yet reached. The two officials closest to ground zero were Assistant Station Master Rajindersingh Meena and his colleague A.K. Sharma, both manning Cabin A.

Meena told the court that, when he stepped out of his cabin, he saw a mob of about 200 to 500 people running towards the train from the back. They were pelting stones. I met Meena in 2007. He told me that, when he came down from Cabin A, he asked the mob why they were chasing the train, and a few of them replied that one of their people had been abducted by the kar sevaks on the train. Meena also said he heard some of them suggesting the coach be set on fire to drive people out of it so they could find the missing person. But he saw no sharp weapons or jerrycans of inflammable material with the mob.

Unable to dissuade the mob, Meena ran back to Cabin A.

The mob reaches a packed coach S-6

By all accounts, coach S-6 was bursting at the seams. It was carrying between 170 and 200 passengers. Its doors and windows were shut. Suitcases and bags of foodgrains were stored near the toilet area. The rexine of the seats, the foam underneath, the paint and adhesive material and the vinyl flooring were all petroleum-based products. The plywood base of the seats was also highly flammable, though these were omitted from the list of coach materials noted in the trial court judgement.

The mob threw stones at S-2, S-4, S-5 and S-7 coaches as well. Burning rags and projectiles were also thrown at S-2, S-4 and S-7. A witness testified that a burning projectile landed inside coach S-4, but the passengers promptly threw it out.

The fire was contemporaneous with the second stop

Passengers inside S-6 confirmed to the court that they saw the mob throwing burning rags, acid bulbs and inflammable material into the coach. They first saw the smoke, then the fire. Many survivors told the court that, after they spotted the smoke, they opened the door on the northern side and started to vacate the coach. The violent Muslim mob was mainly on the southern side. More than a hundred passengers managed to escape the burning coach. Fifty-nine died in the conflagration.

The court testimonies of the railway staff were in keeping with their official records, which showed that the fire was either started at the same time as when the train stopped for a second time, or had started shortly before the stoppage. But the prosecution contended that the fire was started by the accused after the train had been stopped by pulling the chain a second time. As many as three separate official records note the time at which the fire was reported as 7.55 a.m., while the train stopped at Signal Falia at around 7.57 a.m.

The government railway police's wardhy book ('wardhy' means official intimation) contained an entry for 7.55 a.m., which mentioned that the train had stopped at Cabin A, that there was a crowd pelting stones and that a coach had caught fire. These notes were provided by the station master and became an admitted court document. Meena, the assistant station master, deposed in court that the first chain-pulling was rectified and the train restarted at 7.55 a.m. Within three minutes of this, he was informed on his walkie-talkie about the fire, the second stoppage and the stone pelting. He informed the station master, who then recorded a complaint at the GRP post, as evidenced by the wardhy book. The engine driver told the court that when he sensed the train was stopping, he blew the whistle.[5] He then immediately looked back and noticed the fire in S-6.

The preponderance of available evidence suggests that the fire was more or less simultaneous with the second stoppage and that, if anything, it was started a little before the train actually came to a halt. Therefore, the facts recorded by the court do not point to a premeditated conspiracy to set fire to the coach, but to the violent actions of an out-of-control mob, enraged by a previous confrontation with a group of obnoxious kar sevaks and rumours that Muslim women were being abducted by kar sevaks and held captive in the train. The fight spiralled into a riot as rumours spread through the station and the surrounding streets, and growing numbers of angry Muslim men coalesced into a thousand-strong mob that attacked several coaches of the Sabarmati Express, including S-6 with its rowdy kar sevaks, with makeshift weapons, including rags soaked in flammable liquids.

Muslims of Godhra possess 'criminal tendencies': Modi

On the same day that the kar sevaks were murdered by a mob, in a press release, the Gujarat government described what had happened in Godhra as an act of terror. Two days later, while Muslims were being massacred across Gujarat, Modi said that the Muslims of Godhra possessed 'criminal tendencies'. Asked by Zee TV about the Muslims who were now being murdered to supposedly avenge Godhra, he described the massacres as a chain of actions and reactions.

In the first week of March 2002, after many days of bloodletting in Gujarat, the stringent anti-terror laws of the Prevention of Terror Ordinance (which became an Act just a month after the Godhra incident) were applied against the accused in the case, and the train carnage was confirmed as an act of terrorism. However, mob fury alone, without evidence of conspiracy, does not meet the definition of an act of terror. In the press, the Gujarat police speculated loosely about the involvement of Pakistan's Inter-Services Intelligence, the terrorist group Harkat-ul-Jihad al-Islami and even Muslim underworld dons in the conspiracy.[6] The state appeared determined to prove that the carnage in Godhra was the result of careful planning.

The final case built by the police and upheld by the courts was this:

The accused Muslims, driven by communal hatred, hatched a criminal conspiracy on the night of 26 February, in a secret meeting held at Aman Guest House, near Godhra railway station, to burn coach S-6 of the Sabarmati Express (not just any coach, but specifically S-6—the reason for which has not been addressed by either the prosecution or the courts). They bought 140 litres of petrol from a local petrol pump in Godhra and stored it at the guest house on the night before the attack. On the morning of 27 February, the accused, exploiting the spontaneous incident of a brawl between some kar sevaks and Muslim tea vendors, pulled the chain on the train to make it stop at the desired spot near Cabin A, just outside the railway station. How the conspirators would have executed the conspiracy had there been no spontaneous riot and no attempted abduction of a Muslim woman on the platform is a question that has yet to be addressed. They then transported the petrol from Aman Guest House to the railway tracks in seven twenty-litre carboys, climbed onto the train and cut the canvas vestibule between coaches S-6 and S-7 with knives. One accused, it is alleged, kicked the bolted metal door between the two compartments and broke it open, entering S-6 and letting in his fellow accused, who promptly doused the carriage in petrol and set it on fire with burning rags.

It took the police more than eighteen months to arrive at this theory—the result, it would appear, of many arrests and confessions.

By the time the investigation was over, the police had filed a total of nineteen charge sheets, some of which flatly contradicted assertions made in previous charge sheets. It seemed as if the Gujarat police, with its careful polishing and embellishment of detail, and its devotion to conspiracy, was putting together a film script and would not be satisfied until the plot was airtight.

Nine VHP eyewitnesses surface

The police said it arrested fifteen people on the spot in Godhra and another fifteen over the course of the next day and night. Within a fortnight, over forty people had been arrested. The trial court did not believe the police's claim of making on-the-spot arrests. Instead, the judge said, the evidence before the court established that the first fifteen accused had been arrested in an operation by the police late that night.

Between March and April 2002, the police recorded the statements of several passengers and kar sevaks who had been on board coach S-6. None of these witnesses alleged that rioters had entered the coach and set it on fire. The railway police present at the station and the assistant station masters manning Cabin A, with a clear view of the scene, also did not say they saw any men entering the coach with large containers full of flammable liquid.

The first 'independent' witnesses to come forward and identify people from the mob were nine VHP men whom the trial court later disbelieved. Between them, these men identified forty-one Muslims. All nine claimed they had gone to the station to serve refreshments to the kar sevaks. They claimed they saw everything— the assembling of the mob, the sharp-edged weapons and the flammable materials they were carrying—and were witness to the moment when the fire was started. In nine identical statements they said, 'Five to six people who had plastic containers of liquid in their hands had sprinkled the liquid from the said containers upon one compartment and set it ablaze. We all stayed under the cover of Cabin A.' Interestingly, the only variations in the nine statements were the names of the alleged culprits. Each man identified different people from the mob.

BJP–Muslim leader rivarly in Godhra local politics

The testimonies of these nine VHP-affiliated witnesses have a complex political context. Godhra was divided into twelve wards, each with three corporator seats. In the December 1999 municipal council elections, the BJP won eleven seats, independent Muslim candidates got sixteen, the Congress five, and four seats were bagged by pro-BJP independents. Murli Mulchandani, a BJP man, was then the president of the municipal council. In 1999, he contested the municipal election and lost. A party needed nineteen seats to form the majority in the council. The BJP had cobbled together this majority, securing the support of five Congress and three Muslim corporators. Raju Darji, a BJP corporator, was elected president. Deepak Soni, another BJP corporator, was appointed president of the education board formed under the council.

But a year after the elections, twenty-four corporators—sixteen Muslim independents, five Congress and three Hindu independents—joined ranks against the BJP and moved a no-confidence motion. The BJP lost its majority. These twenty-four now elected Mohammad Hussain Kalota as president of the municipal council. During a no-confidence motion debate, a Muslim corporator, Bilal Haji, had beaten up Darji. The latter pressed charges. In 2002, after the burning of the Sabarmati Express, Raju Darji, Deepak Soni and Murli Mulchandani, along with six other witnesses, claimed they saw Kalota, Bilal Haji and three other Muslim corporators 'attack the train'. When cross-examined during the trial, they admitted to the bad blood between them and some of the men they had named.

Stinging two BJP 'eyewitnesses'

In 2007, posing as an adherent of Hindutva, I had stung Murli Mulchandani and Kakul Pathak, two of the nine government witnesses. Haresh Bhatt introduced me to Kakul Pathak, who in turn introduced me to Mulchandani. Both were wealthy merchants and ran flourishing businesses.

I have footage of both of them admitting to having been asleep at home when coach S-6 was set alight. They went on to tell me that the other seven so-called witnesses were not at the station either. Pathak also admitted that though all nine were BJP members, the police passed them off as VHP men to explain their presence at the Godhra station. (The VHP was the catalysing force behind the call to begin building the Ram mandir.)

Yet, the police brought them in as eyewitnesses. These nine men claimed that, at the time of the incident, they were present at the station to serve refreshments to the kar sevaks. Pathak and Mulchandani told me that they, and seven others, had given false statements to serve the cause of Hindutva.

According to Pathak, the police had prepared his testimony in advance and all he had to do was sign. The trial court acquitted all those implicated by the 'VHP' eyewitnesses. By calling them unreliable, the trial judge validated my findings. The statements and subsequent discrediting of these nine men showed that the investigation was not carried out in good faith, that there was a deliberate conspiracy to implicate certain members of the Muslim community in the carnage.

Science and fiction: the forensic reports

The first information report[7] and all investigations until May 2002 were premised on the theory that the train was set on fire from outside. Then, on 3 May, an inspection was carried out by Gandhinagar's FSL. Its report, dated 17 May 2002, concluded that the train could not have been set on fire by flammable liquid that was poured into the coach from outside. At the place where the train stopped, the windows of coach S-6 were seven feet above the ground. Had flammable liquids been thrown into the coach from a bucket or carboy, a major part of the fluid would have fallen on and around the track. This too would have caught fire and damaged the outer and bottom part of the coach. But the coach and the tracks showed no signs of such damage. The forensics team then decided to carry out an experiment with a bucket of water and claimed that '[o]n the basis of the experimental demonstration, a conclusion can be drawn that 60 litres of inflammable liquid was poured towards the western side of the coach by using a widemouthed container and by standing on the passage between the northern door of the eastern side of coach S-6 and the compartment. The coach was set on fire immediately thereafter.' In effect, the state's own forensic report ruled out the claims made by the nine state witnesses that the fire was started from outside, and instead put forward the theory that the flammable liquid was thrown by someone inside the coach.

Manufacturing conspiracy

In the first charge sheet filed on 22 May 2002, the police proffered a fanciful theory. 'The train reached Cabin A at about 8.05 a.m.,' the charge sheet read. 'At that time, in order to fulfil their intentional and illegal conspiracy the accused persons pulled the chain of coach S-6, changed the disc of the train and got the train stopped.' The police claimed that the accused, in the company of a violent mob, then set coach S-6 on fire by using 'petrol-like inflammable liquids'. At the time, the evidence comprised statements from the police and fire personnel, the nine state witnesses, some kar sevaks and other passengers who had survived the attack on the Sabarmati Express, and the forensic report. There were several gaps and contradictions in the narrative that was put together.

The police mentioned the fight between the kar sevaks and the vendors on the platform. However, no reference was made to the fleeting attempt to abduct eighteen-year-old Sofiya, nor of the subsequent rumour that the kar sevaks were taking Muslim girls. That first charge sheet left many basic questions unanswered. Who was being accused of conspiracy? When did the plot come together? Since the train was scheduled to arrive at 2.55 a.m., was the conspiracy hatched in advance, or on the morning of 27 February, or improvised on the spur of the moment? The police had no evidence to show that the accused had pulled the chain, and yet, that was the claim made in the charge sheet. A conspiracy was being alleged by the police without a single plausible detail offered to back that theory.

Noel Parmar and Rakesh Asthana take over

On 27 May 2002, five days after the police wrote up the first charge sheet, a new investigating officer was appointed. ACP Noel Parmar, Vadodara city control room, took over from K.C. Bawa, Western Railways deputy superintendent of police. The deputy inspector general (DIG) in charge of the investigation, P.P. Aagja, was replaced by Rakesh Asthana, a 1984 batch IPS officer. Since taking over the Godhra investigation, Asthana has been given plum postings under the Modi administration—first in Gujarat, and later at the Centre, when he was made the special director, CBI.[8]

Posing as a Sangh Parivar activist in 2007, I met Noel Parmar in his Vadodara office. He freely displayed deep prejudice against Muslims. Here are some examples of his conversations with me that I managed to catch on camera. 'During Partition, many Muslims of Godhra migrated to Pakistan. In fact, there is an area called Godhra Colony in Karachi. Every family in Godhra has a relative in Karachi. They are fundamentalists. This area, Signal Falia, was completely Hindu-dominated but gradually Muslims took over. In 1989 also there were riots. Eight Hindus were burnt alive. They all eat cow meat since it comes cheap. No family has less than ten children.'

The first charge sheet had to be discarded because it was such a mess. To bring some order to the chaos, on 2 July 2002, five months after the burning of the train, the police produced a new star witness: Ajay Kanu Baria, the Hindu tea vendor who saw everything. The police claimed that the accused had forced Ajay to help them burn down coach S-6 and so he had an unrivalled insight into what had happened. In 2007, his mother told me (I recorded her words on my spy cam) that he had been coerced into becoming a police witness and lived under constant police surveillance.

In July, when Ajay was produced as a witness, like a rabbit pulled out of a magician's hat, he was unemployed. But he said he used to be a vendor at Godhra station. According to Ajay, just after the Sabarmati Express pulled into the station, nine Muslim hawkers whom he knew—since they all sold wares at the Godhra station—forcibly took him to the house of Razzak Kurkur, the owner of Aman Guest House. The men went inside and brought out twenty-litre carboys filled with 'kerosene'. He did not say how many carboys. Ajay was ordered to load one into a tempo while the other hawkers loaded the rest. At this point, it should be noted that, in the months and years of police investigations, not a single twenty-litre carboy has ever been recovered, either at the scene of the crime, or in the possession of the accused.

Ajay told the police that the tempo was parrot-coloured but he could not see its registration number. Once the carboys were loaded, the hawkers forced him to go along. They drove up to Cabin A, where the train had come to a stop (for the second time). The accused, he said, then cut the vestibule between coaches S-6 and S-7. Having done that, six hawkers went inside S-6 and poured kerosene on the coach floor. Three others sprinkled kerosene through the windows into the coach. A Muslim vendor then threw a burning cloth into the coach. Neither the police nor Ajay say he was at either of the two meetings that the police claim the conspirators held, nor was he contacted again by any of the accused. Yet, Ajay was integral to the prosecution's case. You could argue he was the prosecution's case.

Of course, Ajay's tale beggars belief. Why would supposed Muslim fundamentalists, seized by hatred towards kar sevaks, induct a Hindu tea vendor into their plot at the last minute, especially with an entire Muslim-dominated locality to draw from right next door? If there were already nine hawkers to load the carboys, why did they need Ajay to load just one? As for the delay in Ajay coming forward, the police said it was because he had been threatened by the accused. There were plenty of holes in Ajay's story for the defence lawyers to pick apart. It is a matter of record that the Sabarmati Express took between three and five minutes to come to halt after leaving the Godhra station for the second time. It is also the prosecution's case, specifically, that it took four minutes for the said tempo, in a fully loaded condition, to start from Aman Guest House and stop near Ali Mosque behind Cabin A. It is a shame that the courts did not press the prosecution on how long it would have taken to unload the carboys and get them to S-6 in order to tip the fluids into the coach.

It is a different matter altogether that neither the engine driver nor his co-driver, nor any of the railway officers stationed at Cabin A, or the railway police, or indeed the local police who arrived at the scene of the crime noticed the tempo or found any trace of it.

A second FSL inspection

On 11 July 2002, the FSL made a second forensic inspection of the burnt S-6 coach. It inspected the open sliding metal door between S-6 and S-7, and the FSL officer told the court that the door was so welded by heat into the groove that it could not be removed. The FSL noted a long scratch on the door, suggesting that it had been forced from the S-7 side.[9] The coach had been examined many times earlier, but this condition of the metal door eluded observation until July 2002.[10]

With the emergence of Ajay Baria and the new FSL report, the police put together a second charge sheet on 20 September 2002, which explained that the coach had been set on fire from the inside. But the anomalies persisted.

Two Muslim vendors pulled the chain

For the police, Ajay's statement got its ducks in a row. They had a witness to explain how the flammable liquids were brought to the spot, how the accused gained entry into the train and how the 'kerosene' was poured inside the coach before it was set on fire. But the police still had to show that it was the conspirators who had pulled the chain a second time so the train stopped near Cabin A. Surely, the conspirators would not have relied on a random passenger to pull the chain so the train would come to a halt, by a happy coincidence, exactly where they wanted it to stop, and then the waiting Muslims could burn it.

Abracadabra, the police came up with two more witnesses, both Muslims. Ilyas Mulla Hussain and Anwar Sattar Kalandar, the police said, had admitted that it was they who had pulled the chain that brought the train to a halt near Cabin A. The statements of these witnesses, both part-time hawkers and truck drivers, were recorded on 9 July and 26 July 2002. Both said they were present at the station when the kar sevaks began brawling with the tea vendors. After the fight, they said, they were told by Razzak Kurkur and Salim Paanwala (a paan seller at the station, who had been absconding since the incident) that the kar sevaks had abducted a Muslim girl from the platform and they had to stop the train. So both men, along with another vendor called Hussain Suleman Gijju (who, according to the police, was also absconding) scaled different coaches, turned the discs and stopped the train.

Both men named the same accused that Ajay had named in his statement. And both claimed to have seen the parrot-coloured tempo parked near the coach. They also said they had seen the nine vendors, who Ajay alleged had set S-6 on fire, near the coach, carrying carboys and later running toward Signal Falia. Ilyas and Anwar added that they had overheard the fleeing hawkers say to each other that the 'train is properly set on fire from inside'. Better yet, unlike Ajay, they had also managed to provide the police with the owner's name as well as the registration number of the rickshaw that the suspects used to transport the carboys to the train. After two weeks of confinement, Ilyas and Anwar were produced in court and their statements were recorded. Despite their close involvement in the conspiracy, neither man was charged with a crime; they were listed as witnesses for the prosecution.

After about a year and a half, Ilyas and Anwar returned to Godhra and retracted their statements in affidavits filed before the Supreme Court. They said that the investigating officer Noel Parmar had told them to leave Godhra and not stay in contact with any local Muslims. In an interview with me in 2007, both men said they were illegally held in captivity and tortured by Parmar and his team. 'Every night, the cops would come and put a log of wood on my legs and then walk over it,' said Hussain. 'I was given electric shocks on my genitals,' said Kalandar. They were allegedly made to memorise a statement handed to them by the police. 'The cops would come and ask us how much we had memorised from the hand-written notes we were given,' both said. During the trial, the prosecution dropped them as witnesses.

A large hole is plugged

On 22 January 2003, the police arrested Jabir Bin Yamin Bahera, an eighteen-year-old hawker at Godhra railway station with a criminal background. Thirteen days after his arrest, the police produced him in court and recorded his confession. On 26 February 2002, Jabir said, he was sitting at a tea stall when three hawkers, including Salim Paanwala, came up to him and said that Razzak Kurkur wanted to see him. When he reached Kurkur's house, Kurkur instructed him to buy petrol. Along with a few other Muslim hawkers, Jabir then went to Kalabhai pump and bought 140 litres of petrol in seven carboys. These were stored in Kurkur's house in Signal Falia, behind Aman Guest House, which Kurkur owned.

After that, at about 11.30 p.m., Jabir said, he was standing outside a shop Kurkur owned when two of the accused—Bilal Haji and Farukh Bhana, both Godhra corporators—arrived. The corporators told him they had just met 'Maulvi Sahab', who conveyed the message that the Sabarmati Express was coming and they were to burn down coach S-6. The two corporators conveyed the message loud enough for Jabir to hear and later tell the police.

Why S-6 and not any other coach has never been explained by the prosecution. Later that night, Salim Paanwala went to the station, the police claimed, to enquire if the train was running late. When he came back with the information that it was late by roughly four hours, Jabir and the other hawkers went home and gathered again at 6.30 a.m., near Aman Guest House.

Jabir said that he watched television for a bit, then came out of the guest house at about 7.15 a.m. He saw a hawker named Mahboob Latika running from the direction of the station, shouting, 'Kar sevaks are beating Muslims!' Jabir went towards the parcel office and saw five Muslim hawkers pelting stones at the train. After that, he, along with the nine Muslim hawkers who had been accused by Ajay of setting the coach on fire, went to Kurkur's house and loaded the petrol-filled carboys into a tempo. Kurkur then told them to take the tempo to a spot near Cabin A.

Kurkur and Paanwala followed on a scooter, with the former riding pillion, carrying a carboy. On reaching Cabin A, they approached coach S-2 first. There, Jabir said, he saw a few hawkers armed with sticks, pipes and sharp-edged weapons trying to break down the train's doors and windows. From coach S-2, they proceeded to S-6, where the hawkers had cut through the vestibule with a pair of scissors. Jabir said he and a few other vendors then entered S-6 with five carboys and poured petrol along the floor of the coach. A stray stone came and hit Jabir on the forehead, and he rushed off to a clinic to be treated. The next day, he said, he came to know that, after he had left the spot, a hawker named Hasan Lalu threw a burning torch inside the coach, which then caught fire. Jabir stated before the court that he visited Maulvi Hussain Umarji over the next few days. On his first visit, the maulvi told Jabir that he was paying Rs 1,500 to everyone who had been arrested. He did not pay Jabir. On his second visit, Umarji told Jabir to run, to get away from Godhra.

In August 2003, Jabir retracted his statement. But since he had made the statement before a magistrate, the court paid no heed. He is now serving a life sentence.

Stitched-up

Armed with Jabir's confession, the police claimed they now knew the five leading conspirators (Maulvi Umarji, Bilal Haji, Farukh Bhana, Razzak Kurkur and Salim Paanwala). They knew where the conspirators had gathered on the eve of the incident (at Kurkur's shop), where the petrol had been bought (Kalabhai pump) and where it was stored (in Kurkur's house, behind his guest house).

Kalota had defeated a BJP candidate to become president of the Godhra municipal council before the incident on the train. Six other prominent members of the area's Muslim community, including four corporators of the municipal council, were charged with terrorism. The other two were advocates. On top of accusing these politically significant Muslims of collusion, the police linked the conspiracy to Maulvi Umarji, Godhra's most notable Muslim religious figure. It was now evident, according to the police, that the burning of the Sabarmati Express and the murder of fifty-nine 'kar sevaks' was not the horrific outcome of a spontaneous riot but a carefully planned plot conceived and executed by Godhra's political and religious leadership, which despised Hindus.

The police booked 134 Muslims of varying descriptions, cutting across social and economic strata. Of these, only ninety-four were tried. (Seventeen absconded, thirteen were released for lack of evidence, five had died and another five were juveniles and not tried.) The trial was eventually conducted in a regular court, after a central review committee revoked the application of POTA to the case.

Of the eight Muslim political figures, the court convicted just two—Bilal Haji and Abdul Rahman Dhantiya, both first-time corporators. Maulvi Umarji was acquitted in 2011, after spending eight years in jail.

According to the police, it was Umarji who was the kingpin of the conspiracy, it was he who wanted the coach to be burnt and it was he who had given instructions to the other accused. If Umarji was acquitted because there was no evidence against him, the court should have asked, what remained of the charge of conspiracy? Sadly, neither court—trial or appellate—asked this question.

A broken, dejected man, Maulvi Umarji died two years after his release from jail in 2011.

Fresh fuel: Fake witnesses on the source of the petrol

This brings me to the two final star witnesses: Prabhatsinh Patel and Ranjitsinh Patel, two salesmen employed at Kalabhai petrol pump at the time of the Godhra incident. On 10 April 2002, a month after the train burning, the two men told the police that they had been at work from 6 p.m. on 26 February 2002, to 9 a.m. on 27 February. Both said they had not sold any loose petrol during that period, much less filled up seven carboys with 140 litres of the stuff. Ranjitsinh Patel was the delivery man, while Prabhatsinh Patel was the cashier at the pump.

But after reading about Jabir's confession in the newspapers, according to the prosecution, the two did a remarkable turn-around on 23 February 2003, when they gave a statement that matched precisely with the police theory. The duo approached the police almost a full year after the events in question to now say they remembered selling the petrol to six Muslim men, including Kurkur, Paanwala and Jabir. The men had arrived at the pump in a parrot-coloured tempo.

In 2007, I tracked Ranjitsinh Patel down to the village he hailed from. I recorded him on my spy cam saying that he had been given Rs 50,000 by Noel Parmar to give false testimony. His colleague, he said, had received the same amount. Ranjit also told me that the police had assured him he would be tutored well in advance and shown the faces of the accused before he took the stand in court to identify them. Even then, neither Ranjit nor Prabhat could identify Kurkur in court. And though the police had taken possession of the stock-register and accounts book of the Kalabhai petrol pump, neither were produced in court to show a record of the purchase. Asgar Ali, the owner of the petrol pump, was never questioned.

By recording Ranjit's admission on my spy cam, I thought I had pulled off a journalistic coup. Here was a major witness for the prosecution, on whose testimony men were convicted, admitting he had been bribed by the police. My report was met with an eerie silence.

During the trial, Ranjitsinh tried to justify his admission to me by claiming that I had bribed him to make a false statement. If that was so, the police should have charged me, because bribing a police witness as crucial as Ranjitsinh, on whose testimony the prosecution case so heavily rested, was a serious offence. Or Ranjitsinh and the investigating officer should have been charged for implicating innocent people. The state did neither. And the courts did not bat an eyelid.

I had met Ranjitsinh on just one occasion. The entire meeting, from first frame to the last, was recorded on spy camera. If there was any question of inducement or bribe, it would have been recorded on the footage. But the footage, in fact, showed how spontaneous our conversation was. Yet, the courts did not hesitate to rely on Ranjitsinh's testimony—a man who had voluntarily 'confessed' to being bribed by the police before a supposed Hindu activist he was meeting for the first time to tell lies about what he saw.

Confessions and retractions

The police also took a statement from sixteen-year-old Sikandar Siddique, a Muslim beggar living with his family along the tracks at that time. Siddique has since migrated to Surat. His statement confirmed the names of the accused and the sequence of events as stated by Jabir. He too claimed that Maulvi Umarji told him he was paying Rs 1,500 to everyone who had been involved in setting the train on fire. However, Siddique also named another religious leader no one else did—Maulvi Yakub Punjabi. Siddique said Punjabi had been shouting provocative slogans from the rooftop of a masjid when the train halted near Cabin A.

Unfortunately for Siddique (or perhaps the Gujarat police), Punjabi, as his passport and visa details proved, was not in the country at the time. So why did Siddique name Punjabi, and on whose instructions? If he could be so wrong about Punjabi, what qualified him to speak authoritatively about Umarji? Were the police using Siddique, and other witnesses, to implicate Muslim clerics in the Godhra fire?

Given the weakness of the nine 'VHP' witnesses, the prosecution's allegations of conspiracy rested on the testimonies of five star witnesses—Ajay, Jabir, Sikandar Siddique, Ranjitsinh and Prabhatsinh Patel. At the time of the Godhra burning, Jabir was an eighteen-year-old petty criminal with a police record, and Sikandar was just sixteen and used to beg at the station and on the streets.

Having gone undercover in 2007 to hear these men tell me their stories first-hand, I was told by Pathak and Mulchandani that the testimonies of these five star witnesses were bogus. Pathak told me that Ajay Baria lived under Parmar's close supervision. The last he had heard of Ajay, Pathak said, he was selling tea near Parmar's office in Vadodara. As noted earlier, Ajay's mother confirmed to me that he was at home and asleep, given the early hour of events at Godhra station, and had seen nothing. She too said that he was now effectively in permanent police custody. When they did occasionally meet, she said, he was always accompanied by two policemen.

The convictions of the key accused and the finding of a conspiracy were secured on the strength of these five witness testimonies. The statements of the other nine witnesses, most of them BJP corporators posing as VHP members, turned out to be fiction, as the court indirectly conceded. My sting operation offered strong indications that the testimonies of these five too were either coerced or bought. Surely any conviction through a trial in which all the key prosecution witnesses are suspect is a travesty.

SIT takes over the investigation

Appointed by the Supreme Court on 26 March 2008, the SIT reopened the Godhra case. Absurdly, Noel Parmar, who had built the prosecution's case, was appointed to this SIT. By this time, Parmar was on his fourth post-retirement extension granted by the Gujarat police. How could an investigating officer be inducted into an SIT to review and investigate his own investigation? Under pressure, the SIT reluctantly dropped Parmar from the team.[11]

Both the sessions court and the Gujarat High Court, seven years apart, agreed with the police that the carnage at Godhra was a premeditated conspiracy hatched by prominent local Muslims. The judgements gave legal ballast to Modi's theory that the Gujarat riots, in which even official figures numbered the Muslim dead at close to a thousand, were a reaction to a provocative action. Eleven Muslims were given death sentences for the Godhra 'conspiracy' and another twenty were jailed for life. Fifty-six people were acquitted, while seven were given the benefit of the doubt. The Gujarat High Court commuted the capital sentences to life in prison. There is an appeal now pending before the Supreme Court. Will the court look at my evidence with a different perspective? Only time will tell.

15

Tendulkar's 100 vs Amit Shah's 267

> [I]t is necessary for a prince wishing to hold his own to know how to do wrong, and to make use of it or not according to necessity ... he need not make himself uneasy at incurring a reproach for those vices without which the state can only be saved with difficulty, for if everything is considered carefully, it will be found that something which looks like virtue, if followed, would be his ruin; whilst something else, which looks like vice, yet followed brings him security and prosperity.
>
> —Niccolò Machiavelli, *The Prince*

In September 2013, when I was running an investigative news portal called *Gulail*, a source handed me a pen drive. It contained hundreds of recorded telephone conversations between Amit Shah—who was minister of state for home in the Gujarat government, working directly with then home minister Modi—and G.L. Singhal, a high-profile Gujarat IPS officer.

Shah, Modi's closest political ally and currently Union home minister, was the junior minister for home in Gujarat for seven years, from 2003 until his arrest in the Sohrabuddin Sheikh extra-judicial killing in 2010.[1] Singhal was a key member of the police hit-squad led by D.G. Vanzara that had gunned down many Muslims in encounters, while passing them off as terrorists.[2]

The tapes in the pen drive offered a close and unsettling encounter with the paranoid Modi model of governance, in which everyone was being watched, all the time. Select police officials were posted in powerful positions in the SIB, the Crime Branch, the commissioner's office and the anti-terrorism squad (ATS). These special wings of the police had sweeping executive powers to intercept phones, develop intelligence networks, detain and interrogate suspects, and were granted large (often unaudited) budgets and human resources. Over time, these officers became a law unto themselves. They frequently crossed the line, legally and professionally, to serve the interests of their political masters. Because they were indispensable to the leaders at the top, they were promoted, rewarded, and shielded from inquiry and scrutiny.[3] Sometimes, given the impunity with which they operated, these top police officers would run extortion rackets and threaten businessmen, builders, even fellow officers who refused to toe the line (the CBI charge sheets in the Sohrabuddin case detail these facts[4]).

It was all methodically arranged. The buck could never stop with the chief minister, even if it sometimes did with Shah. Modi, whom Shah addressed as 'Saheb', seldom dealt with the police officers directly. In fact, he only really interacted with Shah, through whom his writ ran, the tapes showed.

Singhal's luck ran out when he was arrested by the CBI in February 2013. The arrest came after the mother of Ishrat Jahan—a nineteen-year-old student from Mumbra, a suburb of Thane, part of the greater Mumbai region, who was gunned down by the Gujarat police in an encounter—filed a petition in the Gujarat High Court seeking an independent investigation into her daughter's killing. Initially, the investigation into Ishrat's killing was carried out by an SIT of the Gujarat police.[5] Later, the Gujarat High Court asked the CBI to take over. About six months before his arrest, his teenage son had committed suicide.[6] Heartbroken, and anxious to be with his wife and family, Singhal struck a deal with the investigators, a key member of the investigation team told me. He handed over

267 recorded telephone conversations to the CBI that revealed how three key wings of the Gujarat police—the SIB, also known as CID Intelligence, the Crime Branch and the ATS—had, in 2009, stalked one young woman, in her twenties, for more than a month. The CBI drew the panchnama for the recovery of the pen drive on 9 June 2013.

Singhal told the CBI that this odd surveillance operation was mounted on oral orders alone, there was no legal authorisation or paperwork. And the operation was in aid of someone Shah repeatedly referred to as 'Saheb' in the calls that were recorded and subsequently turned in. Singhal also told the CBI about German-made encrypted cell phones used by him and others close to Amit Shah. Four such phones had been procured and distributed among key police officers so that they could talk to each other in complete secrecy.[7] Mostly, Singhal told the CBI, they would talk about the legal strategy to cover up fake encounters.[8]

The CBI was investigating Singhal's involvement in the extra-judicial killings of Ishrat Jahan and three Muslim men, and these tapes about the surveillance of a young woman had nothing to do with the case. Indeed, it had nothing to do with any police case, let alone fake encounters. The reasons for the surveillance were entirely private, Singhal told the CBI. The young woman in question was an architect from a middle-class, Hindu family, a private individual on whom state resources were being lavished. Why?

Singhal had produced the tapes as evidence to show that, whether it was extra-judicial killings or the illegal surveillance of a private person, he was only acting under the instructions of people higher up the food chain. His statement to the CBI read: 'I restate the fact that previously I had been coerced to participate in and help in certain activities intended to obstruct the process of law. Although illegal, unethical and improper, I had not declined to follow instructions because I was under a cloud in this case and Shri Amit Shah used to wield his authority by making it appear that me and my subordinate officers were being protected from incarceration by his and the Chief Minister's efforts.' This statement is part of the CBI charge sheet, but since the trial has not started, it has yet to be tested legally.[9]

In exchange for these tapes and information, Singhal wanted the CBI to not file charges against him within the statutory limit of ninety days after arrest. That would entitle him to be released on bail. Since Singhal was cooperating with the agency, the CBI deliberately delayed filing a charge sheet within the stipulated time period, and in May 2013, he was released on bail.

It took me three months to tie up the various loose ends of this story. I made several trips to Ahmedabad to interview the key characters who figured on the tapes. I identified the woman who was stalked. She was originally from Gujarat but had spent many years working in Bangalore. I learnt that she was now married to an Ahmedabad-based businessman. To safeguard her privacy, I gave her the code name 'Madhuri'.

The illegal spying operation was initiated on Shah's instructions, sometime in July 2009, and continued for several weeks, Singhal told the CBI. For a month in 2009, between 4 August and 6 September, Singhal secretly recorded all of his cell phone conversations with Shah. Perhaps he had an instinct that he might one day need the protection these tapes could provide. He recorded three self-incriminatory statements before the CBI in June 2013. And the CBI prepared a ten-page panchnama while taking possession of the 267 phone recordings. 'In the latter half of 2009, when I was posted as SP [superintendent of police] (operations) in the Anti-Terrorist Squad (ATS) at Ahmedabad,' Singhal told the CBI, 'Shri Amit Shah had directed me several times to watch the movements of Pradeep Sharma, who was then posted as municipal commissioner, Bhavnagar. He had also asked me to surveil a young woman named ****. I had deputed some men of the Crime Branch (as ATS was short of subordinate staff) to follow her, as directed by Shri Amit Shah.'

The tapes indicated that, for over a month, the Gujarat police and its most sophisticated surveillance tools were used in a mysterious operation to closely monitor Madhuri's every movement. She was not a suspect of any kind and yet was tailed so thoroughly that surely laws were being broken. Her conversations were listened in on; she was watched as she went to the mall, to restaurants or to eat ice cream; she was watched at the gym, on trips to the movies; she was watched when she took a flight and stayed at a hotel. When she took a flight out of Ahmedabad, unbeknownst to her, there were orders for a pair of cops to be on the same flight. When she visited her mother in hospital, the Gujarat police was there too, spying on her movements and the people she met, as if she were a dissident in East Germany during the Cold War. It was creepy, and the creepiest perhaps was Shah's apparent interest in the men Madhuri met, and whether she was alone or with a man when she checked into a hotel. Madhuri's phone was illegally tapped, of course, but so were those of her family and friends. All the information that Singhal's men could glean was conveyed to Shah in real time, who in turn would relay it to 'Saheb'.

Such was the importance attached to the surveillance of Madhuri that several senior state police officials were ordered to personally supervise her movements and activities. On the tapes handed over to the CBI, Shah can be heard complaining to Singhal that his men were not doing a thorough enough job as Saheb was obtaining information about Madhuri's activities from independent sources, and that his information network was sometimes faster even than Shah's.

On 9 August 2009, for instance, Shah made a panicky call to Singhal: 'I talked to Saheb and he got to know from someone that they did go outside twice. I think our men are not watching properly. They are still there. They went for shopping as well and also moved out along with that boy who came to see her.' A little later, Shah again rang up Singhal. 'Today they are going out for a meal in a hotel. Saheb received a phone about this. So watch out as she is going with someone. It is the boy who is coming to see her. Pay proper attention. The fact is that Saheb gets all the information, so it leaves us in poor light.'

The tapes also revealed that Shah had instructed Singhal to watch IAS officer Pradeep Sharma, and to tap his phone to find out if he was meeting with Madhuri. Unaware of the existence of these tapes, Sharma had independently filed a writ petition in the Supreme Court in May 2011, alleging that he was being framed in bogus corruption cases by the Gujarat government because he was privy to certain information about a young woman. I discovered that the woman mentioned by Sharma in his petition was the same woman who was kept under watch by Shah.

In one of the phone recordings, Shah tells Singhal to put a man who was meeting Madhuri behind bars. Within three months of this surveillance operation, on New Year's Day, 2010, Sharma was arrested by the Gujarat police on various corruption charges. He was subsequently charged in half a dozen cases of corruption. Sharma has not only maintained his innocence, he has insisted in various TV interviews and court petitions that he was being hounded by the Gujarat administration because he knew of Modi's connection to Madhuri.[10]

Gulail tied up with the investigative journalist Aniruddha Bahal to publish this story. We titled it 'The Stalkers'.[11] The media ended up calling it 'Snoopgate'.[12] We tied up with a weekly news magazine to publish the story. The magazine decided to splash it as a cover story. But by November 2013, opinion polls had started to strongly indicate that Modi would be the next prime minister. The magazine, under pressure from its proprietors, dropped the report at the last minute. Bahal and I then decided to hold a press conference to break the story. Perhaps we should have paid more attention to our timing, because 15 November, the day we chose for our big reveal, happened to be the day that Sachin Tendulkar was playing his last Test match for India. Sachin stepped out to bat at Wankhede Stadium on 14 November, and when he stepped up to the crease the next day, to resume the innings, he was on thirty-eight. Almost the whole country was watching, praying he would get one more hundred before calling it a day. Television news channels were giving a ball-by-ball account of proceedings, even though the match was being screened live.

I belong to a generation of cricket fans that grew up idolising Sachin. When I was younger, every time his wicket fell cheaply in an international match, I would be too distressed to even eat. On that day, though, I confess to secretly hoping Sachin would get out early. Had he gone on to score a century, it would have been his hundred and first international century, and our scoop would have been out for a duck. In the event, Tendulkar fell short at seventy-four. At 3 p.m., at the Press Club in New Delhi, we told the assembled media what we had found on the tapes. The story made it to the front page of every newspaper[13] and was discussed (loudly, of course) on the evening's news debate shows.

The focus of our story was not about Shah and, by inference, his saheb's unseemly interest in a young woman's life; it was about how easily they commandeered the full powers of the state to pursue private interests. They tapped phones, they spied on her, using both technology and manpower. There were no compunctions about putting relatively senior police officers on the job, even getting them to follow the woman across state boundaries. Absurdly, there was correspondence between the Modi government in Gujarat and the B.S. Yediyurappa government in Karnataka over intercepting the young woman's Bangalore cell phone number and keeping tabs on her calls. On one occasion, the Karnataka government turned down Gujarat's request for permission to intercept calls, citing non-compliance with requirements under the Indian Telegraph Act.

By November 2013, the Intelligence Bureau had developed a strong fealty to Modi, no doubt because it expected him to become the next prime minister. I was told by a source that, while I was working on the story, I was followed and my phone was possibly tapped. At any rate, my movements were being watched. A senior IB officer had apparently tipped off the BJP and they were nervous about the fallout from the story. It was not like the Gujarat riots or fake encounters, two topics that only seemed to generate more mass support for Modi among Hindu voters. This investigation was about the completely gratuitous use of state power against a young Hindu upper-caste woman who was being stalked at the behest of a certain Saheb. There was also the impropriety of middle-aged men prying, seemingly voyeuristically, into a young woman's life.

To contain the fallout, the BJP and the woman's father had prepared a press statement. But they slipped up. We had not named the woman or Modi in our story, but the woman's father revealed both her identity as well as that of Saheb, in the press release sent to all the major media houses. He said that Modi was a family friend, and that he had requested the chief minister to keep an eye on his daughter for personal, family reasons.[14]

The BJP, scrambling to defend Modi, publicly acknowledged that he was Saheb, and that he had ordered a surveillance campaign on a private citizen for private reasons—whatever they might be—using public money. It was a breathtaking show of entitlement, and because the story had little to do with politics or ideological conflicts, it offered a frightening insight into how Modi saw himself in relation to the state. The state, and public resources, were subservient to him; they were there to serve him, rather than the other way around. The woman's father's desire to please Modi raised suspicions that he had been bought over, but to debate that was to miss the point. Surely, it did not matter what the father wanted. (Indeed, even if the woman who was being surveilled had consented to it—though there is little evidence to suggest she knew anything about the surveillance—it would still not matter.) The issue in question here was the cavalier abuse of power and the chief minister's disdain for due process.

A key issue, ignored in the general hubbub and prurient chatter around the story, was the use of surveillance technology. Clearly, the violation of privacy issue was important, but the questions that needed asking were much broader. In what circumstances would the government have been justified in tapping phones? Were Supreme

Court guidelines for tapping phones followed? Was the procedure for engaging special agencies followed? Was there a violation of the Indian Telegraph Act? The surveillance operation had been mounted on oral orders. There was no written (and therefore legal) authorisation, and due process was not followed. It was meant only to serve the interests of a 'Saheb'. In a democracy, that should be terrifying.

To deflect attention from these critical issues, the Gujarat state government set up a two-member commission to inquire into the issues raised by 'Snoopgate'. Inquiry commissions are a time-tested strategy in India to bury issues in circumlocution and procedural delays. The commission's terms of reference were tailor-made to divert attention.[15] For one year, the commission asked for, and received, several extensions. Unsurprisingly, the inquiry ended up nowhere. On 30 December 2013, the commission sent me a summons to file a sworn affidavit. I responded with a detailed reply about why I believed the commission was a ploy to shield the Modi government, after which it backed off.[16]

On 10 October 2014, Justice Paresh Upadhyay of the Gujarat High Court scrapped the commission, citing the consent given by the woman and her family to the surveillance operation as the reason.[17] Questions about the infringement of civil liberties and, most especially, the gross misuse of state machinery were not addressed by the bench. The order essentially approved the use of state machinery by a person to put herself under surveillance for her own security. It seemed to say, in effect, that if one is friends with a chief minister or prime minister, one can invoke the might of the state to have one's daughter or girlfriend or wife watched, and no surveillance order has to be written down and no procedure has to be followed in order for this to happen.

The bench did not demand to see if the necessary paperwork had been completed to enable the interception of calls. It did not ask the state about the origins of the 270-odd conversations, nor did it listen to, or analyse, the tapes. Doing so would have revealed the fact that, far from having given their consent, the woman and her family were entirely unaware that they were being watched. Instead, as if it had hit upon a crucial point, the bench raised suspicions about the four years it took for the tapes to surface. Does this mean there is now a (very short) statute of limitations on when whistleblowers can reveal criminal wrongdoing by people in power, or that journalists cannot report malfeasance if it is politically inconvenient? The court's verdict claimed that it had paid heed to the 'feeble voice' of the woman whose privacy had been breached, not by the surveillance itself, but by the inquiry into the use of surveillance.

What the court did not acknowledge was that *Gulail*'s reporting on the tapes had nothing to do with how the young woman lived her life—which was of interest only to Saheb and those like Shah, who did his bidding—but about the alleged abuse of power. For a journalist, the story did not stop at the woman's privacy and questions about whether it was breached or not (quite obviously, it was), but had far larger implications about the use of state power against citizens in a democracy. The High Court reduced what were serious questions with grave national implications into a private affair, even though it involved the use of public resources and the prima facie violation of laws. I wrote strong pieces criticising the judgement. But nothing happened.[18]

In October 2020, I interviewed a key political campaign strategist who had worked for Modi during the 2014 elections. He is no longer involved with Modi or the NDA, but agreed to speak to me, off the record, for this book. I asked him if the Modi camp was nervous when we broke the Snoopgate story. He said: 'Yes, we were rattled. We had four rounds of meetings on how to contain the fallout from the story. We knew five days in advance that you were about to break the story. So we were prepared.'

'How did you contain the damage?'

'At the time,' he said, 'the mainstream media was already more than willing to align itself with Modi and BJP. So we didn't have to work hard on that count. As for the principal actors involved in the story, who, if they had come on record could have substantiated your story, we had already worked upon them.' Then, without prompting, the strategist named a senior political leader from western India who was a key ally of the Congress and a constituent of the UPA at the time. 'We had managed him. He helped us by resisting any move within the UPA and cabinet for the Central government to set up an inquiry commission.'

For several weeks, UPA-II dithered over setting up a commission. 'It took us a few weeks,' a senior member of the cabinet at the time told me in confidence, 'to build the consensus that the issue was way too serious and needed to be probed by a commission headed by a retired Supreme Court judge. Prime Minister Manmohan Singh was hesitant. So were a few allies. But by the time we could get over these hurdles and announce a judicial probe, the Gujarat state government had set up its own commission and that was the end of the story.'

Towards the end of December 2013, UPA-II officially announced a judicial probe. 'But then, we couldn't get a retired judge to head the probe,' said the former cabinet minister. Later, in April 2014, while polling was already underway, the Central government once again tried to revive the probe, but the renewed efforts were met by a veiled threat from Arun Jaitley, who famously said: 'I will be very curious to know the name of the judge who has agreed to "lend" himself to the UPA. I will be surprised if there is one. I hope, for the cause of judicial dignity, no one agrees to be a part of this desperate exercise.'[19]

Finally, in May 2014, just a few weeks before the election results were to be announced, the UPA government junked the probe.[20]

•◆•

'If one were thoroughly honest and wanted to retain one's sense of inner self-worth, there was only one alternative. That was to drop out of the system altogether and become ... professional dissidents. But this meant breaking with the desiring side of life altogether, and exchanging such simple material gratifications as a regular job and apartment for an ascetic life of jail, mental institution or exile,' wrote Francis Fukuyama, describing how totalitarian states demand the complete submission of its subjects.[21] The price of not 'going along' is ruination.

In Modi's Gujarat model, if a bureaucrat or a police officer wanted to rise up the ranks, he had to implicate himself fully in the system's deceit. Those who resisted or tried to fight back were made to pay. And always heavily.

Towards the end of 2010, the Gujarat High Court had inducted Satish Verma, an IGP of the Gujarat police, as a member of a court-appointed SIT assigned to look into the Ishrat Jahan encounter. It was Verma who had refused to obey an alleged order from the chief minister's office to burn the letters written by former (acting) Ahmedabad police commissioner Chitranjan Singh in the Sameer Khan encounter case (see Chapter Three), and had preserved both the originals and the fake letters on file.

The team that was constituted to investigate the Ishrat Jahan case comprised two Gujarat cadre IPS officers, including Verma, as well as one officer from a different state. Satish Verma's investigation showed that Ishrat and her associates were kept in police custody illegally for many days, before being killed in a pre-planned operation by the police. In December 2010, in a major breakthrough, one of the policemen involved in the encounter detailed the whole sequence of events, confirming that Ishrat, along with Javed (alias Pranesh Pillai) and two others, had been murdered in cold blood by police officers. During the field investigation, Verma seized photographic evidence hidden in a computer in the state's Forensic Science Laboratory that showed Ishrat Jahan was shot at close range.

Closely guarded secrets of the Modi regime had begun spilling out of a once tightly closed box. The carefully cultivated public narrative that the teenaged Ishrat and many other ordinary Muslims were terrorists out to target Modi was coming undone. The Gujarat government, as expected, moved to neutralise the SIT. To obstruct Verma's investigation, it initiated an inquiry against him, accusing him of bypassing due process to take photographic evidence from the FSL.

The High Court later observed that, by its actions, including opening an inquiry against Verma, the government had tried to obstruct the SIT.[22] After the court accepted the SIT's finding that Ishrat had been the victim of a custodial killing, it transferred further investigation to the CBI, and directed the Gujarat government to permit Verma to assist the inquiry. Verma's investigation, while he was assisting the CBI, indicated that the political executive in Gujarat might have had prior knowledge of Ishrat's murder. Apart from G.L. Singhal, an accused himself, two witnesses stated before judicial magistrates that Vanzara had declared that both '*kaali daadhi*' and '*safed daadhi*' had cleared the killing. Among the officers, '*kaali daadhi*' was the codename for Amit Shah and '*safed daadhi*' for Narendra Modi. These testimonies form part of the documents in the CBI's charge sheets filed in court in July 2013 and February 2014. Of course, this has not gone to trial yet, and so, whatever evidence there is remains untested in a court of law.

Since 2012, the Gujarat government has given Verma only inconsequential postings, keeping him as far out of the way as possible. After the Narendra Modi government was formed at the Centre in May 2014, Verma was quickly shunted out to Shillong, to work as a chief vigilance officer under the ministry of power. This required the government to certify that there was no adverse material against him, and that he was eligible for such a sensitive posting. Then, in January 2015, the Gujarat government served Verma a charge sheet on counts dating back about three years. It also levelled a charge of absenteeism. Verma argued that he was on duty, but he was in between postings, and the days that he was allegedly absent were part of the grace period given to an officer before he assumes a new charge. Even if the charge of absenteeism was true, it was, by any measure, negligible, even trivial. For the government, though, it was the timing that mattered. The charge sheet was served in January 2015, just three days before a decision on Verma's promotion to the rank of additional director general was to be taken. The petty design was to deny him the promotion and the benefits that would come with a rise in rank.

After 2014, Verma has been posted in the northeast and the south, far away from his family. To further entangle him in administrative inquiries, the government has served him with three more charge sheets—one for stating the facts, in the media, pertaining to the Ishrat Jahan investigation; a second for apparently unauthorised travel while he was a chief vigilance officer in Shillong; and a third for dispatching reports about corruption when he had already been relieved of his post as chief vigilance officer. Verma has challenged the charge sheets in the appropriate tribunal, but the outcome does not concern the government. Its intent is clearly to keep up a campaign of low-level but constant harassment. In administrative matters, an easy way to block a promotion is to issue the officer with a departmental charge sheet. The officer is then considered 'under a cloud', and is denied promotion for as long as the inquiry plods on. Even under the best circumstances, these inquiries can take a long time. And if you have annoyed someone who is both malicious and powerful, the inquiries, however piffling, can take an eternity. To fight his case, an officer may have to hire a lawyer, prepare pleadings and attend hearings.

On the grounds that there are pending inquiries against Verma, the government has continued to deny him the promotion that is his right. His virtual exile illustrates the government's cynical use of state power against officers who stand up to it. Verma's legal cases are still ongoing and while the case of Ishrat Jahan is languishing in the dockets of the court, those who gunned her down have been promoted and rewarded, and those who benefitted politically from her killings are ruling the country.

⋅◆⋅

Verma, sadly, is one in a long line of upright officers whose careers have suffered because they did not toe the government line. Rahul Sharma, a young IPS officer, joined the service in 1992. During the Gujarat riots, he was posted as a superintendent of police in Bhavnagar district. On 2 March 2002, over 400 Muslim children were sheltering in a madrasa in Bhavnagar when a mob comprising thousands of Hindus surrounded the school, baying for their blood. 'The mob was trying to set the madrasa on fire,' Sharma told the authorities later. Many in the mob carried weapons, including swords, pipes and axes.[23] Using a combination of tact and force, Sharma dispersed the mob and saved the children. 'I then shifted about 400 students studying at Akwada Madressa to Ibrahim Masjid Bhavnagar,' Sharma said.[24]

While Gujarat was burning, with seemingly minimal administrative intervention, Sharma led his forces from the front and took decisive action against rioters. By 16 March, eight rioters had been killed in police firing in the district under Sharma's command; five of them were Hindus and two were Muslims. This was one of the rare instances during the riots when the police came to the aid of besieged Muslims.

On 16 March 2002, Sharma received a call from the then minister of state for home affairs. 'Zadafia said that while I had done a good job, the ratio of those who died in the police firing was not proper—he was complaining about there being more Hindu deaths than Muslim. I told him things would depend on the ground situation and the nature of the mob,' Sharma deposed before the Nanavati-Shah Commission. Sharma also told the commission that when he had called K. Chakravarthi, the then DGP, on 1 March, to ask for help, he was told that 'though [the DGP] would send one State Reserve Police Force company the next day and, if possible, some border wing home guards, he told me not to look for more help as the bureaucracy had been completely compromised'.

After the riots, Sharma was transferred from Bhavnagar to the police control room, Ahmedabad (the transfer was effected on 26 March 2002). He was asked by his seniors to assist in the investigation of the Naroda Patiya and Gulbarg Society massacres. Sharma analysed the call data records of all the cell phones active in Ahmedabad during the period of the riots. There were two cell phone companies providing services in Ahmedabad at the time: AT&T and CellForce. The analysis of call data records by Sharma proved vital in the investigation of both massacres. It established the presence of some of the key riot-accused at the scene of the crime. The call records showed that the accused had been continuously communicating with each other while on their killing spree. Still, when Sharma expressed dissatisfaction over the fairness of the investigations in the Naroda Patiya and Gulbarg Society cases, he was removed from the investigating team.

After Sharma produced a CD containing over 500,000 phone call records pertaining to the period between 28 February and 4 March before the Nanavati–Shah–Mehta Commission, the Gujarat government chargesheeted him for having unauthorised possession of the data. When a tribunal quashed the charge sheet as 'tainted by mischief, malafides and coloured by arbitrariness, illegality',[25] the government issued a fresh show-cause notice, asking him to explain why action should not be taken against him for making an 'unnecessary' payment of Rs 3,000 to his driver and gunman. The Gujarat government only withdrew the charge sheet against Sharma after he took voluntary retirement from the service. Sharma now practises law in the Gujarat High Court.

When G.L. Singhal carried out the snooping mission on the young woman, at the behest of Shah, he was a superintendent of police with the ATS, a powerful wing of the Gujarat police. In February 2014, he was arrested in the Ishrat Jahan murder case and suspended from police service, as per the requirements of administrative law. On the day the 2014 Lok Sabha election results were declared and the model code of conduct was lifted, Singhal's suspension was revoked and he was reinstated with effect from 16 May 2014. In 2019, he was promoted to the rank of IGP, though he continues to be an accused in the encounter case. In October 2020, a special CBI court in Ahmedabad refused to discharge him from the case.[26]

Another senior IPS officer, Arun Kumar Sharma, also figured in the snooping tapes. He was later appointed as joint commissioner, crime, in Ahmedabad city, a powerful post. After Modi became the prime minister, Sharma was appointed joint director of the CBI in April 2015. In January 2017, he was appointed joint director of policy, CBI. Abhay Chudasama was another senior officer who was involved in the illegal surveillance of Madhuri. He was arrested by the CBI and charged with staging the encounters of Sohrabuddin Sheikh and Tulsiram Prajapati. His fortunes changed, though, when he was granted bail by the Bombay High Court, a month before Modi became prime minister. By August 2014, Chudasama was reinstated in service by the Gujarat government. In April 2015, a CBI court discharged Chudasama from the fake encounter cases, and in June 2015, he was promoted to the rank of DIG.

As these examples show, a spectacular decline or an equally spectacular rise in your career graph as a policeman in Gujarat, and later at the national level, depends entirely on whether you have served the regime's interests or undermined them.

Seventeen years after Ishrat Jahan was killed in a police encounter and seven years after the CBI filed charges against several Gujarat police officers, a trial has not yet begun. And yet, an Ahmedabad CBI court has seen fit to drop all criminal proceedings against D.G. Vanzara, the notorious front man of those Gujarat police hit-squads, and P.P. Pandey, the former DGP. In October 2019, Ishrat's mother Shamima Kauser wrote a letter to the court: 'I am heartbroken, and my spirit shattered, at the perpetuation of this culture of impunity ... I have lost my will to fight, and can no longer participate in the proceedings before the CBI court.'[27]

Amit Shah, who was once charged by the CBI and briefly incarcerated in 2010 as a main accused in the plot to kill gangsters Sohrabuddin Sheikh and Tulsiram Prajapati, as well as Sheikh's wife Kauser Bi, was discharged by special CBI judge M.B. Gosavi, on 30 December 2014, a few months after he had masterminded Modi's overwhelming general election victory. It was the CBI's case that Shah was part of an extortion racket run by senior police officers like Vanzara and Singhal, both of who were said to be very close to him.[28] Sohrabuddin, the CBI suggested, could have exposed the syndicate, and so, in keeping with Shah's wishes, was killed in a fake encounter.[29] Judge Gosavi summarily held that the charges against Shah were politically motivated, though he did not provide any evidence to substantiate this theory. In fact, it was the Supreme Court which had initiated and then monitored the investigation into the Sohrabuddin encounter. And it was on the Supreme Court's watch that Shah was both arrested and arraigned. But the same court did not bat an eyelid when the case built at its urging fell apart. Shah is currently the Union home minister and, by many accounts, the second most powerful man in India.

16

Walk Alone

If they answer not to thy call, walk alone,
If they are afraid and cower mutely facing the wall
O thou of evil luck
Open thy mind and speak alone.
If they turn away and desert you when crossing the wilderness
O thou of evil luck,
Trample the thorns under the tread,
And along the blood lined track travel alone.
If they do not hold up the light
When the night is troubled with storm
O thou of evil luck
With the thunder flame of pain ignite thine own heart
And let it burn alone.
—*The English Writings of Rabindranath Tagore, Volume 2: Poems*

In early 2013, I was yet again summoned as a witness by an Ahmedabad trial court. The case on trial was regarding the killing of twelve people in Naroda Gam. In Gujarati, a village is called 'gam'. Naroda Gam, barely a kilometre from Naroda Patiya, was an urban village of sorts. As in Naroda Patiya, both Babu Bajrangi and Mayaben Kodnani were the primary accused in the killings next door in Gam. In addition, VHP bigwig Jaideep Patel had been charged by the SIT. A total of eighty-six accused were on trial.

Two days before I was supposed to fly to Ahmedabad, the SIT told me to put off buying my tickets. Apparently, the accused had filed a petition in the Gujarat High Court to prevent my deposition from being recorded. Their argument was that the presiding judge in the Gam case was Jyotsna Yagnik, the same judge who had pronounced the Patiya verdict. And since she had already relied upon my testimony to convict the accused in the Patiya case, she would follow the same reasoning in the Gam case.[1] 'The judge should say "not before me" to the trial of the Naroda Gam case as she has already delivered convictions in the Naroda Patiya case,' the defence lawyers told the press. But the High Court refused to stay my deposition or remove Judge Yagnik. Their petition was dismissed.

On 22 January 2013, I took the witness box as 'prosecution witness 172' in sessions case number 203/09. That day and the following weeks remain firmly etched in my memory.

I had been in and out of the courts in Ahmedabad now for four years. But 2013 was a different year from the others, with change in the air. In December 2012, Modi had routed the Congress yet again in the Gujarat assembly elections. He was sworn in for the fourth time as chief minister of the state. Bollywood stars, industry captains and the BJP top brass all flew down to attend the swearing-in ceremony. At the event, Modi addressed his supporters not in Gujarati, but Hindi. His speech was being telecast live by all the Hindi and English news channels. This was the big stage: Modi was addressing not just the people of Gujarat but the whole of the Hindi heartland. Exuberant anchors speculated that Modi might be preparing to become the next prime minister. 'Unstoppable Modi. Gujarat won, Delhi next?' screamed the headlines.[2]

Manmohan Singh's government was prone, practically comatose. The prime minister himself had become the butt of social media jokes, memes, mocking cartoons, scathing editorials and scornful public commentary. From the moment I stepped into the court room on that winter morning, I could feel India had ushered in a new age: one in which the right-wing would rule not just the streets but also bully institutions.

All the grandiloquence of Indian jurisprudence—high ceilings, polished furniture and oracular pronouncements—are the sole province of the country's higher courts: the Bombay or Gujarat High Court, for instance, and of course the Supreme Court. The milieu of a lower court in India, its typical setting, is grim. For me, it was about to get grimmer. What I would experience was the nadir of our criminal justice system, a subversion of what justice means and should mean to ordinary citizens.

In court, I faced a barrage of insults, petty humiliations and accusations—of being a false witness, a biased journalist, bought over by the opponents of the Modi government—from the defence. The lawyers, unsuccessful in stopping my deposition or getting Judge Yagnik removed, were aggressive, their voices constantly raised to a pitch of hysteria. I had experienced these tactics before. But this time around, even the judge, as much as the witness, was a target of this calculated viciousness. There were at least a dozen defence lawyers, junior and senior, fresh-faced and white-haired, in the courtroom, and they began the day's proceedings with a raucous twenty-minute rant aimed at Judge Yagnik. It was as rude as perhaps any lawyer had ever been to a judge in her own courtroom. She was being harangued about some application the defence wanted a ruling on before the matter could proceed. Impressively, the judge refused to be intimidated.

I had brought with me the transcripts of the sting operation on Babu Bajrangi to produce as evidence before the court. They were about a hundred pages long, but before I could admit them in evidence, the defence argued that I should not be allowed to refer to the transcripts while giving my evidence. Judge Yagnik overruled: 'The witness is depositing before the Court what he heard and recorded in the year 2007. He is not expected to learn by heart all the ninety-six pages of the transcript. It is a well-known principle that the truthfulness and the facts being related by the witness during the deposition is of paramount importance and the process of deposition in the Court is not a test of the memory-power of the witness.'

With the court's permission, I consulted the transcripts and read out the most relevant parts of my conversation with Bajrangi. 'After the massacre,' Bajrangi had said to me, 'I gave all the details over the phone to Gordhanbhai Zadafia, who was the minister of state for home and he advised me to abscond. Police Inspector Mysorewala also informed me of the FIR against me and told me to abscond.' I told the court that Bajrangi had come to Delhi in the first week of September 2007. While in the capital, he asked me if he could meet me and my 'boss' Anandji. He told us that for the four months that he was absconding, Modi, the chief minister of Gujarat, had arranged for him to stay in Mount Abu, a hill station on the state border. Bajrangi also told us that he had planned his arrest with the police—a drama staged to appease public sentiment.

I told the court that, in all my meetings with Bajrangi, between June and September 2007, he had always said, with complete consistency, that had there been no state support, the massacres on that day would not have been possible. Nor, he added, would it have been possible for him to go into hiding for four months. Bajrangi also told me that he had been assured by the state that the investigation into his role in the riots would be deliberately botched so as to protect him from the consequences of his actions. My testimony took all day, and I was told that I would have to appear again on 1 February.

•◆•

I got back on a plane from Delhi to Ahmedabad early morning on 1 February 2013, but thanks to the oppressive fog and pollution that shrouds Delhi in the winter months, I did not arrive in Ahmedabad until the afternoon. Eventually, the delayed proceedings began with me having to identify Bajrangi and Jaideep Patel in court.

The prosecution led by evidence for a few hours, after which defence began the cross-examination. The defence lawyers started by asking me questions that were irrelevant to my deposition, but seemingly designed to test my memory. Questions like: 'On which day exactly did the CBI record your statement? What are the press council rules? Who recorded your statement in the SIT? On which date did you meet SIT Chief R.K. Raghavan? Can you recall the names of the SIT officers who recorded your statements? How long did it take to record each statement?' And after this quiz came the accusations. Apparently, my goal with the sting was to defame the Hindu community. And though this charge was made without evidence, more charges were forthcoming. Apparently, I was also corrupt, greedy, a liar and was not even a journalist. Again, it appeared none of these claims, this casual character assassination, had to be backed up. If the questions were not insulting—'Is it correct that you did the sting operation to earn money? Is it correct that you have not furnished your appointment letter with *Tehelka*? Is it correct that the sting operation was not done by you but by somebody else?'—they were baffling: 'Is it correct that you didn't take the permission of the Gujarat police before doing the sting operation?'

Such questions stretched the session out till the end of the day, and then I was asked to return on 4 February. As we resumed, after the weekend, the defence continued to ask questions apparently crafted to delay, annoy and confound rather than get to any truth. 'In addition to whatever stated by you in the context of the sting operation,' the defence lawyer intoned gravely, 'what else do you want to say?' I scratched my head, metaphorically, wondering how to answer this question when the judge intervened: 'Such wide and vague questions are meaningless. Further, such questions are designed to confuse the witness, and thus should be disallowed. Please ask specific ones.'

The defence asked a more specific, if not necessarily more meaningful, question: 'Were all the statements that you gave to the SIT recorded on 19.01.2009?'

'My statements were recorded in at least four different cases, by different investigation officers, on different dates, about three to four years ago. How can I remember the exact date of each of my statements?'

'How many hours did it take for the statement in the Naroda Gam case to be recorded?'

'I was called by the investigating officers of various cases more than twelve times,' I responded, exasperated, 'and I do not remember such details.'

The defence argued that, by claiming to have forgotten each time, I was answering the questions in the same way and that my response should not be recorded each time. Again the judge spelt out the law on evidence. Given, she pointed out that 'the learned defence advocate has repeated the questions, therefore the witness also has repeated his reply. Not recording his reply is not in the interest of justice.'

Then it was back to trying to portray me as somehow disreputable.

'Is it true you do not pay respect to the Honourable Justices of the Court?'

'It is not true that I do not pay respect to the Hon'ble Justices of the Court,' I replied.

'In one of your columns have you written that one Honourable Justice was pressurizing you to give your reply to suit the conveniences of the defence side?'

'If I am being asked this question in the context of Gulbarg Society case,' I responded, 'then at the relevant time, it appeared to me that the behaviour of the Hon'ble Judge towards me as a witness was not fair and proper.' And the cross-examination continued in this way until I was asked to appear again the next day.

On each day, a new defence lawyer would question me. As if to underline the farcical nature of what was happening in that courtroom, one of these defence lawyers had been appointed by the state as a public prosecutor in the Naroda Patiya case. He was a card-carrying member of the VHP. At least, by appearing for the defence, he was more plausibly a part of the proceedings here.

The defence asked why did I not submit a report to the Gujarat police once the sting operation was over.

'A journalist reports to his Editor. Once his reports are vetted editorially, they are published, to be read by the people. In my career in journalism I have never seen or heard any journalist reporting to the police,' I answered.

On 6 February, the defence was still asking me questions. Seeking to further delay the hearing, the defence lawyer got a bee in his bonnet about some other frivolous application that he insisted the court consider before he would continue his cross-examination of me. Wearily, the judge recorded in the court proceedings that the defence lawyer had been shouting aggressively and had 'levelled wild allegations against the Court like—"You are pre-determined, you are issuing bogus orders, the whole world knows it" ... Since the witness was present, the defence was told to proceed with cross-examining. Yet the learned lawyer is not cross-examining the witness.' After a half-hour tantrum, the defence continued to question me. They played the sting footage, which at least gave me the opportunity to explain how the tapes were made. At which point, the defence asked me why I could not be seen in the videos, forcing me to explain that hiding a camera behind a shirt button necessarily meant my face would not be seen, though my voice was present in all sixty hours of footage. It was only the judge's willingness to stand up to barrack-room tactics that enabled my responses to be properly recorded.

Later, I was told by the SIT that the defence did not want Yagnik to have the opportunity to deliver a verdict because they knew she had only ten months left before she was due to retire. It explained their truculence.

When I approached Yagnik, who is now retired, for an interview for this book, she said: 'I have studied and taught law all my life. I know the limits of cross-examination. The defence has the right to ask all the relevant questions. What they don't have is the right to humiliate or threaten witnesses. Witnesses are the guests of the court. And since I had drawn a line for cross-examination in my court, the defence didn't like it.'

To delay proceedings, the defence pulled every trick out of their bag. They filed dozens of applications, nearly all of them frivolous. They approached the High Court to challenge several of Yagnik's orders. And when none of that worked, they spent whole sessions asking nasty, insinuating questions and behaving as boorishly as possible. On 11 February, I was asked to appear again.[3]

―•―

As soon as I left the courtroom on 6 February, however, another form of vilification began. A Hindi newspaper and a website began to publish false reports that I had become hostile. 'Khetan Ban Gaya Shaitan' read one headline. 'Bayan Se Mukre Khetan' claimed another, as if I had retracted my sting, which was, in any case, presented as proof of my diabolic nature. I started receiving phone calls from other reporters. On social media, there were jokes and memes about me being a liar. I tried to get in touch with the newspaper editor who was in charge of the publications in question to explain what the implications of me turning hostile were, but it was a hit job and I got nowhere.

So I wrote to the SIT head, R.K. Raghavan. It was his job to ensure that witnesses were not harmed and their reputation not tarnished. In my lengthy complaint, I pointed out the attitude of the defence lawyers, I told him about the campaign begun by the newspaper and how, when I had complained, I was threatened with more adverse coverage. The story was that I had retracted my testimony, and the result was a strident social media campaign that made me out to be a liar. It was galling and could not be further from the truth. Raghavan responded that day with a couple of consoling lines, but it was clear that he was not going to do a thing to help. In fact, what helped me cope was to remember how Judge Yagnik had handled the bullying—by maintaining her calm at all times.

On 11 February, I appeared in court again for more inanity and aggressive prevarication.

For the several days that I testified in the Naroda Gam trial, I watched the defence diminishing the office of the judge every day. And yet, this was no ordinary trial. It was supposedly being monitored by the Supreme Court. Those proceedings in that courtroom, unbeknownst to me at the time, offered an indication of the future, a time not far away when institutions would offer little refuge from swaggering thuggery.

Despite Judge Yagnik's desire to keep the process rolling, whatever the provocation, she retired without being able to complete the trial. Seven years since Yagnik's retirement, three more judges—K.K. Bhatt,[4] P.B. Desai,[5] M.K. Dave[6]—have come and gone, but the trial is still far from over. 'The wheels of justice turn slowly but grind exceedingly fine'—we are assured when we despair about justice delayed. But sometimes, in India, the wheels do not turn at all, stuck as they are in mud and grime and quicksand.

·•·

It has been eighteen years since the Naroda Gam massacre. In all these years, the victims have filed multiple petitions before the higher courts, complaining of injustice and delays in the trial. And multiple times the higher courts have intervened. But the other side knows how to arrange an unending obstacle race. You jump through one hoop only to bang your head on a brick wall. If you get a fair hearing in the Supreme Court, you won't get a fair judge in the lower court. If you get a fair judge in the lower court, you won't get a fair public prosecutor. If you get both, you won't get a fair investigating officer. If you are lucky to get all three, the system chokes you in traffic.

Since the Naroda Gam massacre on 28 February 2002, it took until March 2008 for the Supreme Court to hand the investigation over from the Gujarat police to a specially appointed SIT. At the end of September 2009, eighty-six people accused of having a role in the massacre were chargesheeted. After the Supreme Court replaced the public prosecutors with new appointees in June 2010, it took until March 2011 for just two prosecution witnesses to be examined in court. For over a year after, until July 2012, not a single witness was examined in court. The public prosecutors then resigned, and another set of prosecutors was appointed in April 2013. My own examination began on 22 January 2013 and was completed weeks later in the middle of February. The examination of the investigating officer began on 23 September 2013 and continued until 31 December when Yagnik retired. Her replacement, K.K. Bhatt, scheduled proceedings for only two days a week. By the time he retired on 30 September 2014, the investigating officer was still on the stand.[7] It had taken over a year to question a single witness.

A new judge, P.B. Desai, was appointed on 15 October 2014 and, finally, in February 2016, over two years since the cross-examination began, the investigating officer was finally allowed to step down from the witness stand. Desai retired on the last day of 2017, to be replaced by M.K. Dave. The prosecution concluded its arguments on 8 August 2018, and it took until 16 October 2019 for just the first of the defence lawyers to rest his case. On 9 March 2020, Dave was transferred and a new judge, Subhadra Baxi, was appointed. On 22 March, the courts were closed as part of the lockdown and are, at the time of writing, yet to reconvene.

In the meantime, as the victims have had to persevere with this tortuous process, the accused have been on bail for over seventeen years.

Bear in mind that this is still the sessions court. Even if they are found guilty, the accused will (as is, and should be, their right) appeal first before the High Court and then the Supreme Court. It could take another decade or more before the process is exhausted.

At least there have been convictions in some of the other trials. The conviction of Babu Bajrangi and two of his associates for murder and conspiracy to murder in the Naroda Patiya massacre, primarily on the basis of my evidence, was for me a vindication of my work as a journalist. The court relied on my evidence to assess guilt and hand out stringent sentences. There is no precedent in the history of Indian journalism where a reporter's story has led to the conviction of mass murderers.

Of course, Bajrangi appealed Judge Yagnik's verdict, as did Maya Kodnani and others. It took five years for the High Court to conduct hearings in the matter. On 20 April 2018, a two-judge bench delivered its verdict in a lengthy 3,422-page judgement.[8]

The High Court wrote more than 200 pages analysing my evidence under the heading 'XXVIII THE STING OPEARTION'. It found my evidence to be reliable, trustworthy and unbiased, and the sting operation authentic. In paragraph 333.19 the court noted that the 'testimony of this witness regarding the confession made before him is coherent and has not been in the slightest degree shaken in the cross-examination'.

The only question that arose for consideration, the court noted, was about the admissibility of the sting operation video footage under the Indian Evidence Act. The court went on to note that the CBI officer and the FSL Jaipur scientists who had investigated the authenticity of the video footage had found that the tapes were genuine and had not been tampered with. The CBI and FSL personnel had also deposed that the voice samples of the accused, which were taken during the investigation, matched with the voices on the sting tapes.

But the court also found that the special public prosecutor had messed up the technical procedures mandated under the law while producing electronic evidence and its transcripts. The court said 'the transcripts produced on record do not appear to have been admitted in evidence and exhibited, which clearly reflects on the lack of ability or gross negligence on the part of the Special Public

Prosecutor appearing on behalf of the prosecution before the trial court'. The court also said that 'the contents of the DVDs and CDs, which are in the nature of electronic documentary evidence, have not been proved in the manner provided under Section 65B of the Evidence Act'. Blaming the public prosecutor for the error, the court observed, 'It is difficult to believe that the learned Special Public Prosecutor who conducted the case did not possess the elementary knowledge about how documentary electronic evidence is required to be proved. Thus, while there is important evidence in the nature of the Sting Operation on record, the same is not admissible in evidence as it has not been proved in accordance with law.'[9]

I was crestfallen. Years of work, including months of questioning by the SIT and courts, and having to endure a hostile and gruelling cross-examination and snide media coverage, all of this would come to nothing because of a technicality. The High Court also observed: 'A perusal of the recording contained in the DVD reveals that right from the time the person who is recording the sting enters, till he leaves the place the recording is continuous. The conversation is so natural that it leaves no scope for any doubt as regards its authenticity. However, in view of the non-compliance with the provisions of Sub-section (4) of Section 65-B of the Evidence Act, the electronic documentary evidence contained in the DVDs and CDs is not admissible in evidence and cannot be looked into.'

A clear admission of guilt and the naming of co-conspirators could not be used as evidence because forms had not been filled out correctly and technical procedures had not been followed by a prosecutor who should have known better.

But in its see-saw verdict, the High Court went on to rely on my oral testimony and upheld the convictions of Bajrangi and the co-accused:

> If the contents of the DVDs and CDs cannot be looked into, is the entire evidence of the sting operation inadmissible in evidence? In the opinion of this court the answer is in the negative ... the extra-

judicial confession of the accused is not sought to be proved only through the electronic record, but a significant part of what has been spoken by the accused before the witness has also been deposed by the witness in his testimony. The accused have made extra-judicial confession before PW 322 Ashish Khetan, who has clearly deposed regarding the same, including facts stated by the accused to him. Since everything has been recorded by the witness, he has prepared transcripts based on such recording and has deposed on the basis of such transcripts.

I had spent long days and nights preparing those transcripts in a one-bedroom apartment in Andheri, Mumbai, that I shared with my wife and six-month-old daughter. She would be sleeping in her cot, and in my earphones, for hours, I would hear almost boastful admissions of the most horrible murders, pleasure taken in unimaginable mayhem. I had emailed those transcripts to my editors and had preserved all of my correspondence.

The court noted this obvious fact: 'The entire transcripts prepared by the witness have been produced on record vide list Exhibit 2266. This witness is not inimical to the accused. He had gone to Vadodara to cover some other incident and upon meeting the concerned persons, got a link about the riots related to the Godhra incident and found that it was worth uncovering, accordingly, with the permission of the higher ups, he went ahead with the sting operation, covering those persons whose names were disclosed during the operation. The witness, in his deposition, comes across as a truthful witness. He had no specific agenda when he embarked upon the sting operation, except to unearth the truth.'

All of a sudden, my work was not in vain.

After citing several Supreme Court judgements, the High Court noted, 'In the facts of the present case, the witness before whom the extra-judicial confession has been made is a trustworthy and credible witness and, therefore, the extra-judicial confession to the extent deposed before the court, deserves to be accepted.'[10]

The court also called out the 'inept manner' of the investigations by both the police and SIT and the prosecution. It 'speaks volumes about the intentions of all concerned', said the court, damningly.

It appeared that the court was as angry about the wastage of my footage as I was. After accepting that I was 'unbiased', it went on to say that 'to discard' my oral testimony 'would amount to playing into the hands of a dishonest prosecution, which has not taken care to see that such important evidence is proved in accordance with law'.[11]

For all the irritation the court showed for the way in which the prosecution's case was put before it, little could be done. Either the government was squandering public money on substandard investigators and prosecutors, or the prosecution was invested in failing.

After exposing the prosecution's shoddy work and even hinting at a deliberate attempt on the part of the SIT to sabotage evidence, the High Court said 'the upshot of the above discussion is that ... the oral evidence adduced by PW 322 Mr Ashish Khetan regarding the extra-judicial confession made before him is admissible in evidence'.[12]

The court thus relied on my testimony to uphold the guilt, on various charges, of Babu Bajrangi, Suresh Richard and Prakash Rathod. It said that the three men had entered into a conspiracy to attack and kill the Muslims of Naroda Patiya: 'The evidence of PW 322 Ashish Khetan before whom the accused (Babu Bajrangi) made an extra-judicial confession as narrated here in above, clearly indicates the active involvement of the accused in the entire incident'.[13] Judge Yagnik had sentenced Bajrangi to rigorous imprisonment for the remainder of his life, subject to remission or commutation at the instance of the government, which the High Court reduced to rigorous life imprisonment for twenty-one years without remission. Judge Yagnik had condemned Richard and Rathod to long prison sentences, both of which were upheld by the High Court.

In a moment of personal vindication, Rathod was convicted purely on the strength of my testimony. 'None of the witnesses have implicated Accused No 21 Prakash Rathod,' noted the court. 'However, from the testimony of PW-322 Ashish Khetan, the extra-judicial confession of this accused has been proved, which indicates his complicity and participation in the offence in question. The court has found this accused guilty of the offence of criminal conspiracy punishable under Section 120B of the Indian Penal Code and therefore, on the principle of agency he is liable for all the offences committed at different stages of the crime.'

This is a curious twist as far as my evidence in the Gujarat cases is concerned. The Gulbarg Society trial court judge had rejected my oral testimony on irrelevant grounds (see Chapter 8), the appeal against which is now pending before the High Court. Now, since the High Court has relied on my deposition to find the guilt of the Naroda Patiya accused, on the principle of precedent, a coordinate bench of the same court may rely on it to convict some of the Gulbarg accused who got away and also find a charge of conspiracy against the accused, which the trial court had dropped.

·•·

In March 2019, a Supreme Court bench headed by Justice A.M. Khanwilkar granted bail to Babu Bajrangi on medical grounds.[14] He claimed to be '100% blind' and his medical certificates were verified by the Gujarat government. The apex court, relying on the Gujarat government's certification, granted him bail. Curiously, when I last identified him in the Gujarat court in 2013, he seemed absolutely fine. In fact, he would give me death stares and grind his teeth, each time our paths crossed in the court complex.

Be that as it may, Bajrangi is out on bail while his appeal against his conviction in the apex court is pending. Maya Kodnani, given the benefit of the doubt by the High Court, was acquitted in the Naroda Patiya case, though she is still in the dock for Naroda Gam. As the latter case still winds its exceedingly slow way through the sessions court, Kodnani is out on bail. In January 2019, an Ahmedabad court relaxed the conditions of her bail sufficiently to enable her to travel outside Gujarat.[15]

After a harrowing last few months facing down abusive defence lawyers, Judge Yagnik retired and now teaches law in a college in Ahmedabad, where she lives with her son and her husband. In 2015, she wrote to the SIT that she had received as many as twenty-two threatening letters and blank phone calls at her home while she was presiding over the Naroda Patiya case and after her verdict.[16] A section of the right-wing continues to carry on a social media vilification campaign against Yagnik.[17] Some right-wing commentators have even demanded her prosecution in TV interviews.[18]

In June 2020 and then again in October, I spoke to her on the phone. She declined an extensive interview, but I wanted to know what had kept her going when so many in the system had failed the victims of the Gujarat riots. 'To keep my head high before my own conscience,' Yagnik replied. 'To truly observe the oath of upholding the constitution I had taken when I became a judge. That's what kept me going.' It would have been easy to back down. Yagnik received many threats to herself and to her family. She would be burnt alive, the anonymous callers and letter-writers said, just like the Muslims in Gujarat. 'My religion was that of a judge,' Yagnik told me, 'detached from all caste, creed or ideological complexions. While I was hearing the Patiya case, there were all kinds of pressures, mostly subtle, indirect. There were also temptations. But then as a judge you need to insulate yourself from such pressures and allurements ... I firmly believe that the judges should be barred by law from accepting any post-retirement posts or assignments.'

Yagnik said she still fears for her life and the safety of her son. 'Unfortunately, the police have not tracked down or identified the people behind the threats I received. But then, that's the price one should be willing to pay to uphold the majesty of justice.' She told me that she believed riots were 'nothing but terrorism of one kind'.

In India, there are many heroes. We worship many idols from Bollywood and the cricketing world. But for the victims of the Gujarat riots, Yagnik is a hero. She may be obscure now, mostly forgotten—except by the lunatics who threaten her safety. But she did a great service to her country by showing us that, with a little backbone, it remains possible to hold people accountable for their gruesome crimes. Even when many in the system fall in line behind the criminals.

Epilogue
Riot after Riot

On the night of 25 August [1947], the small town of Sheikhupura, near Lahore—with a population of 10,000 Muslims and 10,000 Hindus and Sikhs—exploded into a massive pitched battle, for no reason anyone could ascertain. It had previously been known as one of the quietest spots in the West Punjab. Twenty-four hours later, several thousand people, mostly Sikh and Hindu, had been murdered in a frenzy of stabbing, shooting, beating and burning, and parts of town were ablaze. No effort had been made to quell the violence. The Muslim police actually aided it. A journalist who visited Sheikhupura the next day found a civil hospital in a disgusting state, with flies teeming thickly over the blood-soaked rags that substituted for bandages, and the stench of death in the muggy monsoon air.

— Alex von Tunzelmann, *Indian Summer: The Secret History of the End of an Empire*

Foolishness, sir. How can old wounds heal while maggots linger so richly? Or a peace hold for ever built on slaughter and a magician's trickery?

— Kazuo Ishiguro, *The Buried Giant*

Love jihad: Hindu right-wing organisations coined this phrase sometime in the early noughties. It describes a scenario in which Muslim men conduct religious warfare by marrying Hindu women who then convert to Islam and produce Muslim children. To prove the existence of such a conspiracy, every inter-faith marriage in which the man happens to be Muslim and the woman Hindu is cited as evidence. Around that decade, the Sangh Parivar launched a massive programme to mobilise Hindus—from UP to Gujarat and Karnataka to Kerala—to be aware of and wary of 'love jihad'. Volunteers distributed provocative pamphlets, organised meetings and held seminars to discuss this clear and present danger. Humming underneath all this was a project that had been in motion since the late 1980s, of sowing resentment and victimhood among Hindus—supposedly at the receiving end of the Muslim aggression, even as minorities were being appeased by the secular elite at the expense of the majority community.

After he was released on bail in 2003, Babu Bajrangi, by his own admission, took up the cause of fighting back against love jihad. When I met him at his office in Ahmedabad in June 2007, he paraded before me half a dozen Hindu women whom he had 'rescued' (see Chapter 9). These rescue operations involved the forceful abduction of a Hindu woman from the home she had made with her Muslim husband or lover, beating the man up and imprisoning the woman in her parents' house.

By 2013, western UP became the prime battlefield in a nationwide war against love jihad. They didn't stop at Hindu women, of course, but also made saving the Indian cow from abattoirs of Muslim butchers a 'crusade'. Everywhere, Sangh Parivar activists armed with pamphlets or loudspeakers were reminding Hindu men of their patriarchal responsibility to save their women and their cows.

Confrontation was inevitable. In September 2013, a private dispute between two small groups of Hindus and Muslims spilt over into region-wide communal rioting, engulfing four districts—

Muzaffarnagar, Shamli, Meerut and Bagpat. At least sixty-two people died in the fighting and tens of thousands were displaced.

At the time, I was running *Gulail*.[1] An intrepid, young reporter (name withheld at her request) had recently joined my team. We decided to investigate the charge of love jihad, look at the reality of inter-faith marriages in UP and at how these marriages are perceived, particularly in the Hindu community.

For almost a year, she travelled across western UP, Karnataka and Kerala. Posing as a researcher, the most convenient and plausible cover for a young woman reporter, she secretly filmed more than a dozen BJP MLAs and VHP and RSS leaders, who admitted on spy cam to using the fear of love jihad to unleash a reign of terror and violence against Muslims.

Gulail's year-long investigation showed that the anti-love jihad campaign was a potent mix of communal politics and patriarchal oppression. We did not find any evidence of a conspiracy by Muslim men to convert Hindu women. What we did find was compelling evidence of a conspiracy by major Hindutvawadi outfits and their leaders to build a false narrative about love jihad and use the heightened emotions it generated to mobilise Hindus against Muslims. The campaign by Hindutvawadi outfits not only demonised Muslims but also treated Hindu women as chattel, not much higher in status than the cows they also had to rescue from covetous Muslim men.

The story also confirmed that secular liberals had lost more ground than ever before in the losing battle they were fighting against Hindutva. Whatever its manifest absurdities, a very large number of grassroots Hindu activists believed that love jihad was real, and what's more, it needed to be actively resisted. The agenda we heard repeated by mid-level and ground-level Sangh Parivar workers across regions comprised three action points: build the Ram temple in Ayodhya; revoke Article 370 in Kashmir; convert India into a Hindu Rashtra. This was in 2013; seven years later, the first two objectives have been achieved.

We filmed leaders and members of the RSS, VHP and BJP speaking at great length about how they manipulated, intimidated and blackmailed Hindu girls who chose to marry Muslims. These right-wing leaders also admitted to weaponising the legal system to target Muslim men. Many of them bragged about registering false cases of rape and kidnapping to ensure both the annulment of inter-faith marriages and long prison sentences. The Hindu partners of these men were coerced into giving false testimonies about their marriages.

A BJP MLA from Thana Bhawan constituency in UP, Suresh Rana, told the *Gulail* reporter how he had made a girl tell lies in order to have Muslim boys charged with rape. We had senior BJP leaders from the region presenting alarming levels of hate and rage directed at the Muslim community. Sanjeev Balyan, who was elected to the Lok Sabha from Muzaffarnagar in 2014 and 2019, and is currently minister of state for animal husbandry, dairying and fisheries said, 'In the beginning, (Muslim) boys would roam around on motorcycles in front of schools and Plus Two Colleges,' he said, 'using Hindu names like "Sonu", "Monu", with a kalawa (sacred thread) tied around their wrists, pretending to be Hindus. A girl who falls in this trap would come to know only later, after eloping with the boy, that she is not with a Hindu. There have been a lot of such cases.'

Another BJP politician, Umesh Malik, currently an MLA, told the *Gulail* reporter that if 'our mother's and sister's honour is at stake, our daughter-in-law's and our daughter's honour is at stake, then I say that if we can die, we can kill also'. Spinning his web of conspiracy, he added: 'Those people have eight children, ten children and they send one or two of them to Deoband. There, the handsome ones are selected and trained to trap Hindu girls. They are told if they do this, Allah will be pleased with them. Their religion says this. They do this work of trapping our girls and making them elope. In the last four months alone, twenty-seven girls have eloped.'

When we investigated some of the love-jihad cases that Balyan and Malik had mentioned, we found that they were all fabricated;

ordinary inter-faith marriages had been maliciously distorted to represent examples of love jihad. We interviewed young inter-faith couples, lawyers and policemen in UP and Karnataka. We found that, in some districts, Hindu outfits kept vigil at the city magistrate's office to see if there were any Hindu women who had registered to marry a Muslim man. To stop such marriages from being solemnised, a mob of Hindu activists would descend upon the magistrate's office and cause havoc. They would then persuade or force the police to register fabricated criminal cases against the Muslim man and sometimes even beat him up. If a Hindu woman was not willing to give a statement against her Muslim partner, the mob would even use physical force to make her fall in line. More often than not, a Hindu woman, under sustained pressure from her community, her family, the Hindu outfits and even the police, would eventually agree to make a false statement of rape and abduction against her partner. In north Kerala, we came across a counselling centre run by Hindu activists, where they used to administer medicinal treatment to Hindu women to cure them of 'love jihad'.

Hukum Singh, then a BJP member of parliament from Kairana, UP, told our reporter that love jihad required a concerted effort from the community. If 'the girl gives a statement in the police station that she wants to stay with the boy,' he said, 'what strategy are we possibly going to use then?' The only solution in his mind was to 'change the psychological atmosphere ... let Modi come to power, then no Mohammedan will dare look at any Hindu girls let alone touch them'.

These conversations between the *Gulail* reporter and Singh happened towards the end of 2013, still some months to go for the Lok Sabha elections. Not long after, the slogan *'Desh, bahu aur gai ko bachana hai to Narendra Modi ko lana hai'* began to ring across UP.

Modi did become prime minister in 2014, of course, and three years later, Yogi Adityanath, the firebrand Hindu cleric, became UP chief minister. In 2015, *Gulail* broke this story in collaboration with Aniruddha Bahal's *Cobrapost*. (As we did the 'Snoopgate' story, in which the surveillance capabilities of the Gujarat government were used to stalk a young woman at the behest of 'Saheb'.) We called it 'Operation Juliet: Busting the Bogey of Love Jihad'.[2]

We had almost twenty-five hours of footage featuring conversations with over two dozen RSS, VHP and BJP members from three states—Kerala, Karnataka and UP. Its revelation of a planned attempt to stoke communal hatred using the scaremongering chimera of love jihad was ignored by the police and the courts. Disappointingly, the mainstream media too shied away from reporting on our investigation, even though it was a story they would have ordinarily jumped on. Only *India Today*,[3] the *Deccan Herald*,[4] *Scroll*[5] and the *Wire*[6] covered the story to some extent. There seemed to be a diminished appetite in the mainstream media to take on subjects that were critical of the idea of militant Hindutva and its effect on our once-cherished national ideals. Muscular Hindu nationalism was the new normal. The hard liners and radicals in the BJP and the Sangh were no more the fringe. They were now the core. And any report critical of them was suddenly to be treated with abundant caution.

Among those whom *Gulail* had captured on camera was an extremist who ran a 'Hindu Helpline' in Ernakulam, Kerala. He outlined a sinister strategy to create a conducive environment for a Hindu–Muslim riot.[7] On camera, he said, 'We cannot initiate a riot. That never happens. What I can do is I can make all the circumstances ready. When we create a consciousness amongst the community, the element of hatred comes. Then society is ready for a riot.' He bemoaned the prevalence of law and order in Kerala. Any incident he could invent to provoke a riot would have a far greater chance of succeeding in UP because 'there people are armed. They are not controlled by the government.'

December 2019. It was a winter of hope and of revolutionary poetry. Thousands of Indians were marching on the streets, staging sit-ins, and singing songs of love, peace and justice while waving the tricolour. Students from the Indian Institute of Management, Ahmedabad, the Indian Institute of Technology, Kanpur, the Indian Institute of Science, Bangalore, and Savitribai Phule University, Pune, recited Faiz Ahmed Faiz's stirring 'Hum Dekhenge'.[8] It's a poem that voices the resolve of the oppressed to one day throw off the shackles, so that the ruled and downtrodden can take control of their own destiny.

This spontaneous outpouring was against the Citizenship Amendment Act, which grants Indian citizenship to people who have fled neighbouring Afghanistan, Bangladesh and Pakistan because of religious persecution. On the face of it, the Act was benign—except that Muslims alone were denied the right to apply for Indian citizenship on the grounds of religious persecution. Those who opposed the law argued that it was a pretext to deny citizenship to many Indian Muslims who might not be able to furnish documents to prove their Indian origins, and would then be declared foreigners in their own land. The lack of similar papers among those of other religions would not necessarily be a bar to citizenship.

Ground zero for this Act was the decades-old agitations in Assam over the threat represented to the indigenous Assamese, including land rights, language and culture, by illegal immigration from Bangladesh. Student agitations led to the Assam Accord in 1985, which made various promises that subsequent governments in Delhi had failed to keep.

The CAA was passed after a sustained political campaign led by then BJP president Amit Shah, in which Muslims in the northeast were repeatedly labelled as infiltrators whom the BJP vowed to throw out of the country.[9] The BJP had declared in its manifesto for the 2019 Lok Sabha elections that it was committed 'to protect[ing] the linguistic, cultural and social identity of the people of North East'. The manifesto said 'there had been a huge change in the cultural and linguistic identity of some areas due to illegal immigration, resulting in an adverse impact on local people's livelihood and employment'. It went on to promise the completion and implementation of a National Register of Citizens which it would expand 'in a phased manner in other parts of the country'.[10]

Shah laid out the roadmap for identifying and deporting these Bangladeshi intruders. In an election speech in West Bengal in May 2019, he said: 'First we will pass the Citizenship Amendment bill and ensure that all the [non-Muslim] refugees from the neighbouring nations get Indian citizenship. After that NRC will be made and we will detect and deport every infiltrator from our motherland.'[11] To the BJP's core constituency, Shah pitched the CAA as a precursor to the NRC. That is why many people read the two as connected, with the CAA being a magic bullet for non-Muslims who might not be able to prove their Indian citizenship through the paperwork demanded. Muslims who had lived in India all their lives would, if their paperwork was deemed insufficient, be left stranded as infiltrators and 'illegal' immigrants.

Paradoxically, a discriminatory law, devised to divide people, united many instead, particularly young people, women and students. A spontaneous and exuberant movement began to take shape on campuses and on the street. Walls near campuses and elsewhere were covered in paintings, graffiti and poetry. Social media was full of young people making impassioned speeches, and using words, in songs, rap and spoken-word poetry, to express their resistance to the BJP's narrow, sectarian worldview.

The anti-CAA protests attracted ideological co-travellers. Human rights activists, sundry organisations working for the rights of Dalits, minorities, women, farmers and the like glommed onto this fresh movement with its exciting impetus. Barring a few sporadic incidents of violence, the protests were largely peaceful, marked by joy and inclusion rather than hate, anger and exclusion. On 16 December 2019, the Delhi police alleged that protestors assembled near Jamia Milia Islamia in Delhi, set a few public buses and private vehicles on fire and pelted stones at police personnel.[12] The police in Meerut, UP and Mangaluru in Karnataka also claimed that they were attacked by protestors.[13] Civil rights activists countered that the violence during the protests in UP, in coastal Karnataka and Bihar (all three were BJP-ruled states) were provoked by police brutality, by the gratuitous force used when trying to break up anti-CAA protests. The police crackdown on protestors took a particularly vicious turn in UP, where more than a dozen Muslim protestors were killed by police firing and dozens of police were also injured.[14] More than a thousand protestors were jailed and/or tortured in UP, including minors.[15]

Just as it seemed the anti-CAA protests would lose momentum, crushed by baton and trigger-happy police, a group of middle-aged and elderly Muslim housewives began a neighbourhood sit-in in Delhi. In fact, the sit-in had begun not long after the passage of the CAA through both houses of parliament on 11 and 12 December, but it began to attract nationwide attention some days later, probably because it provided such a model of contrast to the unrestrained anger on the streets, particularly from the police and right-wing groups opposed to the anti-CAA protests. Soon, Shaheen Bagh, a suburb in southern Delhi, became the epicentre of the anti-CAA protests, a social movement that expressed not just opposition to a prejudiced law but offered an alternative vision for India, a fairer, more inclusive country, less masculine and less predatory. It became a space where Muslim women, of all age groups, levels of education and social backgrounds discovered their political voice and found an accommodating space. Young mothers brought tiny babies, the elderly sat fearlessly among their friends and strangers, some women came in veils, others in jeans, and around the edges were people of all faiths and classes who quickly became enveloped in the warm embrace of Shaheen Bagh.

A young poet composed a beautiful hymn, 'Jamia ki Ladkiyan'. Without quite capturing the music of the original, here's a loose English translation of a few lines: 'They unmask tyrants / with gestures of revolution / the girls of Jamia / shredding the cloaks of patriarchy'. Rather than insisting on always referring to women as mothers, sisters, wives and daughters, the poet wrote that 'They live their lives / they also smoke cigarettes / some are drifters / these are the girls of Jamia / and keep your opinions to yourself / keep a hijab handy if you need it'.[16]

Soon, Shaheen Bagh began to be replicated in other parts of the country. Muslim women, so easily dismissed as adjuncts to their men, were both the voice and the heart of the protest. Brandishing flags, copies of the Constitution and singing the national anthem, they refused to allow their love for India to be slandered by Hindutva nationalists who sneered about Pakistan and biryani. Shaheen Bagh was also the model for anti-CAA protests in other parts of Delhi, in Jaffrabad, Chand Bagh, Khajuri Khas, Old Mustafabad, Seelampur, Turkman Gate, Kardam Puri, Sundar Nagari, Lal Bagh, Inderlok, Nizamuddin, Hauz Rani and Sadar Bazar. From 15 January onwards, at least seven protest sites emerged in northeast Delhi alone.

...

By then, however, the atmosphere had already been vitiated by the BJP's communal rhetoric. An early salvo was fired by the prime minister himself. Speaking at a BJP election rally in Dumka, Jharkhand, Modi said that those who were protesting against the CAA could be recognised by their clothes, a direct reference to the headgear of Muslim men and the veil worn by Muslim women.[17] A *Guardian* staffer described Modi's remark as a 'blaring foghorn', not just a dog whistle.[18] In the election campaign for the Delhi assembly elections, scheduled for 8 February 2020, the BJP made the citizenship law and the Shaheen Bagh protest its core election issue. The Delhi election was compared by BJP leaders to a cricket match between India and Pakistan. Anti-CAA protestors were used as shorthand for traitors and anti-nationals. Press the EVM button with such anger, Home Minister Amit Shah told Delhi voters in the last week of January, that Shaheen Bagh feels the current.[19] There were incessant references to that other BJP strawman, the 'tukde-tukde gang' of rebels who apparently want to break up India, but is used loosely now to refer to anyone who disagrees with the BJP and the tenets of Hindutva. Yogi Adityanath said terrorists should be fed 'with bullets not biryani',[20] terrorists being an oblique reference to protestors. And Minister of State for Finance and Corporate Affairs Anurag Thakur chanted an expletive-ridden slogan calling for traitors to be shot. Traitors, again, in this case, meaning anyone who disagrees with the BJP.[21]

On 28 January 2020, in a televised interview, Parvesh Verma, a young BJP MP, said: 'The people of Delhi know that the fire that raged in Kashmir a few years ago, where the daughters and sisters of Kashmiri Pandits were raped, caught on in UP, Hyderabad, Kerala, the same fire is raging in a corner in Delhi. Lakhs of people gather there. This fire can reach the residences of Delhi anytime. People of Delhi will have to decide wisely. These people will enter your houses, rape your sisters and daughters, kill them. There's time today, Modi-ji and Amit Shah won't come to save you tomorrow.'[22] On the same day, while addressing a crowd at a community centre in west Delhi, Verma said he would demolish all the mosques in his constituency if the BJP won the elections: '… give me one month … however many masjids have been built on government land … I won't leave even one of them standing'.[23]

On 29 January 2020, Tarun Chugh, national secretary, BJP, tweeted: 'We will not let Delhi become Syria and allow them to run an ISIS-like module here, where women and kids are used. They are trying to create fear in the minds of people of Delhi by blocking the main route. We will not let this happen.'[24] The tweet carried the hashtag #ShaheenBaghKaSach. And on 30 January 2020, a Hindu radical named Rambhakt Gopal fired his gun, in full view of the Delhi police, at protestors gathered at the gates of Jamia Milia University, injuring one student.[25] A couple of days later, another Hindu radical Kapil Gujjar entered the Shaheen Bagh protest site with a gun and opened fire, though nobody was hurt.[26]

The BJP's ugly rhetoric had hit its mark, and suddenly Shaheen Bagh was no longer a site of peaceful protest but a den of traitors deliberately holding up the traffic. Some in the press wondered whether the jams were being caused by the protests, or by deliberate action taken by the Delhi police to close roads they could have left open.[27] Still, some well-meaning activists warned the Shaheen Bagh protesters that the BJP was using the inconvenience caused to the general public to whip up communal frenzy.[28] Sensing that the protests were beginning to become unpopular, Arvind Kejriwal, running to become chief minister for a third time, said four days before the polls, 'if the police reported to me, I would have cleared the protest sites in two hours'.[29]

But the protestors, understandably, did not want to retreat. Portraits of Babasaheb Ambedkar, Mahatma Gandhi, Bhagat Singh, Savitribai Phule and Ashfaqulla Khan adorned the site in an open display of allegiance to the vison of India expressed by the freedom fighters and the country's Constitution.[30] This was the legacy that belonged to all the defiant protestors at the site. They waved the national flags and recited the Preamble to the Constitution as if it were scripture, but perhaps they overestimated the appeal of such idealism. The BJP's darker, more fearful narrative held the country in its grip.

The BJP, as it turned out, was soundly thrashed by the Aam Aadmi Party at the polls held on 8 February. But the monsters had been let loose. The charged Delhi air was rent with increasingly vicious calls to arms. On 22 February, a group of anti-CAA demonstrators staged a sit-in near the Jafrabad metro station, causing the closure of the metro station and of one carriageway of a major road, leading to resentment among some locals. The police claim that the sit-in was in response to a call for a Bharat bandh given by Chandrashekhar Azad Ravan, founder of the radical Ambedkarite group, the Bhim Army. Some anti-CAA protestors responded by blocking more roads the next day, claimed the Delhi police.[31]

On 23 February, AAP-turned-BJP leader Kapil Mishra called for supporters of CAA to gather in Maujpur Chowk to mark their protest against the Jafrabad sit-in, which was less than a kilometre from the spot where Mishra and his supporters finally assembled. Early in the evening, Mishra, with the local DCP in full riot gear standing by his side, warned that, as long as then US president Donald Trump was in India (until 25 February), Mishra's supporters would be peaceful. But 'after that, if roads are not cleared out, we won't even listen to you (police)'.[32] Many people have interpreted this as a call to violence. Facebook chief executive Mark Zuckerberg, in a video interaction with his employees in June, referred to Mishra's speech as incitement to violence.[33] Zuckerberg said, 'There have been cases in India, for example, where someone said, "Hey, if the police don't take care of this, our supporters will get in there and clear the streets." That is kind of encouraging supporters to go do that in a more direct way, and we took that down.' Facebook did take down Mishra's speech after it went viral, but it continued to spread on WhatsApp, which, incidentally, Facebook owns.[34]

·•·

The police have not carried out any credible investigation into the impact of Mishra's provocative words as a catalyst for the riots, but the fact remains that, shortly after his speech, violence did break out between a mob supporting the CAA and those who were opposed to it. The police have also accepted this sequence of events in their affidavit filed before the Delhi High Court.[35] Both pro- and anti-CAA protestors, said the police, fought pitched battles from the afternoon of 23 February well into the night. The violence soon spread out to other areas in northeast Delhi. For four days, mobs of men armed with daggers, sticks, stones and guns patrolled the narrow lanes and streets in that part of the city. A twenty-six-year-old employee of the Intelligence Bureau, Ankit Sharma, was stabbed, his corpse left in an open drain. A forty-two-year-old Delhi police head constable, Ratan Lal, was shot dead. Shahid Khan Alvi, a twenty-two-year-old autorickshaw driver, was shot in the stomach and left to bleed to death. Anwar Qassar, a fifty-eight-year-old, was set on fire. By the time the violence was brought under control, fifty-three people had died, forty of them Muslim, and many hundreds were wounded. Most of the violence took place in a working-class part of the city, and so, most of the dead were either poor or very poor; wealthier parts of the city were unaffected.

As the violence raged in the neighbourhoods of northeast Delhi, on 26 February 2020, Justice S. Muralidhar of the High Court of Delhi asked the police to take a 'conscious decision' within twenty-four hours to register an FIR against BJP leaders Kapil Mishra, Anurag Thakur and Parvesh Verma for hate speech. Justice Muralidhar expressed 'constitutional anguish' that the city was burning, and questioned the Delhi police on its delay in initiating action and its lack of acknowledgment of the communally provocative speeches as crimes. The solicitor general of India, Tushar Mehta, appearing for the police, told the court that the FIRs would only be 'registered at an appropriate stage'. The matter was reverted to a different bench for a hearing on the next day, and the new bench granted the state four weeks to file its reply. Justice Muralidhar was immediately transferred to the Punjab and Haryana High Court.[36] At the time of writing, several months after the riots, no FIR has been registered against these BJP leaders. So normalised did the slogan '*Desh ke gaddaron ko / Goli maaro saalon ko* (Shoot the traitors)' become that, on 29 February, six men wearing saffron tee-shirts and kurtas chanted the slogan in a train on the Delhi Metro's busy Blue Line and then again at the Rajiv Chowk metro station. Many other passengers joined in.[37]

On 5 October, the Delhi government's home department flagged a set of seven video clips to the Delhi police, which included two policemen purportedly throwing bricks alongside rioters and egging them on during the riots.[38] Amnesty International—which ceased its India operations in September 2020, citing an 'incessant witch-hunt by the Government of India'—released a report that analysed video footage widely available on social media to argue that the Delhi police were not just ineffective at stopping the riots, they joined in alongside the Hindutva mobs.[39] In one viral video,

Delhi police officers were filmed kicking and hitting a group of five wounded Muslim men, poking them with rifles and asking them to sing the Indian national anthem. The video was shot on 24 February; two days later, one of the men, Faizan, died of his injuries. The police on its part has alleged that its personnel, including senior officers like DCP Shahdara Amit Sharma and ACP Gokulpuri Anuj Kumar, were attacked by anti-CAA protestors.

Even before the riots broke out in northeast Delhi, the police were accused of using excessive force when dealing with anti-CAA protestors, while treating right-wing pro-CAA activists with kid gloves, even after they had violently attacked protestors. The police had beaten up students at Jamia Milia Islamia, and on 5 January 2020, a masked right-wing mob rampaged through the prestigious Jawaharlal Nehru University (JNU) campus for around two hours, beating up students and manhandling professors. The police took no action.

The police have registered a total of 751 FIRs in 665 incidents of violence during the northeast Delhi riots, arresting 1,430 persons from both communities.[40] While it appears as if the police has been even-handed, arresting hundreds of alleged rioters from both communities, the Delhi police, in its reports filed in courts, have claimed that the riots were a conspiracy engineered by anti-CAA protestors. More than a dozen anti-CAA activists have been booked under the Unlawful Activities (Prevention) Act (UAPA), a legislation mostly intended to deal with terrorists, and which denies prisoners what would otherwise be inalienable rights.

The police case is that anti-CAA dharnas, speeches by the likes of activist Umar Khalid, a former PhD student at JNU, calling for people to protest in large numbers on the streets during Trump's visit, and the blockading of public roads were intended to provoke communal riots. Protest is fundamental to democracy. But in the new playbook of the Modi regime, planning and staging protests is equivalent to preparing for and inciting communal violence, even if the leaders of these demonstrations repeatedly plead for peace.

But at the same time, deliberately communal language, incendiary sloganeering, divisive election campaigning and calls for violence (*goli maaro saalo ko*) are legitimate free speech.

There are curious giveaways in the police records, however.

A general diary entry made at Gokulpuri police station on 24 February at 19:42:34 hours records that a violent mob of pro-CAA activists, 400–500 in number, armed with sticks and iron rods were shouting provocative slogans in the A-block Gokulpuri area. The mob had blocked the A-21 Main Gokulpuri Road, and had set many vehicles and shops on fire. Even after police reached the spot, the mob continued to set more shops and vehicles on fire.

Another general diary entry dated 24 February, made at 20:05:30 hours, records a mob of 100–150 pro-CAA activists setting shops and vehicles at a tyre market near Kapoor petrol pump in Gokulpuri on fire.

More such diary entries recording violent behaviour, including arson, by pro-CAA activists form part of the charge sheet filed against twelve anti-CAA protestors charged under the UAPA legislation. Almost every FIR pertaining to the northeast Delhi riots speaks of clashes between pro-CAA and anti-CAA activists.[41] Why then are the likes of Umar Khalid alone charged as provocateurs, and those shouting '*Goli maaro saalon ko*' are not even investigated by the police, let alone arrested? Why is there not even an FIR regarding the inflammatory language of BJP leaders and the ugly actions of their supporters?

Human rights activists, who in the past were catalysts for justice in Gujarat, Assam, Uttar Pradesh and other parts of the country, have been accused by the police of fomenting violence in Delhi. People like Harsh Mander,[42] who have dedicated their whole lives to working for the public good, have been accused by the Delhi police of instigating rioters. It is as if words and deeds no longer matter, and anything you say can be twisted to fit a certain narrative—anti-national and conspirator if you are a critic of the government, and patriotic son of the soil if you are aligned with the government and its agenda.

On 16 December 2019, addressing the students of Jamia Milia Islamia, Mander had said: 'If someone is darkening the future of the country, and we reply in the same language, then we will only be amplifying the darkness. Darkness can be fought only with light. We have only one answer for their hate, and that is love. If they use violence, they will compel us to use violence as well, but we will never choose the path of violence. You must understand their motive is to arouse you to become violent, so that if you are two per cent violent, they can respond with a hundred per cent violence. We have learnt from Gandhi-ji how we must respond to violence and injustice. We will fight with non-violence. Whoever encourages you to use violence is not your well-wisher.'[43]

According to the Delhi police's report to the court, Mander 'used a facade of peace in his speech' to instigate the protestors to resort to violence.[44] These claims—seemingly plucked out of thin air, given that there is no evidence in the speech that Mander is making a subversive call for violence—were amplified by pliant television anchors. Mander had earlier petitioned the Delhi High Court, asking for an independent probe into the riots. It was while hearing this petition that Justice Muralidhar criticised the Delhi police for its inaction and selective hearing when it came to certain BJP leaders.[45]

It is a matter of public record that Umar Khalid, now named by the Delhi police as the 'mastermind' behind the riots, has appealed only for peaceful protests.[46] But the police insists that, behind these cries for peaceful civil disobedience, lies an infinitely more devious, secessionist message—a plot to destabilise the Indian government.[47] Delhi university Hindi professor Apoorvanand is a vocal critic of the BJP and its majoritarian politics. In his many columns in the national press and on news websites, he has written of his disdain for the BJP's vision for India; he too, despite his very public life, has been called in by the police to answer to the allegation that he provoked Muslims to protest and then become violent.[48] Among others the Delhi police made persons of interest in the investigation, based on the statements of witnesses, were CPI (M) General Secretary

Sitaram Yechury, the former psephologist and Swaraj Abhiyan founder Yogendra Yadav and the well-known economist Jayati Ghosh. All of them have been accused of 'provoking and mobilising' anti-CAA protests, though none have been formally charged with committing any criminal offence. So far at least.

India has a long, shameful history of communal rioting. But after every riot, diverse groups of citizens have come together to seek justice for the victims. Human rights activists, lawyers and journalists among others joined forces in both 1984 and 2002 to try and force the government and other pillars of the institution to snap out of their indifference and pay heed to the suffering of citizens. It has taken decades, but some victims of the riots of 1984 and 2002 have received at least partial justice and partial closure.

The northeast Delhi riots are different because such coalitions of citizens have been accused of being complicit in the violence and charged with serious crimes. The script is Orwellian: civil disobedience and legitimate dissent are taken to mean sedition and anti-national treachery; human rights activists and intellectuals are no longer do-gooders but the altogether more dangerous 'urban naxals'. By smearing supporters of free speech, secularism and democratic values as people who wish to harm India, the government has taken yet another stride towards being a fascist state. The Delhi riots and its aftermath show that justice and the rule of law are arguably at their lowest ebb in our democracy.

We are living in a time of spectacular malevolence. If, or rather when, this phase eventually passes (as it must), the question will be: did we do enough to resist?

Notes

PREFACE
1. Report of the Delhi Minorities Commission Fact Finding Committee on the North East Delhi Riots of 2020, headed by the Supreme Court lawyer M.R. Shamshad, 27 June 2020.
2. Elie Wiesel, *Night*, Hill and Wang, New York.

INTRODUCTION
1. https://cjp.org.in/incriminating-video-transcripts-yet-untested-as-evidence/.
2. https://www.thehindu.com/news/national/other-states/Godhra-case-Witness-claims-police-tortured-him/article16816454.ece.2.
3. Lucas Chancel and Thomas Piketty, 'Indian Income Inequality, 1922–2015: From British Raj to Billionaire Raj?', World Inequality Database (5 September 2017).
4. https://timesofindia.indiatimes.com/city/ahmedabad/Modi-kicks-off-Gujarat-Gaurav-Yatra/articleshow/21590967.cms.
5. https://scroll.in/article/658119/film-maker-releases-a-dozen-clips-of-controversial-modi-speeches-made-just-after-gujarat-riots.
6. https://timesofindia.indiatimes.com/city/ahmedabad/Tapes-capture-rabid-speeches-made-by-Modi/articleshow/22294236.cms.
7. https://www.rediff.com/election/2002/dec/01guj.htm.
8. https://indianexpress.com/article/explained/explained-justice-bedi-report-on-gujarat-fake-encounters-5530501/ and https://www.thehindu.com/news/national/Ishrat-Jahan-killing-also-a-fake-encounter-probe-report/article16879866.ece.

9. https://www.indiatoday.in/latest-headlines/story/sohrabuddin-got-what-he-deserved-modi-21494-2007-12-05.
10. https://www.thehindu.com/news/national/Modi-is-back-at-it-—-name-calling/article12434596.ece.
11. As per an analysis of 254 incidents of hate crimes by Hate Crime Watch tracker. The tracker was shut down: https://www.newslaundry.com/2019/09/12/factchecker-shuts-down-hate-crime-watch-samar-halarnkars-stint-with-india-spend-ends. However, its findings are summarised here: https://scroll.in/article/901206/new-hate-crime-tracker-in-india-finds-victims-are-predominantly-muslims-perpetrators-hindus. This tracker records lynchings in India: https://www.thequint.com/quintlab/lynching-in-india/.
12. According to the union home ministry's reply to the Lok Sabha on 6 February 2018.
13. https://theprint.in/india/4-retired-judges-2-ex-civil-servants-set-to-independently-probe-delhi-riots/521563/ and https://thewire.in/communalism/delhi-govt-flags-seven-videos-of-police-complicity-in-february-riots.
14. https://thewire.in/rights/fundamental-rights-free-speech-protest.
15. https://www.thehindu.com/opinion/lead/a-dangerous-new-low-in-state-sponsored-hate/article30427527.ece.
16. In lectures delivered in Uttar Pradesh in December 1949, M.S. Golwalkar likened the efforts to bring about Hindu–Muslim unity to converting the nation into a dharmashala, calling the Muslims 'parakiya' or outsiders. (Jyotirmaya Sharma, *Hindutva: Exploring the idea of Hindu Nationalism*, HarperCollins, 2015, p. 177.) An important idea within the Hindu nationalist discourse was the need to make Hindus more masculine, violent and aggressive in order to make them to fight their enemies. (*Hindutva*, p. 179.) Golwalkar and the RSS made the question of cow protection and the ban on killing cows for meat a central plank of their organisational agenda since Independence. (*Hindutva*, p. 182.)

The stigma attached to beef-eating and its association with Muslims became increasingly fraught and occupied a pre-eminent place in the Indian nationalism context (Therese O'Toole, 'Secularising the Sacred Cow: The Relationship between Religious Reform and Hindu Nationalism' in Antony Copley (ed.), *Hinduism in Public and Private: Reform, Hindutva, Gender and Sampraday*, Oxford University Press, 2003.)

The Jaganmohan Reddy Commission on the Ahmedabad riots (1969) and the Madan Commission on the Bhiwandi riots (1970) condemned the RSS and its political wing, the Bharatiya Jana Sangh, the BJP's ancestor, for their alleged role in riots. Justice Vithayathil's report on the Tellicherry riots (1971) censured the RSS for 'rousing up' communal feelings and for 'preparing the background for the disturbances'. Justice Jitendra Narain's report on the Jamshedpur riots (1979) castigated the RSS supremo M.D. Deoras personally for the communal propaganda that had caused the riots. The RSS had held a conference there 'only four days before the Ram Navami festival (when the riots erupted) and the speech delivered by Balasaheb Deoras contributed their full share in fomenting these communal feelings'; the RSS had created 'a climate for these disturbances'. The report of Justice P. Venugopal of the Madras High Court on the riots in Kanyakumari (1982) found the RSS guilty of fomenting anti-Christian feelings: 'It has taken upon itself the task to teach the minority their place and if they are not willing to learn their place, teach them a lesson. The RSS has given respectability to communalism and communal riots and demoralise (sic) administration.'

17. The charge sheet was filed in the Karkardooma Courts, Delhi, FIR no. 37 dated 27 February 2020.
18. The State of Gujarat vs I.R.C.G. on 29 August 2017, Supreme Court of India.
19. https://economictimes.indiatimes.com/news/politics-and-nation/setback-for-narendra-modi-sc-upholds-justice-ra-mehtas-appointment-as-gujarat-lokayukta/articleshow/17853445.cms.
20. https://www.news18.com/news/india/from-bjps-birth-in-1980-40-years-of-indias-political-history-defined-by-ayodhyas-ram-mandir-hindutva-2743593.html.
21. https://www.economist.com/leaders/2020/01/23/narendra-modi-stokes-divisions-in-the-worlds-biggest-democracy.
22. https://thewire.in/rights/uttar-pradesh-yogi-adityanath-fake-encounters-un.

1. A STING IN THE TALE
1. The lead story, titled 'State Forgot to Hang Killer Sentenced to Death in '96', was published in the Lucknow edition of *Hindustan Times* on 8 January 2004.

2. THEATRE OF MASCULINITY
1. Zahira Habibulla H. Sheikh and Anr vs State of Gujarat and Ors on 12 April 2004, Supreme Court of India in appeal (crl) no. 446–449 of 2004, author: J. Arijit Pasayat, bench: Doraiswamy Raju and Arijit Pasayat.
2. Zahir Sheikh's interview to Pankaj Shankar of Doordarshan News: https://www.youtube.com/watch?v=5OhBhOSJhOs.
3. https://timesofindia.indiatimes.com/india/Zahira-turns-hostile-in-court/articleshow/967163.cms.
4. The conversation below is from the transcript published in *Tehelka*, December 2004.
5. Inquiry report in crl M.P. nos. 6658–6661, 11884–11887, 12515–12518 and 12519–12522, in appeal (crl) no. 446–449/2004, Zahira Habbullah H. Sheikh and Anr vs State of Gujarat and Ors.
6. https://www.indiatoday.in/magazine/indiascope/story/20060313-best-bakery-case-nine-accused-get-life-imprisonment-783565-2006-03-z13.
7. https://cjp.org.in/countering-all-allegations/.

3. THE TEN-FOOT-TALL OFFICER
1. https://www.indiatoday.in/mail-today/story/how-mumbai-police-foiled-ajit-dovals-operation-dawood-290050-2015-08-25.
2. https://indianexpress.com/article/cities/kausar-bi-was-raped-before-killing-exats-officer-to-cbi/.
3. https://www.outlookindia.com/website/story/should-we-run-relief-camps-open-child-producing-centres/217398.
4. What follows is from the transcript published in *Tehelka*, May 2007.
5. https://www.hindustantimes.com/india-news/justice-bedi-panel-indicts-9-cops-says-3-out-of-17-gujarat-encounters-fake/story-suLPKhReRcnfFEmPfp1cPN.html.

4. PAINTING WITH FIRE
1. https://timesofindia.indiatimes.com/city/vadodara/fine-arts-alumnus-sets-msu-head-office-on-fire/articleshow/62761877.cms.
2. Bail order passed by the High Court of Gujarat in misc. application no. 16559 of 2018, dated 14 September 2018.

5. ALONE IN THE DARK

1. https://indianexpress.com/article/opinion/columns/godhra-2002-riots-train-burn-sabarmati-express-communal-violence-in-uttar-pradesh-fifteen-years-back-still-alone-4547065/.

6. TRUTH ON TRIAL

1. By the judgement rendered in 'NHRC v. State of Gujarat' in (2009), 6 SCC 767, the apex court had ordered a slew of measures for instilling a sense of confidence in the mind of the victims and their relatives, and to ensure that witnesses depose freely and fearlessly before the court. Besides ensuring safe passage for the witnesses to and from the court precincts and providing security to the witnesses in their place of residence wherever considered necessary, the court had asked the SIT to even relocate witnesses to another state wherever such a step was necessary.
2. *Tehelka*, Vol 4, Issue 43.
3. https://www.aajtak.in/india/story/truth-of-2002-gujarat-riots-30523-2008-09-08; https://nhrc.nic.in/press-release/nhrc-sends-notice-government-india-lending-services-cbi-investigating-authenticity.
4. https://timesofindia.indiatimes.com/india/NHRC-seeks-CBI-probe-into-Tehelka-tapes-on-Godhra-riots/articleshow/2918406.cms.
5. Testimony of Ashish Khetan in sessions case no. 152/02, with 167/03, 279/03, 190/09, 191/09, 193/09, 194/09, 195/09, 279/09, prosecution witness no. 313, ex. 1091.
6. https://www.thehindu.com/news/national/2002-gujarat-riots-state-govt-to-table-justice-nanavati-mehta-commission-report-in-assembly-today/article30274396.ece.

7. CONSPIRATORS AND RIOTERS

1. http://archive.indianexpress.com/news/gujarat-govt-counsel-quits/233175/.
2. Zahira Habibulla H. Sheikh and Anr vs State of Gujarat and Ors on 12 April 2004, Supreme Court of India.
3. https://indianexpress.com/article/india/gujarat/hc-quashes-appointment-of-public-prosecutor-for-his-role-in-2002-best-bakery-case/.

4. https://www.himalmag.com/the-judge-the-prosecutor-and-best-bakery/.
5. https://www.hindustantimes.com/india-news/delhi-riots-prez-approves-l-g-s-list-of-11-spl-public-prosecutors/story-OgMJkCBQy4vpNrSdjR036M.html.
6. https://indianexpress.com/article/cities/delhi/delhi-high-court-riots-police-6519060/.
7. https://www.hindustantimes.com/india-news/accusations-in-police-affidavit-unwarranted-delhi-hc-on-delhi-riots-case/story-wECtaOPtFUiH1YI1lhbbEJ.html.
8. https://www.thehindu.com/news/cities/Delhi/probe-targeted-only-towards-one-end-in-riots-case-says-delhi-court/article31699048.ece.

8. THE GULBARG MASSACRE

1. Page 264 of the judgement dated 17 June 2016 by Justice P.B. Desai, special judge of designated court for speedy trial of riot cases, city sessions court, Ahmedabad.
2. Page 104 of the judgement.
3. Page 262 of the judgement.
4. Page 122 of the judgement.
5. Page 120 of the judgement.
6. The conversations that follow are unedited transcripts which were submitted before the SIT, then produced in court and were also read out by me in court during my deposition.
7. https://www.rediff.com/news/interview/gulbarg-society-case-prosecutor-speaks-out/20100325.htm.
8. https://www.thehindu.com/news/national/New-judge-for-Gulberg-Society-case/article15411840.ece.
9. Page 383 of the judgement.
10. Page 1,196 of the judgement.

9. THE KILLING FIELDS

1. Alex Alvarez, 'Militias and Genocide', *War Crimes, Genocide & Crimes against Humanity*, vol. 2 (2006), 1–33.
2. The Prosecutor of the Tribunal vs Zeljko Raznjatovic, also known as 'Arkan' (26 September 1997), International Criminal Tribunal for the Former Yugoslavia Indictment, case no. IT-97-27-I.

3. Page 15 of the judgement.
4. Page 527 of the judgement.
5. https://www.indiatoday.in/magazine/society-the-arts/films/story/19981221-issues-on-which-bajrang-dal-sparked-controversies-827549-1998-12-21.
6. 'Politics by Other Means: Attacks against Christians in India', Human Rights Watch (September 1999).
7. 'Politics by Other Means', Human Rights Watch.
8. Common judgement in sessions case nos. 235/09, 236/09, 241/09, 242/09, 243/09, 245/09, 246/09 and 270/09, pronounced by special court, designated for conducting the speedy trial of riot cases, situated at Old High Court building, Navrangpura, Ahmedabad.

10. THE SALIENT FEATURE OF A GENOCIDAL IDEOLOGY

1. Page 316 of the trial court judgement: Final order and judgement dated 19 April 2008 by the special judge for Greater Mumbai, Justice U.D. Salvi, in sessions case no. 634 of 2004, the State of Gujarat v. Jaswantbhai Chaturbhai Nai and others.
2. Paras 191, 357, 371 and 372 of the judgement dated 4 May 2017 by Justice V.K. Tahilramani and Justice Mridula Bhatkar of the High Court of Bombay in appeal (crl) no. 1020 of 2009, Jaswantbhai Chaturbhai Nai and Others v. the State of Gujarat, with appeal (crl) nos. 1021, 1022 and 1023 of 2010 and appeal (crl) no. 194 of 2011.
3. https://thewire.in/books/bilkis-bano-gujarat-2002.
4. The CBI officer also named his boss who wanted to botch up the probe. But since it was given off the record, I am withholding the name.
5. The officer has requested that his name not be disclosed as he is still in service.
6. The ages of the accused are as of the day the trial court delivered the judgement in 2008.
7. Saadat Hasan Manto, translated by Aatish Taseer, 'Khol Do', *Manto: Selected Short Stories*, Random House India (2012).
8. Sunil Khilnani, *Incarnations: India in 50 Lives*, Allen Lane (2016), 466.
9. Page 159 of the trial court judgement.
10. Page 154 of the trial court judgement.
11. Page 222, para 204 of the trial court judgement.

12. Page 337, paras 379–381 of the trial court judgement.
13. Pages 195–205 of the trial court judgement.
14. The judgement dated 4 May 2017 by the division bench of the High Court of Bombay, comprising Justice V.K. Tahilramani and Justice Mridula Bhatkar, in appeal (crl) nos. 1020, 1021, 1022 and 1023 of 2009.
15. Order of the Supreme Court of India in writ petition (crl) no. 118 of 2003 with appeal (crl) nos. 727–733 of 2019.
16. Note dated 20 January 2011, submitted by senior advocate and amicus curiae Raju Ramachandran in special leave petition (crl) no. 1088 of 2008.

11. THE ARTFUL FAKER

1. https://www.india-seminar.com/2002/513/513%20ashis%20nandy.htm.
2. https://www.srisriravishankar.org/blog/post/my-first-meeting-with-narendra-modi.
3. The report dated 20 January 2011 submitted by Raju Ramachandran to the Supreme Court in special leave petition (crl) no. 1088 of 2008.
4. https://cjp.org.in/zakia-jafri-case/.
5. Supreme Court order dated 27 April 2009 in special leave petition (crl) no. 1088 of 2008.
6. Supreme Court, by its order dated 15 May 2009 in special leave petition (crl) no. 109 of 203, reconstituted the SIT by bringing in two retired CBI officers, A.K. Malhotra and Paramvir Singh. These two retired officers were entrusted by SIT chief R.K. Raghavan to inquire into Zakia Jafri's complaint. After Singh quit the SIT in February 2010, Malhotra was the lone officer who carried out the probe. The nature of this probe was of a preliminary inquiry and not a criminal investigation as contemplated by the CrPC, 1974.
7. The charge sheet dated 19 April 2004, filed by the CBI, Special Crime Branch, Mumbai, in the Bilkis Bano case.
8. The reports dated 20 January 2011 and 25 July 2011 filed by amicus curiae Raju Ramachandran in special leave petition (crl) no. 1088 of 2008.
9. Zahira Habibulla H. Sheikh and Anr vs State of Gujarat and Ors on 12 April 2004, Supreme Court of India.

10. The preliminary report dated 12 May 2010 by SIT member A.K. Malhotra admitted to the controversial transfers and postings but contended that no criminal culpability could be fastened for such actions.
11. Special leave petition (crl) no. 1088 of 2008 filed in the Supreme Court on 18 December 2007.
12. The questioning was not videographed, but only recorded in a question-and-answer form, and was submitted by A.K. Malhotra as part of his preliminary inquiry report dated 12 May 2010 to the Supreme Court.
13. https://www.outlookindia.com/website/story/should-we-run-relief-camps-open-child-producing-centres/217398.
14. In March 2014, filmmaker Rakesh Sharma released a dozen clips of controversial Modi speeches made just after the Gujarat riots: https://scroll.in/article/658119/film-maker-releases-a-dozen-clips-of-controversial-modi-speeches-made-just-after-gujarat-riots.
15. https://www.thehindu.com/news/national/BJP-produces-Modi-degrees-AAP-finds-discrepancies/article14310247.ece.
16. https://indianexpress.com/article/india/pm-degree-row-acharyulu-stripped-of-hrd-charge/.

12. THE SMOKING GUN

1. The SIT preliminary inquiry report dated 12 May 2010.
2. Page 67 of the SIT report.
3. Page 69 of the SIT report.
4. Page 153 of the SIT report.
5. Page 13 of the chairman's comments in the SIT report.
6. Speech given at Becharji, Gujarat, on 9 September 2002.
7. Page 160 of the SIT report.
8. Page 12 of the chairman's comments in the SIT report.
9. Pages 7–8 of the chairman's comments in the SIT report.
10 Page 35 of the SIT preliminary inquiry report submitted by A.K. Malhotra.
11. Pages 44–51 of the SIT report.
12. https://thewire.in/politics/narendra-modi-delhi-polls-shaheen-bagh-jamia-protests-anti-caa.
13. There are several instances of this. A couple of examples: https://thewire.in/media/from-sturmer-to-sudarshan-indian-media-should-

realise-incitement-of-hatred-is-a-crime and https://www.firstpost. com/india/hate-speech-in-india-medias-rabble-rousing-doesnt-help-cause-proves-counter-productive-to-free-speech-5182231.html.
14. Pages 79–86 of the SIT report.
15. Pages 101–105 of the SIT report.
16. Page 13 of the SIT report.
17. https://www.thehindu.com/news/national/Proceed-against-Modi-for-Gujarat-riots-amicus/article12828442.ece.
18. Pages 20–23 of the amicus curiae report dated 25 July 2011.
19. Page 5 of the chairman's comments in the SIT report.
20. Page 14 of the SIT report.
21. Para 27 of the amicus curiae report.

13. DRUM ROLLS OF AN IMPENDING MASSACRE

1. The SIT in its preliminary inquiry report dated 12 May 2010 claimed on page 13 of the report that police wireless messages for the period pertaining to the riots of 2002 were not provided to the SIT as they had been destroyed. Subsequently, former Ahmedabad police commissioner P.C. Pande submitted a voluminous data containing Ahmedabad police control room messages before the SIT on 15 March 2011. The SIT, then, also retrieved SIB messages. These messages are now in the court records, part of the Zakia Jafri protest petition filed before the 11th metropolitan magistrate, Ahmedabad. In the following notes, each message is referenced to file and annexure number as they appear in the protest petition dated 15 April 2013 filed by Jafri. In some places, the numbering is uneven, but this is how they are numbered in the petition and the official records.
2. http://timesofindia.indiatimes.com/articleshow/1992871437.cms.
3. https://thewire.in/video/video-gujarat-burning-army-vehicles-former-lieutenant-general.
4. https://www.freepressjournal.in/cmcm/2002-gujarat-riots-sit-report-on-army-deployment-is-blatant-lie-says-retired-lt-general-zameer-uddin-shah.
5. https://www.indiatoday.in/buzztop/buzztop-national/story/gujarat-riots-2002-godhra-sudden-spontaneous-backlash-frantic-police-warnings-ignored-158882-2013-04-15.

6. A bandh, or strike, is the most common form of political protest in India. While it literally means 'voluntary closure', in reality, bandhs are often marked with violence, arson and damage to public property. The cadres of whichever political party, left or right, has called the bandh, go out onto the streets to enforce it, refusing to allow businesses to open, and often beating up people and smashing vehicles and shop fronts. In 2018, the Supreme Court ruled that organisations that called bandhs would be legally liable for 'loss of life or damage to public or private property either directly or indirectly' caused by such demonstrations.
7. Page 134 of the SIT closure report dated 8 February 2102: 'Shri Vijay Badheka, Under Secretary to Home Department, has stated before the SIT that both Gujarat bandh on 28.02.02 and Bharat bandh on 01.03.02 were supported by the BJP.'
8. Naroda Patiya trial court judgement in sessions case no. 235/09 with 236/09, 241/09, 242/09, 243/09, 245/09, 246/09 and 270/09; The Gulbarg massacre judgement dated 17 June 2016 by Justice P.B. Desai, special judge of designated court for speedy trial of riot cases, city civil and sessions court, Ahmedabad.
9. SIB, annexure III, file XVIII, D-160 at 188, 27 February 2002.
10. SIB, annexure III, file XXI, D-166, p. 365, message no. 73/02, sender: ACP (Intelligence), Surat, 9 a.m.–10 a.m., 28 February 2002. This message also stated that at this meeting, Kapil Swami from the Swami Narayan Sect was present as chief guest.
11. SIB, annexure III, file XIX, p. 273, fax message no. 273, sender: B.M. Mohit, Anand Centre, 5.45 p.m., 27 February 2002.
12. SIB, annexure III, file XIX, D-161 part-II, pp. 356–360, message no. 531, sender: ACP (Intelligence), Ahmedabad, recipient: ADG (Intelligence).
13. SIB, fax message no. 311/02, page no. D-1/ HA/Jaher Sabha/ Junagadh, sender: CID, Bhavnagar, recipient: IG, Gujarat and Intelligence Bureau, Gandhinagar.
14. SIB, annexure III, file XIX, D-161 part-II, pp. 356–360, message no. 531, sender: ACP (Intelligence), Ahmedabad, recipient: ADG (Intelligence).
15. I.C.R. no. 78, annexure III, file XIV, p. 5768, 28 February 2002, area: Odhav, Ahmedabad.

16. SIB, message at 8.30 p.m., 27 February 2002.
17. SIB, message at 9.30 p.m., 27 February 2002.
18. PCR message at 12.30 a.m., 28 February 2002, area: Odhav, Ahmedabad.
19. PCR message at 2.05 a.m., 28 February 2002, annexure IV, file XIV, p. 5757.
20. '50 kar sevaks on special bus from Ahmedabad reached Modasa, Vadagam village at 6:30 pm. Police presence insufficient to maintain order. 10 shops owned by Muslims & several vehicles set ablaze by mobs.' SIB, fax message: Com/HM/550/Out no. 398, sender: ACP, Gandhinagar Region, recipient: IG, Gujarat and Intelligence Bureau, Gandhinagar, 11.59 p.m., 27 February 2002.
21. 'Eight Bodies of VHP workers will be brought to Kalupur Railway station, Ahmedabad. Dead bodies will be carried in funeral processions. VHP gave a bandh call. High possibility of riots in Ahmedabad. Take preventive action.' SIB, annexure III, file XIX, D-161 part-II, pp. 356–360, fax no. 525, 12.30 p.m., 27 February 2002. Later at 8.46 p.m., a message was received that the eight bodies had arrived at 3 p.m. at Kalupur station, and from there they were taken to Dhanvanti hospital (owned by VHP leader Praveen Togadia) for the Bajrang Dal activists to pay homage.
22. PCR message, annexure IV, file XIV, p. 5750, 1.54 a.m., 28 February 2002.
23. PCR message, annexure IV, file XIV, p. 5790, 4 a.m., 28 February 2002.
24. PCR message, annexure IV, file XIV, p. 5796, 7.14 a.m., 28 February 2002.
25. PCR message, annexure IV, file XIV, p. 5894, 11.55 a.m., 28 February 2002.
26. PCR message, annexure IV, file XV, p. 6162 of 11.55 a.m., 28 February 2002.
27. PCR message, annexure IV, file XV, p. 6172, time not shown, 28 February 2002.
28. PCR message, annexure IV, file XIV, p. 5907, 11.58 a.m., 28 February 2002.
29. SIB message (Khedbrahma, Sabarkantha) Com/538, annexure III, file XIX, p. 258, 28 February 2002.
30. SIB message (Khedbrahma, Sabarkantha), annexure III, file XIX, p. 262, 28 February 2002.

31. SIB message (Khedbrahma, Sabarkantha) Com/574, annexure III, file XIX, p. 254, 3.32 p.m., 28 February 2002.
32. Pande's statement recorded on 24 March 2010, p. 7.
33. PCR message, 4.28 a.m., 28 February 2002.
34. PCR message, 2.38 a.m., 28 February 2002.
35. SIT Closure Report, pp. 36–37, 8 February 2012.
36. National Human Rights Commission interim and final reports, 2003 and 2004.
37. https://www.telegraphindia.com/business/lockdown-contain-contagion-spend-smartly-says-joseph-stiglitz/cid/1793985.
38. The assessment by the National Sample Survey Office (NSSO), conducted between July 2017–June 2018, showed that the unemployment rate stood at 6.1 per cent, the highest since 1972–73. The report showed that joblessness stood at 7.8 per cent in urban areas compared with 5.3 per cent in the countryside. The NSSO data showed that consumer spending fell for the first time in forty years. In January 2019, the Centre for Monitoring Indian Economy, a leading independent think-tank, said India lost as many as 11 million jobs in 2018. In April–June 2020 quarter, GDP contracted by a massive 23.9 per cent year-on-year (YoY), the first GDP contraction in more than forty years. In the seven quarters before the April–June 2020 quarter, the growth rate was already in a steep decline.

14. THE GODHRA CONUNDRUM
1. Page 652 of the judgement dated 9 October 2017 by Justice A.S. Dave and Justice G.R. Udhwani of the High Court of Gujarat in criminal confirmation case nos. 1, 2 and 10 of 2011.
2. Page 755 of the High Court judgement.
3. Page 174 of the High Court judgement.
4. Chargebook of Harimohan Rajindersingh Meena, assistant station master, Godhra. Entry dated 27 February 2002 notes coach no. 90238 as requiring correction, but no record shows that the correction was made.
5. The alarm chains are connected to the main brake pipe of the train. This brake pipe maintains a constant air pressure, helping the train move smoothly. When the emergency chain is pulled, the air stored in the brake pipe escapes through a small vent. The drop in air

pressure leads to the slowing down of the train. More information on how alarm chains work: https://blog.railyatri.in/facts-about-chain-pulling-in-train-you-never-knew-before/.
6. https://www.outlookindia.com/website/story/role-of-the-media/218050.
7. C R no. 9/02, Godhra railway police station. The complainant was R.R. Yadav, engine driver.
8. As of 10 October 2020, Asthana was serving as director general of the BSF and of the NCB.
9. Page 353 of the High Court judgement.
10. Nitya Ramakrishnan, 'Godhra: The Verdict Analysed', *EPW* (9 April 2011) vol. xlvi, no. 15.
11. http://archive.indianexpress.com/news/godhra-celebrates-exclusion-of-noel-parmar-from-team-assisting-sit/302984/.

15. TENDULKAR'S 100 VS AMIT SHAH'S 267

1. In the Indian cabinet system there's a provision for creating two kinds of positions for ministers, a senior minister and junior minsters. Modi was the senior minister for home and Shah was his junior home minister.
2. Fake encounters are staged killings by the police, usually of people in custody, made to appear as though they occurred in gun battles. The Gujarat police led by D.G. Vanzara killed many Muslims in such encounters. Some of these 'fake encounter' cases led to court-monitored investigations, because of which Vanzara, Singhal and many other police personnel were subsequently arrested and charged. One such case was of a nineteen-year-old girl named Ishrat Jahan, who, along with three men, was killed by the police on the outskirts of Ahmedabad city on 15 June 2004.
3. For instance, on 21 April 2011, the High Court of Gujarat observed in the hearing of matters relating to the Ishrat Jahan encounter case that authorities of the Gujarat state appeared complicit in disobeying the earlier orders issued on 28 January 2011 by the court for transferring P.P. Pandey, then additional director general of police, CID (Intelligence), and others.
4. An order by M.B. Gosavi, special judge for the CBI, Greater Bombay, dated 30 December 2014, records on page 4 and page 60 the charges

levelled by the CBI against Amit Shah and certain police officers—that they were running an extortion racket through Sohrabuddin, and that Shah instructed the police to kill Sohrabuddin in a fake encounter as he could have exposed the extortion racket. The court discharged Shah of all charges, while some other accused officers charged by the CBI are still on trial.

5. On 24 September 2010, the High Court of Gujarat constituted an SIT for the investigation of Ahmedabad city DCB PS I CR no. 8/2004 (Ishrat Jahan encounter case), as per the judgement and order in criminal miscellaneous application no. 9832 of 2010 in special criminal application no. 1850 of 2009 with criminal miscellaneous application no. 10621 of 2010. Satish Verma, IPS (1986, Gujarat), IGP, was nominated by the court as a member of this three-member SIT.

6. https://ahmedabadmirror.indiatimes.com/ahmedabad/cover-story/ips-officers-teenaged-son-hangs-himself-in-satellite/articleshow/36194684.cms.

7. Singhal's statement dated 11 April 2013, recorded by chief investigating officer, CBI, deputy superintendent of police G. Kalaimani: 'In 2009, Shri A.K. Sharma had procured four special mobile phones manufactured by a German company Enigma. These phones could scramble/encrypt voice signals for secrecy even if the phones were intercepted. One each of these instruments was given by Shri Sharma to Shri G.C. Murmu, Shri P.P. Pandey and me, while he used the fourth one. The sim cards were taken by us individually, often in the name of a subordinate. I had the number 9712901345. We used to talk regarding the encounter cases and our tactics over these phones.'

8. As per Singhal's statement to the CBI, which is part of the charge sheet.

9. Singhal's statement to the CBI while he was in police custody has limited legal validity. Under Section 27 of the Indian Evidence Act, 'when any fact is deposed to as discovered in consequence of information received from a person accused of any offence, in the custody of a police officer, so much of such information, as relates distinctly to the fact thereby discovered, may be proved'. Essentially, any statement made by an accused before the police is inadmissible. But if such statement enables the police to discover facts directly related to the crime under investigation—for instance, the recovery of a weapon used in a murder or recovery of stolen goods—then such

information is admissible in court. In this case, Singhal's statement led to the discovery of taped phone conversations that in turn indicate an elaborate conspiracy of surveillance and illegal snooping. However, this remains to be tested in court.

10. https://www.youtube.com/watch?v=_5wi7KkP26Q; https://www.youtube.com/watch?v=RB-fJAMTIuA.
11. https://cobrapost.com/blog/stalkers-amit-shahs-illegal-surveillance-exposed/904.
12. https://timesofindia.indiatimes.com/india/Order-central-probe-into-Snoopgate-Congress/articleshow/27696702.cms; https://www.business-standard.com/article/politics/all-you-need-to-know-about-snoopgate-113112700241_1.html; https://www.youtube.com/watch?v= Xz8BoEtapbM.
13. https://www.financialexpress.com/archive/narendra-modi-aide-amit-shah-used-police-to-spy-on-woman-at-sahebs-behest-accuse-cobrapost-gulail/1195397/; http://archive.indianexpress.com/news/ narendra-modi-aide-amit-shah-used-police-to-spy-on-woman-at-sahebs-behest-accuse-cobrapost-gulail/1195397/.
14. https://www.business-standard.com/article/politics/snoopgate-what-links-the-soni-family-and-gujarat-govt-113112100023_1.html; https://www.indiatoday.in/magazine/cover-story/story/20131202-narendra-modi-snooping-scandal-illegal-surveillance-gujarat-government-amit-shah-768811-1999-11-30.
15. https://economictimes.indiatimes.com/news/politics-and-nation/snoopgate-gulail-com-asked-to-file-affidavit/articleshow/28141884.cms?from=mdr.
16. https://economictimes.indiatimes.com/news/politics-and-nation/snoopgate-gulail-com-asked-to-file-affidavit/articleshow/28141884.cms?from=mdr.
17. The order and judgement dated 10 October 2014 passed by the High Court of Gujarat at Ahmedabad in special civil application no. 14389 of 2014.
18. https://magazine.outlookindia.com/story/objection-milord/292280.
19. http://timesofindia.indiatimes.com/articleshow/34507459.cms?utm_source=contentofinterest&utm_medium=text&utm_campaign=cppst.

20. https://timesofindia.indiatimes.com/india/Snoopgate-probe-totally-junked/articleshow/34896195.cms.
21. Francis Fukuyama, *The End of History and The Last Man*, Fress Press, New York.
22. On 8 April 2011, the High Court of Gujarat, during the court proceedings, expressed serious displeasure regarding the complaint filed against Satish Verma immediately after the seizure of evidence from FSL on 3 March 2011. The court also directed the state to transfer certain police officers within a week.
23. Sharma gave a sworn affidavit before the Nanavati–Shah Commission on 2 July 2002, in which he gave a detailed description of at least a dozen instances where he and his officers protected the lives of Muslims by taking strict action against the Hindu rioters.
24. 'During all this action, the road towards Madressa was closed because of burning tyres, big stones, wooden hurdles etc. due to which very much hardship was caused to police in reaching to Madressa and returning from there. While taking residents of Madressa and coming back in the way stone pelting was made on buses and other government vehicles,' Sharma stated in his affidavit dated 2 July 2002.
25. The order dated 22 January 2016 passed by the Central Administrative Tribunal, Ahmedabad.
26. https://www.thehindu.com/news/national/other-states/cbi-court-refuses-discharge-plea-of-3-officers-in-ishrat-case/article32931425.ece.
27. https://www.deccanherald.com/national/west/ishrat-jahans-mother-gives-up-hope-for-justice-765415.html.
28. https://punemirror.indiatimes.com/news/india/amit-shah-extorted-6-crore-after-sohrab-killing/articleshow/32312328.cms; https://thewire.in/rights/sohrabuddin-fake-encounter-case-chief-investigating-officer-claims-accused-had-no-motive.
29. Order by M.B. Gosavi, special judge for the CBI, Greater Bombay, dated 30 December 2014.

16. WALK ALONE
1. https://www.dnaindia.com/india/report-plea-seeks-replacement-of-naroda-gam-case-judge-1780507.
2. https://www.indiatoday.in/assembly-elections-2012/video/gujarat-assembly-poll-2012-narendra-modi-wins-hat-trick-405821-2012-12-20.

3. https://timesofindia.indiatimes.com/Journalist-Ashish-Khetan-is-to-depose-before-the-special-SIT-court-in-the-Naroda-Gam-case-A-defence-lawyer-is-to-cross-examine-him-on-the-sting-operation-he-had-undertaken-/articleshow/18443631.cms.
4. https://www.deshgujarat.com/2014/10/17/a-new-judge-designated-for-naroda-gam-gulberg-society-ahmedabad-serial-blast-modasa-blast-cases/.
5. https://www.newindianexpress.com/nation/2017/dec/30/special-sit-judge-hearing-2002-naroda-gam-riots-case-retires-1740620.html.
6. https://www.thehindu.com/news/national/judge-hearing-2002-naroda-gam-riot-case-transferred/article31014915.ece.
7. https://timesofindia.indiatimes.com/city/ahmedabad/100-days-on-cop-still-recording-testimony-in-Naroda-case/articleshow/44844386.cms.
8. Judgement dated 20 April 2018 by Justice Harsha Devani and Justice A.S. Supehia in appeal (crl) nos. 1713/12, 1708–1711/12, 1740/12, 1862/12 and 1812/12.
9. Para 334.9 of the High Court judgement.
10. Para 334.13 of the High Court judgement.
11. Page 3037 of the High Court judgement.
12. Para 335.4 of of the High Court judgement.
13. Paras 432–447 of the High Court judgement.
14. https://timesofindia.indiatimes.com/india/gujarat-riots-supreme-court-bail-for-babu-bajrangi/articleshow/68328164.cms.
15. https://indianexpress.com/article/cities/ahmedabad/naroda-gam-riots-kodnani-can-travel-out-of-gujarat-for-another-6-months-5821517/.
16. https://thewire.in/law/judge-who-convicted-modis-minister-in-riots-case-now-fears-for-her-family.
17. https://www.facebook.com/HinduNews/posts/biased-judge-jyotsna-yagnik-needs-to-be-dismissed-immediatelyjustice-jyotsna-yag/435201123262089/.
18. https://www.facebook.com/IndiaToday/videos/newstodayjudge-jyotsna-yagnik-should-be-tried-for-writing-that-idiotic-judgement/10156324741477119/.

EPILOGUE

1. I started *Gulail* in May 2013. But due to paucity of funds, the website was shut down and the team was disbanded in early 2014. Though, we decided to continue researching the love-jihad story for a few more months after shuttering our office.
2. https://www.cobrapost.com/blog/OPERATION%20JULIET:%20 BUSTING%20THE%20BOGEY%20OF%20'LOVE%20JIHAD'.
3. https://www.indiatoday.in/india/story/sting-operation-busts-the-love-jihad-bogey-266739-2015-10-06.
4. https://www.deccanherald.com/content/504728/bjp-vhp-rss-nexus-against.html.
5. https://scroll.in/article/760021/investigation-uncovers-coercive-tactics-hindutva-groups-use-to-battle-love-jihad.
6. https://thewire.in/communalism/bjp-rss-leaders-caught-using-love-jihad-bogey-to-fuel-communal-polarisation.
7. https://thewire.in/communalism/bjp-rss-leaders-caught-using-love-jihad-bogey-to-fuel-communal-polarisation.
8. Faiz Ahmed Faiz wrote 'Hum Dekhenge' during General Zia-ul-Haq's oppressive martial law regime. In 1985, when Zia-ul-Haq issued a decree prohibiting women from wearing sarees, Pakistan's renowned singer Iqbal Bano, clad in a black saree, protested against the decree. She sang this nazm of Faiz's in front of a crowd 50,000 strong in a Lahore stadium. The stadium echoed with chants of 'Inqilaab Zindabad'.
9. The Citizenship Amendment Bill (CAB) was passed by both houses of parliament on 9 and 11 December 2019, and after the assent of the President of India on 12 December, the Bill assumed the status of an Act.
10. https://images.indianexpress.com/2019/04/bjp-election-2019-english.pdf.
11. https://scroll.in/article/947436/who-is-linking-citizenship-act-to-nrc-here-are-five-times-amit-shah-did-so.
12. FIR 242/2019 dated 16 December 2019, Police Station New Friends Colony, New Delhi, and FIR 298/2019 dated 16 December 2019, Police Station Jamia Nagar, New Delhi.

13. https://www.hindustantimes.com/india-news/up-police-releases-video-of-meerut-violence-showing-protesters-shooting-at-cops-during-anti-caa-protests/story-5xOg9bK52sY3eAKeb6pxoJ.html.
14. https://indianexpress.com/article/india/uttar-pradesh-citizenship-law-protests-yogi-adityanath-6185483/.
15. https://frontline.thehindu.com/dispatches/article30828344.ece.
16. Jamia alumnus and poet Aamir Aziz: https://www.thehindu.com/entertainment/music/meet-the-poets-of-dissent-who-critique-the-establishment-and-call-for-change/article30470619.ece.
17. https://economictimes.indiatimes.com/news/politics-and-nation/those-indulging-in-arson-can-be-identified-by-their-clothes-narendra-modi-on-anti-caa-protest/articleshow/72687256.cms.
18. https://thewire.in/communalism/narendra-modi-citizenship-amendment-act-protests-clothes.
19. https://www.news18.com/news/politics/press-evm-button-with-such-anger-that-shaheen-bagh-feels-the-current-says-amit-shah-in-delhi-election-rally-2474583.html.
20. https://www.ndtv.com/india-news/delhi-elections-yogi-adityanath-slams-citizenship-amendment-act-protesters-at-rally-says-their-ances-2173342.
21. https://scroll.in/video/951289/watch-anurag-thakur-minister-of-state-for-finance-lead-goli-maaro-saalon-ko-slogans-at-rally.
22. https://www.financialexpress.com/india-news/delhi-election-2020-bjp-mp-says-shaheen-bagh-will-be-cleared-in-an-hour-if-bjp-comes-to-power/1837215/.
23. https://www.firstpost.com/politics/will-remove-shaheen-bagh-protesters-mosques-on-state-land-west-delhi-bjp-mp-parvesh-vermas-poll-promise-7965961.html.
24. https://www.republicworld.com/india-news/politics/tarun-chug-wont-let-delhi-become-syria-and-allow-them-to-run-an-isi.html
25. https://www.thequint.com/news/india/rambhakt-gopal-man-shoots-jamia-student-at-anti-caa-rally-new-delhi.
26. https://timesofindia.indiatimes.com/city/delhi/now-shaheen-bagh-man-fires-in-air-caught-by-cops/articleshow/73858581.cms.
27. https://scroll.in/article/954072/the-road-that-opened-near-shaheen-bagh-had-been-blocked-by-delhi-police.

28. https://www.thehindu.com/opinion/op-ed/its-time-for-the-shaheen-bagh-protests-to-end/article30720669.ece.
29. https://www.ndtv.com/india-news/arvind-kejriwal-to-ndtv-amit-shah-wants-to-fight-delhi-election-on-shaheen-bagh-bjp-doesnt-want-issu-2174453.
30. https://www.livemint.com/mint-lounge/features/shaheen-bagh-s-revolution-highway-11580373131891.html.
31. Page 35 of the Delhi Police affidavit dated 13 July 2020, filed in the writ petition (crl) nos. 556, 588, 565, 665, 669, 670 and 700 of 2020, Rahul Roy vs GNCTD and others.
32. https://www.thequint.com/news/bjp-mla-kapil-mishra-denies-inciting-north-east-delhi-violence-maujpur-jaffarabad.
33. https://www.telegraphindia.com/india/on-the-mark-zuckerberg-on-kapil-mishra-not-donald-trump/cid/1778748.
34. https://indianexpress.com/article/opinion/editorials/face-it-facebook-hate-speech-politics6558937/.
35. Delhi police affidavit dated 13 July 2020, filed in the writ petition (crl) nos. 556, 588, 565, 665, 669, 670 and 700 of 2020, Rahul Roy vs GNCTD and others.
36. https://www.livemint.com/news/india/row-erupts-over-transfer-of-judge-hours-after-he-pulls-up-delhi-cops-11582853787313.html.
37. https://theprint.in/india/goli-maaro-slogans-chanted-inside-busy-rajiv-chowk-metro-station-in-delhi/373320/.
38. https://indianexpress.com/article/cities/delhi/delhi-riots-police-complicity-videos-6716673/.
39. Investigative briefing, Amnesty International India, 28 August 2020.
40. Page 6 of the Delhi police affidavit dated 13 July 2020, filed before the Delhi High Court in writ petition (crl) no. 556 of 2020.
41. FIRs have been included in the final report, filed under Section 173 of the CrPC before the court of Special Justice Amitabh Rawat, Karkardooma Courts, Delhi, in the conspiracy case filed under UAPA.
42. https://www.opensocietyfoundations.org/who-we-are/boards/human-rights-initiative-advisory-board/member/harsh-mander.
43. https://amp.scroll.in/article/965111/with-harsh-mander-named-in-delhi-riots-chargesheet-indian-democracy-has-slipped-into-a-dark-hole.

44. The police final report under Section 173 of the CrPc, filed in the court of Justice Pawan Singh Rajawat, CMM, northeast, Karkardooma Courts, Delhi, in FIR no. 65/2020, dated 26 February 2020, district northeast police station, Dayalpur, 2020.
45. Harsh Mander vs Government of NCT Delhi & Ors, writ petition (crl) no. 565/2020.
46. https://timesofindia.indiatimes.com/india/academicians-activists-condemn-umar-khalids-arrest-call-it-witch-hunt/articleshow/78109373.cms.
47. https://scroll.in/latest/967605/anti-caa-protests-had-secessionist-motives-delhi-police-claims-in-affidavit-on-february-violence.
48. https://www.aljazeera.com/opinions/2020/9/1/framed-and-hanged-how-the-indian-state-persecutes-dissent/.

Acknowledgements

All good journalism happens in the broader institutional framework put in place by a media organisation. The editor, the editorial vision and the energy in the newsroom drive reporters to produce high-quality reporting. This is the reason why some publications generate good quality journalism month after month, year after year.

Tehelka was one such organisation. The collective idealism, commitment to truth and justice, and passion to break new ground in reporting inspired ordinary reporters like me to carry out extraordinary work. I, therefore, would like to thank Tarun Tejpal for creating the news platform Tehelka, which inspired a whole generation of reporters and copy editors to produce high-quality long-form writing and interventionist reporting.

I would like to thank Sankarshan Thakur, Vikram Kilpady, Ramesh Sharma, S. Srikanth, Shyama Haldar, Manjula Narayan and Anand Naorem for supporting my work on the ground. I would like to especially thank Christina Fernandes for being the first editor of all my work. I owe gratitude to Aniruddha Bahal, who in my view has been one of the best investigative reporters this country has seen, and who has unending desire to go after big stories, for helping me editorially. Ananda Yagnik, the Ahmedabad-based human rights lawyer, deserves a special mention for his perseverant legal battles representing the disadvantaged minorities in Gujarat. I want to thank Harsh Mandar for being a doughty champion of the poor, the marginalised and the disadvantaged, and for fighting legal battles for the riot survivors of Gujarat; Harinder Baweja, the editor who didn't look at my degrees, but at my stories before offering me a job; senior lawyer Mihir Desai, who has always been there as a pillar of support for the victims and survivors of Gujarat riots. Lawyer Suhel Tirmizi has never flinched from taking up human rights cases even at great personal costs. Shabnam Hashmi, for always staying positive and supplying insights into human rights abuses over unending cups of tea and cigarettes. Shoma Chaudhury, one of the finest political commentators, for editing, shaping and sharpening my copies. Somnath Vatsa, the Ahmedabad-based human rights lawyer, whose academic and critical approach to Gujarat riots cases, has helped me in appreciating the legalities associated with them. Teesta Setalvad, for meticulously documenting the communal crimes in Gujarat and for presenting the facts before different legal forums and untiredly and unceasingly fighting for justice for the victims of the 2002 riots. I would also like to thank the many brave and upright police officers from Gujarat who bore the wrath of a very malevolent and vindictive regime but still chose the difficult path of upholding the law. They, although I could not name them as they wanted anonymity, at various stages helped me understand the complex issues of law and criminal investigation. I would like to make a special mention of R.B. Sreekumar, the former DGP of Gujarat police, who documented the connivance of various state actors with the riots accused and testified against the Gujarat chief minister and other senior officials before different judicial and quasi-judicial forums.

I would like to especially thank Shougat Dasgupta, a very fine writer and commentator on current affairs, for the sharp and fastidious editing of this work. My special thanks also to V.K. Karthika and Ajitha G.S., without whom this book would not have been possible.